49.95

BALKAN BABEL

◆

Politics, Culture, and Religion in Yugoslavia

BALKAN BABEL

♦

Politics, Culture, and Religion in Yugoslavia

Sabrina Petra Ramet

Westview Press

BOULDER • SAN FRANCISCO • OXFORD

The map on p. xvii is reprinted from *Problems of Communism,* March-April 1983, by kind permission of *Problems of Communism,* United States Information Agency.

Published in 1992 in the United States of America by Westview Press, Inc., 5500 Central Avenue, Boulder, Colorado 80301-2847, and in the United Kingdom by Westview Press, 36 Lonsdale Road, Summertown, Oxford OX2 7EW

Library of Congress Cataloging-in-Publication Data
Ramet, Sabrina P., 1949–
    Balkan babel : politics, culture, and religion in Yugoslavia /
Sabrina Petra Ramet.
        p.   cm.
    Includes bibliographical references and index.
    ISBN 0-8133-8184-3
    1. Yugoslavia—Civilization—20th century.   I. Title.
DR1308.R36   1992
949.702—dc20   91-33354
                                                                                          CIP

Printed and bound in the United States of America

The paper used in this publication meets the requirements
of the American National Standard for Permanence of Paper
for Printed Library Materials Z39.48-1984.

10   9   8   7   6   5   4   3

To Susan McEachern,
my editor, my friend

Contents

Foreword, Ivo Banac ix

Preface xv

Introduction 1

Part One
Politics

1   Political Debate, 1980–1986 7

2   The Gathering Storm, 1987–1989 21

3   Brotherhood and Unity, 1989–1991 37

Part Two
Culture

4   The Press 57

5   Rock Music 81

6   Women and Men 105

Part Three
Religion

7   The Catholic Church 121

8   The Serbian Orthodox Church 145

9 Islam   165

    Epilogue   175

Notes   183
For Further Reading   211
Index   215

Foreword: The Politics of Cultural Diversity in Yugoslavia

THE COLLAPSE OF SOVIET AND EAST EUROPEAN communism has upset all the political and ideological conventions in the countries concerned. One noticeable consequence has been the revival of nationalism—that much misunderstood mutant ideology whose many faces have tested a legion of analysts. The nationalisms of Eastern Europe, in particular, have long been a stumbling block for U.S. observers. The example of a stable civil society like the United States, where an assimilationist political culture mitigated the effects of ancestry, really cannot inform the "ethnic" relations of East European multinational states. The latter—and Yugoslavia is a prime example—are really conglomerates of historical nations, each with its own internal subnational—or, if you prefer, ethnic—problems. Yugoslavia is currently in the midst of the most dramatic phase in its perennial nationality question. It is not likely that it will survive as a state. For insight into its future, and by extension into the future of other multinational states in Eastern Europe, it might be wise to look at the political implications of cultural diversity in Yugoslavia. It is to Sabrina Ramet's great credit that she understood the cultural context of South Slavic nationality relations at a time when most of her colleagues promoted entirely unrealistic readings of the subject.

The cultural diversity *among* the nationalities of Yugoslavia has frequently been so acute that there is a tendency to underestimate the elements of diversity *within* each single nationality. Take the Serbs, for example. Vuk Karadzic (1787–1864), the foremost Serb cultural reformer, was probably not the first Serb scholar to recognize the vast cultural—not just linguistic—differences between the Serbs of the Habsburg Monarchy and those of the Ottoman Empire. Jovan Cvijic (1865–1927), a noted Serbian geographer, developed a whole system for the classification of Serb "cultural belts," having personally identified three Serb "psychological types" (really, cultural types). And, indeed, there are vast differences between the disciplined "imperial sons" from the former Habsburg Military Frontier, the exponents of urban Byzantine Orthodoxy from southern Serbia, the patriarchal and natural Orthodox highlanders of Hercegovina and Montenegro, the latitudinarian clergy and burghers from the Vojvodina and their no less latitudinarian kinsmen from the harbors of the Montenegrin littoral, not to forget the Serbs who live in areas of predominantly Muslim influence. One could go on like this and demonstrate to what extent the perennial calls for Serb unity (including cultural unity) address the real fears of cultural fragmentation in one of Yugoslavia's reputedly more homogeneous nationalities. Slobodan Milosevic, currently the paramount Serbian leader, is therefore as keen as any of his non-Communist predecessors to foster the homogenization of Serbs throughout Yugoslavia, that is, beyond the Serb heartlands in eastern Yugoslavia.

Yugoslavia's extreme cultural diversity stems from the fact that this relatively small country is situated at the cultural crossroads of the Old World. The continental crusts of Rome and Byzantium have been colliding here for a millennium. The subcontinent of Islam dashed at the emerging landmass half a millennium ago. There is a Central European Yugoslavia (Slovenia, northern Croatia, the Vojvodina) and a Mediterranean Yugoslavia (the littorals of Slovenia, Croatia, and Montenegro). There is a Muslim Yugoslavia and an Eastern Orthodox Yugoslavia. And sometimes they come together. In Mostar, Hercegovina, one can sip Viennese coffee and read newspapers mounted on wooden frames, listening all along to a muezzin's call in the shadow of a Franciscan church (where the chant is Latinate), and then wander into a fig grove that surrounds a Byzantine-style church (where the chant is Slavonic). None of this is imported for the tourists. It raises no native eyebrows. And it does not prompt intolerance.

Because Yugoslavia's cultural diversity is really religiously based, there have been numerous attempts to link the country's divisions to religious intolerance. In fact, South Slavic interconfessional relations never occasioned religious wars on the scale of those fought in Western Europe after the Reformation or along the banks of the Tigris for the length of the Islamic era. The tragic events of World War II, when some of the massacres committed by the contending sides became religiously based, occurred in the context of occupation, not of religious or even civil war (a much misused term). The hold of religious culture is strong, but not stronger than the practicality of the usually practical South Slavs. An epic Croat folk song tells of how the war party of the Uskoks of Senj, a sixteenth-century martial community that lived on piracy and plunder, was faced with an unexpected spell of cold weather. Instead of permitting his men to freeze, the Uskok leader offered the following solution:

> I do not know of a stone cave [where they presumably could hide];
> But I know of Saint George's church.
> We shall break the door of the holy church,
> We shall burn fire in it,
> So that God will send us his luck,
> So that we shall warm our flesh,
> And safely return to Senj.
> We shall then build a better church,
> And secure it with a new door,
> Made of silver and purest gold.

I mention the question of cultural diversity and its misapplications because diversity, as such, is not the fuel of current national hostilities. I personally have been a strong exponent of the idea that the nationality question in Yugoslavia and other East European countries does not derive from religious differences, cultural diversity, or even from the problems of unequal economic development. Rather, I have argued that the nationality question was shaped by the dissimilar structure and goals of various national ideologies that have emerged within the political culture of each of Eastern Europe's national groups. Quite obviously, these national ideologies are historically determined, which is to say that each one of them also contains elements of historically determined cultural diversity. From that point of view, it might be useful to trace the postwar Communist experience in order to discover how Communist ideology operated within the context of Yugoslav cultural diversity, thereby reshaping the national ideologies of Yugoslavia's principal national groups.

The Yugoslav Communists promoted the interests of their respective national groups a great deal more than is usually imagined, and not just since the death of Tito in 1980. The Communists have debated the Yugoslav nationality question from the beginning of their party in 1919 and "solved" it in turns as revolutionary centralists and unitarists, separatists, federalists, and, increasingly in recent years, as confederalists. They emerged from the war with the program of "new Yugoslav socialist culture," which was intended to eliminate the nationality question by eradicating its historical sources. This proved impossible from the beginning. The permitted, mainly traditional, cultural cults could not easily be harmonized and frequently expressed fundamentally irreconcilable cultural and national aspirations. Worse yet, the Communist cults of "new Yugoslav socialist culture" were no more harmonious.

Two of the foremost literary figures of socialist Yugoslavia, Nobel laureate Ivo Andric and Miroslav Krleza, were the living embodiment of Communist cultural diversity. They were not just stylistic antipodes; their communism itself covered the diapason of Yugoslav Marxist patterns. Like most intellectuals, Krleza came to Leninism from the shipwreck and carnage of Central European civilization, which collapsed on the fields of Galicia in World War I. His principal literary motif was his profound skepticism about the historical mission of the Central European bourgeoisie. The fog that enveloped Croatia (and Eastern Europe) could only be lifted "when whole flotillas of nations and classes start sailing" toward the Leninist beacon. But that beacon, too, was fundamentally chimerical. Krleza's Lenin-types, for example his Christopher Columbus, are crucified by the mindless masses. Nevertheless, Krleza's pessimistic revolutionism brought the intelligentsia to the Communist party. In terms of nationality programs, it was an expression of a steadfast federalist project, built on the premise, which Krleza shared with many of his non-Communist fellow Croats, that Yugoslavia's cultural diversity (the Rome-Byzantium cleavage) could not easily be filled. In Andric we have a veteran of the nationalist and mythopoeic Bosnian Youth—the movement that cast forth the Sarajevo assassins—a Yugoslav integralist of profoundly authoritarian bent, a prewar diplomat, and an associate of right-wing cultural journals, who missed the Chetnik train by a very small margin. His postwar membership in the Communist party was typical of the premium paid to the unitarist intelligentsia by the cultural architects of the new state.

The building of the "new Yugoslav socialist culture" also ended as a failure among the generation of literary Partisans—the veterans of Tito's wartime insurgency. Members of the Partisan generation failed to integrate Yugoslavia culturally. Moreover, prominent Partisan writers became the ideologists of Yugoslavia's new national divisions and contributed to the collapse of Yugoslav cultural unitarism that can be dated from the mid-1960s. The changing nature of official Yugoslav ideology and statecraft, the growing delegitimation of the Communist movement (with the accompanying need to seek national underpinnings of legitimacy), and real national grievances (but also the attempts to explain and cure them) are among the other factors that contributed to the failure of cultural unitarism.

Tito's answer to this failure was a more consistent federalism that substituted democracy with formal axiomatic constructions (the rotation system of leadership, parity in leaderships, constitutional reforms, the refederation of Serbia's two autonomous provinces, and an indirect system of elections). These constructions and changes necessarily prompted resistance, which exploded after Tito's death and reached its culmination in the current war between the republics. It is important to note here that the content of Communist thinking in all of Yugoslavia's six territorial parties came to resemble, indeed duplicate, the national ideologies that have evolved and prevailed in the given party-state before the war. In other words, Serbia's leading Communist, Slobodan Milosevic, has more in common with the prewar Radical Party, the party of Serbian supremacy, than with Slovene or Croat Communists. Yugoslav communism, national since 1948, has become further nationalized along internal national divisions. A similar process has occurred in the Soviet Union, where, for example, the pre-August 1991 discourse between Lithuanian and Russian Communists resembled the old contention between the Lithuanian national movement and the imperial Russian state.

It has recently been observed that never before in its seventy-year history has Yugoslavia been more divided than it is today, that never before have the peoples of Yugoslavia shared such deep resentment of one another. As bitter as this assessment certainly is, it is also entirely true. The Yugoslav project is finished, root and branches. At this late date, after the ex-Yugoslav army unleashed a war of conquest on Croatia, thereby wrecking the prospect of meaningful negotiations among the republics, the emerging independent successor-states of Yugoslavia will have to be judged by their attitude toward the minorities. The equality and territoriality of each of ex-Yugoslavia's nationalities must be protected, as must the legitimacy of the links between the minority nationalities and their matrix-states. For example, the Serbs should be able to enjoy their independent statehood without obstructing the national institutions and the democratic rights of Serbia's minorities. The protection of minorities, especially their cultural unity, could in time be extended to the whole of Eastern Europe, thereby lessening the importance of some of the region's more irrational borders, and perhaps even contributing to their change. Moreover, the full legitimation of the national cultures would necessarily legitimate diversity, which must prevail if peace is to return to the South Slavs.

Ivo Banac

Preface

IT GIVES ME GREAT pleasure to be able to collect some of my previous writings on Yugoslavia and reissue them in book form. Of the nine chapters printed herein, six are revised and updated incarnations of earlier publications of mine. Three chapters (Chapters 3, 5, and 6) are new.

I took up the study of Yugoslavia in 1977 while still in graduate school—I had become excited about ethnic relations in that country while engaged in master's research on my mother's country, Austria-Hungary. Since then, I have visited Yugoslavia repeatedly and spent time in all of the republics except Montenegro. Inevitably, most of my work has taken me to the cities—above all to Ljubljana, Zagreb, and Belgrade, but also, on occasion, to Sarajevo and Skopje. I have also had occasion to visit villages in Slovenia, Croatia, and Serbia and to get some idea of the differences between city and countryside in the Yugoslav setting.

My impressions of Yugoslavia have been formed by the people I met and interviewed in Yugoslavia and through their writings. I have tried, in my own writings, to convey something of the "spirit" of Yugoslavia—what makes its people tick, what issues concern them, and how they think. That spirit, for me, is the lifeblood of political history.

In bringing together these essays, I hope to suggest a vital inter-connection and interaction among the political, cultural, and religious spheres and show how changes in one sphere are accompanied by parallel changes in the other spheres.

Chapter 1 was previously published in *Crossroads,* No. 23 (1987). Chapter 2 was previously published in *Global Affairs,* Vol. 5, No. 1 (Winter 1990). Chapter 4 was previously published in John B. Allcock, John J. Horton, and Marko Milivojevic, eds., *Yugoslavia in Transition: Choices and Constraints* (Oxford and Hamburg: Berg Publishers; New York: St. Martin's Press, 1991). Chapter 7 was previously published in Pedro Ramet, ed., *Catholicism and Politics in Communist Societies*

(Duke University Press, 1990). Chapter 8 was previously published in Pedro Ramet, ed., *Eastern Christianity and Politics in the Twentieth Century* (Duke University Press, 1988). And Chapter 9 was previously published in *Religion in Communist Lands* (a publication of Keston College), Vol. 18, No. 3 (Summer 1990). I am grateful to the editors of these publications and to the respective presses for permission to reuse this material. I am also deeply grateful to Karen Walton for coding this manuscript and assisting in other ways.

Some of these essays appeared originally under my former name, Pedro Ramet. I changed my gender and my name in December 1990: Pedro and Sabrina are one and the same person.

Sabrina Petra Ramet
Seattle, Washington

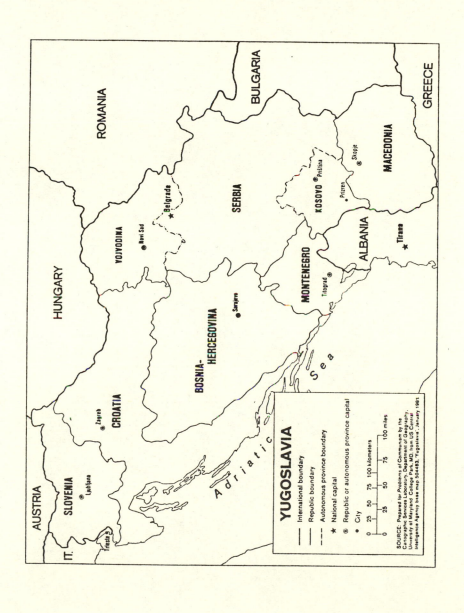

AUSTRIA

IT.

HUNGARY

ROMANIA

BULGARIA

GREECE

SLOVENIA
• Ljubljana

Trieste •

CROATIA
• Zagreb

VOJVODINA
• Novi Sad

SERBIA

Belgrade ★

BOSNIA-
HERCEGOVINA
• Sarajevo

KOSOVO ⊚ Pristina

Prizren •

MACEDONIA
⊚ Skopje

MONTENEGRO
Titograd ⊚

ALBANIA
Tirana ★

Adriatic Sea

YUGOSLAVIA

— International boundary

— — Republic boundary

- - - Autonomous province boundary

★ National capital

⊚ Republic or autonomous province capital

• City

0   25   50   75   100 kilometers

0   25   50   75   100 miles

SOURCE: Prepared for Problems of Communism by the
Cartographic Services Laboratory, Department of Geography,
University of Maryland College Park, MD, from US Central
Intelligence Agency base map 504453, Yugoslavia, January 1981.

Introduction

THERE WAS NO YUGOSLAVIA before 1918. Until then, Serbs and Croats had never lived in the same state. Until then, Slovenes had, for centuries, been attached to Austria, and in cultural terms, looked north, to Vienna, rather than south, to Belgrade, for kinship. Kosovo, remembered by Serbs today as the heartland of the medieval Serbian kingdom, was ruled by Turkey for some 500 years, and by the time Serbia regained rule over Kosovo, in 1913, the province had a decisive Albanian majority. Yugoslavia's prophets (in the nineteenth century) had conceived of the state as a land in which related peoples—the South Slavs—could build a common life. Many of Yugoslavia's early rulers, however, were essentially the rulers of the former Serbian state, and conceived of the new state as an extension of old Serbia.

Since 1918, there has been a constant tension between Serbs and non-Serbs in this polyglot country, as Serbs have repeatedly tried to Serbianize and/or dominate the non-Serbs, and non-Serbs have doggedly fought such domination. This struggle between Serbs and non-Serbs lies at the heart of the instability for which Yugoslavia is famous. It has never been the *only* source of Yugoslav instability, but it has been a crucial component in that syndrome.

Yugoslavia is a multi-national country in which every national group is a minority. The Serbs, for example, are the largest group, numbering 8.1 million out of a total 22.4 million persons, representing 36.3 per cent of the population in 1981. Croats are the second largest group, with 4.4 million or 19.7 per cent of the population. Ethnic Muslims numbered 2.0 million or 8.9 per cent of the population. The fourth largest group in 1981 was the Slovenes (1.8 million, or 7.8 per cent), followed by the Albanians (1.7 million, or 7.7 per cent). All other groups numbered less than 1.5 million persons (i.e., less than 7 per cent of the total population). These other groups include Macedonians, Montenegrins, Hungarians, Gypsies, Turks, and others.

Yugoslavia is also a multi-confessional country. The three largest religious groups are the Serbian Orthodox Church (which claims to have some 10 million adherents), the Catholic Church (which claims to have some 7.3 million adherents), and the Islamic community (which claims some 3.8 million adherents). All of these figures are inflated, and do not take account of the secularization of the population. This reflects the tendency of these respective organizations to claim the allegiance of the entire membership of each national group traditionally affiliated with the given religion (as if all Serbs and Montenegrins were Orthodox, or all Slovenes and Croats were Catholics). Fortunately, sociological studies have been conducted which reveal more accurately the proportion of each ethnic group reporting religious belief. These figures are given in chapter 7. Taking these figures into account, we may estimate that, in real terms, there were probably about 2.5 million Catholics, 1.2 million Muslims, and 1.1 million Serbian Orthodox in Yugoslavia in 1981. Given general population growth and a modest religious revival among all groups, these figures would be somewhat larger for 1991, possibly in the range of about 3 million Catholics, 1.5 million Muslims, and 1.2 million Serbian Orthodox. The Catholic Church is, by this revised estimate, easily the largest religious body in the country. There are also smaller numbers of Protestants, Jews, Jehovah's Witnesses, Hare Krishnas, and others. There are also many agnostics, atheists, and religiously uncommitted.

Yugoslavia is also a multi-cultural country, and in fact the cultural differences are often so wide that different groups cannot understand each other at all. The difficulty that Serbs and Slovenes have understanding each other is in part a function of the vast differences separating their respective cultures.

And finally, Yugoslavia is also—if one may use the expression—a multi-political country, by which I mean that politics in its diverse regions has always differed, one to the other. This has been especially true of the period since Yugoslav President Tito's death in 1980.

This book is about politics. It is also about culture and religion. I have brought these topics together, because I am convinced that no country's politics exists independently of its cultures or its religions, and that without an understanding of the culture and religion, one can *never* understand the politics. Those Western analysts who have made the most sense of Yugoslav politics have been those who have understood Yugoslavia's culture and its religious climate.

Culture and religion are about values, about prescribed behavior, about social expectations. These components cannot but impinge on politics and infuse politics from below. I might even be so bold as to say that culture should be understood as the source of values, and hence of conflicts over values—which is to say that without culture (of which religion is a constituent part), there can be no politics. Or to put it differently, religion and politics alike were born at the same point in time as offspring of a common mother—and that mother is culture in the broad sense.

This book is pessimistic about Yugoslavia. In fact, I have always been pessimistic about Yugoslavia, even when I gave it credit for its achievements. As of mid-1991, Yugoslavia is dead—in cultural terms: it has no more unifying energy, only divisive energy rooted in a complete and total breakdown of inter-cultural contact and exchange. The cultural death of a country is bound to lead to its political death, in due course, even if the Great Powers intervene to delay the moment of truth. The only escape is through an Ataturk, who is able to create a new consensus on the basis of a new culture. There is no Yugoslav Ataturk in sight in July 1991.

Yet to be pessimistic about Yugoslavia is not to be pessimistic about its parts. All of Yugoslavia's peoples have experienced cultural reawakening in recent years (as explained in chapter 2). On this foundation, the prospects for at least some of them to succeed (the most likely being Slovenia and Croatia but with Macedonia having some important, if less well understood, cultural strengths) would seem to be quite good, were it not for the incipient civil war already unleashed by June 1991. Unless that war can be defused and pacified, Yugoslavia may perish less peacefully, amid vast carnage and destruction.

PART ONE

Politics

CHAPTER ONE

◆

Political Debate, 1980–1986

JOSIP BROZ TITO RULED Yugoslavia for some 37 years, guiding the country through a major crisis in relations with the Soviet Union, steering it through four constitutions, and creating a political formula centered on self-management (in the economy), brotherhood and unity (in nationalities policy), and nonalignment (in foreign policy). Despite the internal crises that shook the country in 1948–49, 1961–65, and 1970–71, Tito created a network of institutions that many hoped would prove stable and resistant to destabilizing change. Yet, for reasons quite different from and independent of those affecting other countries in Eastern Europe, Yugoslavia's political institutions ultimately proved vulnerable to pressures for change. Such pressures built up gradually and steadily, from the grassroots, from the intellectuals, from feminists, environmentalists, pacifists, and liberals. Political change was adumbrated first in the cultural sector,[1] and borne along by small independent organizations set up from below.

The ruling party, the League of Communists of Yugoslavia (LCY), was aware even as Tito was dying, that his political formula needed revision. The result was a political debate which raged for nearly a decade. The debate went through three broad phases: 1980–87 (internal party debate), 1987–89 (internal party debate pitting Milosevic supporters against his antagonists), and 1989–91 (inter-party debate between the remnants of the old communist party and the new noncommunist parties in Slovenia, Croatia, Bosnia, and Macedonia over the future of the country). This chapter is concerned with the first phase, and argues that the system was so constituted that substantive change was precluded by the very nature and structure of the system. At the core of the problem was the party's insistence on narrowing the debate, by excluding discussion of pluralization; the preservation of its power monopoly was taken for granted. This proved to be an unexpected source of bottlenecks, as I shall show.

7

After Tito's death in May 1980, critical voices began to be heard, in a way they had not been in Tito's time. Gradually, in the course of the 1980s, Yugoslavia saw the abandonment of the party's claim to have devised an exportable model, abandonment of the central concept of the withering away of the state, abandonment of the idea that self-management is the font of the system and the key to the solution of all policy issues, redefinition of nonalignment in terms of *Realpolitik,* and abandonment of the idea that the LCY had a historic or superordinate claim to rule, and rejustification on the grounds that any alternative would lead to civil war (though increasing numbers of people rejected even this rejustification, in order to argue for the establishment of a two-party or multi-party system in Yugoslavia). This post-Tito disintegration of ideology in Yugoslavia followed on the heels of a devolution of powers to the constituent republics and provinces that revived, on a nationwide basis, the autonomist logic of the Cvetkovic-Macek *Sporazum* of 1939.[2]

POLITICAL DECAY

In the course of the years 1980–86, leading Yugoslav party functionaries and news organs charged almost every major social institution with malfunctioning. Only the army was exempted from criticism at that time. Other organizations were variably charged with unconstitutional practices, corruption, rampant inefficiency, unresponsiveness to people's needs, etc.

Problems in the functioning of the party remained central to these concerns, of course. Here the pivotal concern was the manifest inability of the eight regional party organizations of Yugoslavia's eight federal units (six republics, and two autonomous provinces) to coordinate their policies or agree on strategies. This, in turn, gave birth to the realization that the LCY had already ceased to exist and an organizationally unified and politically meaningful unit: the LCY had become merely the institutional arena in which the real powers in the system—the regional party organizations—met and discussed their common concerns.

Within the party itself, the real channels of authority often diverged considerably from the formal channels: the secession of the provincial party organizations of Kosovo and Vojvodina from the effective jurisdiction of the Serbian republic party organization was only one example of this. While the party as a whole was weak and disunified, local branches sometimes showed a resilient capacity for intrusion into domains lying outside their jurisdiction. Local party members often joined out of sheer opportunism, and used their positions for private gain, often, evidently, in disregard of the law.[3] Even *Socijalizam,* the party theoretical organ, admitted in summer 1984 that the LCY was having difficulties with members who ignored party directives and behaved in an irresponsible fashion.[4]

But while the federal party organization had become totally divorced from governmental functions—to the extent that it experienced considerable difficulty in making any headway in applying the 1982 recommendations of the Krajgher Commission on the Economic System—the regional party organizations retained a firm grasp on power, thus provoking complaints of "republican etatism." A striking illustration of the balance of power came in the second half of 1984, when the Fourteenth Central Committee (CC) Plenum was held. Under party statutes, the eight regional party organizations (of six republics and two autonomous provinces) were obliged to meet to compare their own policies with the latest CC resolution (which dealt specifically with the economy and the failure to implement the Krajgher Commission's recommendations). In actual fact, not a single regional party organization bothered to meet in this connection[5]—a sure sign of the flimsiness of central party discipline.

The self-managing interest communities likewise got out of control. Created in late 1974 with the idea of involving citizens in monitoring public services in education, health, social welfare, childcare, employment, sports, information, and so forth,[6] the communities (known collectively as "SIZ," from the initials of the Serbo-Croatian, *Samoupravne interesne zajednice*), quickly mushroomed in number and scope. The resulting system, in which two parallel structures exercised jurisdiction in the same area, was mocked as "SIZ-ophrenia" (a pointed pun on "schizophrenia"). But under the constitution, the self-managing communities were supposed to be created by local bodies of citizens, and not by republic or provincial legislation; in practice, on the contrary, all such communities owed their existence to republic or provincial legislation. Moreover, instead of functioning as consumer advocates—their supposed portfolio—the new institutions quickly adopted the behavior of government agencies.

Finally—where political institutions are concerned—the Socialist Alliance of Working People of Yugoslavia (SAWPY), a front organization designed to involve non-party people in supportive activity, had long been little more than a marionette of party barons.

The malfunctioning of political organizations might not have become a problem had it not been for repeated charges to that effect and for an attendant shrinkage of public confidence in the system. But neither the malfunctioning of institutions nor the shrinkage of confidence would have garnered much attention had it not been for the economic mire, which probably deserves to be credited, in the first place, as the chief catalyst of the crisis of confidence. Precipitated by a combination of uncoordinated investments, unbridled trade imbalances, and over-borrowing throughout the 1970s, by the mid-1980s, economic problems included, by 1985, a spiraling inflation in excess of 100 per cent annually and a growing gap between the cost of living and real wages. The latter gap was compensated by the growth of a barter economy and of smuggling and black-marketeering.

The party's strategy, in creating the Krajgher Commission, was the try to correct the economic problems without tampering with the fundamental political institutions which some Yugoslavs blamed for the problems in the first place.

CRISIS AND POLARIZATION

That post-Tito developments in the economic and political spheres were pushing Yugoslavia into a very real crisis was at first denied by party spokespersons. Only in 1983—four years after the economic situation began to deteriorate, two years after the province-wide riots by Albanians in Kosovo, and a year after the controversial Twelfth Party Congress—did party elders finally concede that there was a "crisis" in Yugoslavia and even that a "Polish situation" could develop in the country.[7]

This hesitation in turn constricted party participation in the political debate that started in Yugoslavia soon after Tito's death. At first, the chief participants were scholars and journalists. The Twelfth Party Congress, insofar as it opened the floodgates to debate within the party itself, was a turning point.

In the initial phase of the debate (1980–81), the economic difficulties were not yet far advanced and discussion therefore centered on press policy, supervision of the universities, and general political democratization. Within this context, there were two broad positions: one partial to liberalization and one opposed. Later, as economic deterioration forced Yugoslavs to confront the sources of strain, four clear factions emerged, as constituted by the dual issues of liberalization vs. retrenchment and recentralization vs. preservation of the decentralized system. While almost every constituent regional party organization was factionalized to some extent, liberal recentralizers were dominant in the Serbian Party, conservative recentralizers in the Bosnian and Montenegrin parties, liberal decentralists in the Slovenian and Vojvodinan parties, and conservative decentralists in the Croatian, Macedonian, and Kosovar parties.[8] Needless to say, this double polarization prevented any broad coalition from being formed, since there were at least three parties on either side of each of the issues. The result was that while the disintegration of the center allowed the burgeoning of political debate and the generation of sundry prescriptions, it simultaneously prevented, under conditions of double polarization, the imposition of a new solution on the system, even though there was widespread consensus that *something* needed to be done. Ultimately, of course, this irresolution would contribute to breaking the communist party's hold in four republics (Slovenia, Croatia, Macedonia, and Bosnia) in 1989, which in turn resulted in opening up new strategies for dealing with the crisis.

The weakening of the center after Tito's death allowed the Serbian, Slovenian, and Vojvodinan parties to further liberalize their policies in the spheres of culture, the media, and even religion. Controversial plays such as Jovan Radulovic's *Pigeonhole* and Dusan Jovanovic's *The Karamazovs*—which touched on politically delicate subjects—were staged in these republics, though the former play was eventually suppressed under pressure from the more conservative Croatian party organization. Serbia's most popular weekly magazine, *NIN,* actively encouraged the awakening of popular interest in Goli Otok,[9] the prison in which the Communist Party had incarcerated and tortured its political enemies in the late 1940s. The media in these federal units, and to a certain extent also in Croatia, launched a new era of investigative journalism in Yugoslavia—sometimes even to the point of muckraking.[10] And where religious policy was concerned, Slovenia and Vojvodina achieved a rare tranquility in Church-state relations, while in Serbia, the Serbian Orthodox Church was allowed (in 1984) to lay the foundation stone for a new theological faculty in Belgrade, and continued its lively publication activity with the first *official* Orthodox Church translation of the New Testament in Serbo-Croatian. Since liberalization was dependent on the slackening of authority at the center, it was understandable that few liberals could be found among recentralizers at that stage.

In Croatia and Bosnia, by contrast, conservative forces remained dominant. One expression of this more conservative political climate came in the shape of a series of petty harassments of clergymen in these two republics (above all of Catholic clergymen and Muslim ulema and officials). But while Bosnian and Montenegrin conservatives were also recentralizers—with the Montenegrin Central Committee suggesting, in November 1981, that regional party organizations should be shorn of their power to select their own representatives to the LCY Central Committee[11]—the internally divided Croatian party moved from a position partial to system standardization in 1982,[12] to a position of jealously safeguarding Croatian autonomy (by 1984).

In Kosovo, finally, local provincial party barons tried, in the years 1974–81, to maximize their autonomy not merely from the federal administration but also from the Serbian Republic, to which both autonomous provinces (Kosovo and Vojvodina) were nominally subordinate. They sought to accomplish these above all by restricting the publication of Serbo-Croatian accounts of party meetings and by constricting the flow of information to Belgrade. The result was that Belgrade was largely unaware of the activities of Albanian irredentist organizations in Kosovo at this time, even though the provincial government in Pristina was monitoring them. The unconstitutionally broad extent of Kosovar autonomy could only be safeguarded by repressing open discussion of issues, and hence, in Kosovo, devolutionary policy was wedded to cultural and political conservatism.

THE SEARCH FOR SOLUTIONS

That the political debate had, by the mid-1980s, revived certain themes first bandied about in the late 1960s suggested that the underlying problems were anything but new. As early as 1967, for instance, M. Caldarevic had urged that the principle of democratic centralism was outmoded in conditions of self-management.[13] These same sentiments were voiced by Zagreb journalist Antun Zvan in 1981, when he argued that since democratic centralism only applied to party members, its effect was to make party members "less free" that nonmembers.

Again, the idea of pumping life into SAWPY and transforming it into a second party had a long history.[14] The revival of this idea in the mid-1980s was a measure of discontent with the political status quo.

By the time party elders convened the Twelfth Party Congress in summer 1982—the first congress since Tito's passing—there were strong expectations that the occasion would prove a breakthrough in terms of the political direction of the system. But all radical proposals for organizational "reform" (most of them inspired by hopes of reconstituting the center) were blocked, including Rade Koncar's rather dramatic proposal, on the floor of the Congress, that the republic-based federal organization of the party be scrapped and replaced with organization on the basis of lines of production.[15] The upshot was that while decentralists and liberals alike could gloat over their defeat of the sundry centralizing proposals presented at the Congress, the rivalry between the recentralizers and the decentralists in the party had not been resolved, and hence, the pressure for change had not been removed.

Although the Twelfth Party Congress thus accomplished little or nothing, it did signal the impotence of the center, which naturally further encouraged republican and provincial elites to ignore exhortations emanating from the center. A subsequent CC resolution (in April 1983) urging its own members not to misconstrue themselves as representatives of their respective republics or provinces was, for instance, ignored by all concerned. In early summer 1984, the party leadership made another attempt to restore resilience to the central organs. The CC Presidium drew up a report on relations between the central and regional party organizations. The report found that ". . . decisions adopted unanimously at the national level are being carried out only half-heartedly [at the republican and provincial levels], and execution is largely limited to those aspects which suit the particular region at the moment."[16] This report was submitted to the Thirteenth Session of the Central Committee for action. But, despite the urgings of those who warned of the creeping "federalization" of the party itself,[17] the Committee demurred and decided to pass the text on to the 70,000 basic organizations of the party for discussion and to delay final action until the Thirteenth Party Congress, in June 1986.

By then, recentralization was no longer rationalized in terms of the vanguard role of the party as the political instrument of the working class. Recentralization was presented, on the contrary, as a pragmatic consideration.[18] Ideologically deflated, the Yugoslavs quietly abandoned their earlier claims to greater fidelity to Lenin.[19] Former Partisan general Peko Dapcevic, for instance, told the Twelfth Party Congress that Leninism was outdated—a conclusion presumed by Zvan's earlier effort to scuttle democratic centralism, and seconded, in 1983, by Svetozar Stojanovic,[20] and in 1985, by sociologist Vladimir Arzensek and party theorist Vladimir Goati.[21] Indeed, Arzensek charged that Leninist ideas remained a serious impediment to necessary change throughout Eastern Europe. Likewise, where the Yugoslavs were once fond of claiming that their system was neither a one-party system nor a "bourgeois" multi-party system, but rather something unique,[22] *Socijalizam* now openly conceded that Yugoslavia had been set up as, and hence still was, a one-party system.[23]

The realization that the system had dead-ended gave birth to an astonishingly wide range of reform proposals. Famed economist Branko Horvat, for example, suggested in 1984 that "all political parties" (i.e., the communist party in its sundry regional organizations) be abolished and that Yugoslavia be reorganized as a "partyless" socialist system operated through citizens' associations.[24] Two political scientists from Belgrade suggested in 1983 that a multi-party system be restored[25]— an alternative specifically repudiated at the June 1984 Session of the 163-member LCY Central Committee. In reflecting upon the evident support for this remedy, Radoslav Ratkovic drew a distinction between "the pluralism of self-managing interests" and political pluralism, calling it erroneous to think that the legitimacy of the former could legitimate the latter.[26]

Despite the party's obvious reluctance to share power with non-Communists, sociologist Miroslav Zivkovic did not hesitate, in spring 1985, to call for the establishment of a full-fledged "social democracy" in Yugoslavia.[27] Still others (such as Cedo Grbic) called for a more liberal attitude toward private enterprise, or for the restoration of strong-arm (cvrsta ruka) rule, or—more tamely—for the complete rewriting of Communist party statutes.[28] Multi-candidate elections were also a popular idea, especially as a device to defuse support for multi-party elections.[29]

Within the context of this debate, then, SAWPY appeared as both temptation and, ostensibly, opportunity. Its advocates were able to argue, plausibly, that the organization was entitled, under the constitution, to a greater role in public life and that the LCY control of SAWPY was an "unnatural partnership."[30] Perhaps drawing lessons from the Polish crisis of 1980–81, Rados Smiljkovic told the Zagreb weekly magazine *Danas* in 1984, that the "marginalization" of SAWPY deprived non-Communist citizens of legitimate political channels and risked pushing them into the illicit "politicization of nonpolitical organizations and associations." Indeed, for Smiljkovic, "new political groups appear, and they will keep appearing" until legal structures would be offered, because "if people are not satisfied with the existing organizations, they create new ones, or [lapse into] a catastrophic political apathy."[31]

The difficulty, according to high-ranking party official Cedo Grbic, was that SAWPY had been controlled by "semi-legal coordinating groups and commissions" which excluded the public from any voice in personnel questions and perpetuated the organization's docile subordination to party hierarchies.[32] Seconding this assessment, Grlickov noted that non-Communists had only slight chances of being promoted to republic-level leadership posts in SAWPY. His remedy was to allow 30–50 per cent of responsible posts in the Socialist Alliance to be filled by non-Communists and to expand its jurisdiction. Going one step further, Serbian political scientist Mihailo Popovic told a party symposium in spring 1984 that SAWPY should be allowed to reorganize itself as an independent party, in order to provide an independent, critical voice, in the role of permanent opposition. And finally, Svetozar Stojanovic outlined a program in which SAWPY would gain organizational independence from the LCY, have a separate membership, and share power with a still dominant LCY.[33]

The radical tenor of some of these proposals was a measure of the seriousness with which the participants in the Yugoslav debate viewed the political situation. But any structural or systemic reorganization, as well as any far-reaching revisions of the statutes of the LCY, the regional parties, or the SAWPY, could only be achieved on the basis of a broad consensus among the leaderships of the eight regional party organizations (or nine, if the army's party organization was included). Such consensus was lacking. In early 1984, for example, the Slovenian leadership took the small step of suggesting that it might propose three candidates for its single seat on the collective state presidency, and allow a popular vote to determine the outcome. The other republican leaderships objected, and Slovenia withdrew its proposal and simply named Stane Dolanc to the post.

THE SERBIAN SOLUTION

The most comprehensive "reform" package to be proposed by a regional party organization in the first five years after Tito's death came in October 1984, when the Serbian party organization issued a four-part draft reform program, calling for the strengthening of the role and autonomy of economic enterprises, the strengthening of the federal government, the democratization of the electoral system, and a roll-back of the prerogatives and overall autonomy of the two autonomous provinces. The last of these points was assured of popularity among Serbia's Serbs, who were becoming disgruntled over the provinces' power to veto legislation. Serbs complained that their republic had unique difficulties in passing important legislation and blamed obstructionism on the part of the autonomous provinces. As part of the package, the Serbs also resurrected the 1981 proposal to divest republican parties of the power to select their representatives on the Central Committee.

The regional party organizations of Kosovo, Vojvodina, Slovenia, and Croatia were enraged. Kosovo and Vojvodina, in particular, had been fighting (since the April 1981 Albanian riots in Kosovo) to stay the Serbian backlash. But Slovenia and Croatia were likewise concerned about the threatened erosion of their hard-won autonomy. Slovenian-Serbian differences came into full view at the Fourteenth CC Plenum in October 1984, when the aforementioned Dragoslav Markovic attacked the Slovenian deputies for their opposition to the Serbian package. Markovic also called into question the propriety of requiring unanimity among the eight organizations before a decision could be taken. This challenge in turn impelled Slovene Andrej Marinc to take the podium, observing inter alia that the principle of unanimity was a long-standing procedure in the LCY and that Markovic's view had been specifically repudiated at a previous session. Marinc added that continued public discussion about changing the system could lead to "a political crisis, to a crisis of society."[34] The Serbian party leader, Slobodan Milosevic, replied to Marinc the following month:

We have been threatened with a political crisis if we continue to discuss these problems. All right, let us enter that political crisis. This crisis is going to produce a great uproar about the question of unity or separatism. In such a crisis, separatism will not prevail, because the people have accepted unity. Those leaders incapable of seeing this will lose the public's confidence. If separatism is not opposed, our country will have no prospects for the future. It can only disintegrate.[35]

The equation of advocacy of the federal status quo with "separatism" was a polemical punch that had some clout in Yugoslavia at that time. But with four other regional parties antagonistic, in varying degrees, to the Serbian draft, and a fifth (the Bosnian) at best "restrained" in its support, the prospects for adoption of this package seemed, and indeed, proved to be, were slight.

In the wake of this exchange, a new term crept into Yugoslav polemical vocabulary: "autonomism." Used by Serbian recentralizers as a pejorative term for the Vojvodinan party's desire to maintain the political status quo, the term was incorporated into a draft resolution of the Serbian Central Committee in April 1985, where it was placed in the same category with "Serb nationalism" and "Albanian nationalism."[36] When Vojvodina's press responded to criticism with counter-criticism of its own, some Serbian politicians grumbled that Vojvodina's newspapers were launching "an attack on the reputation of the Serbian Assembly"—a charge which suggested a desire to curb the independence of the provincial press.[37]

THE CONSTITUTION AND THE SYSTEM

In October 1984, *Borba* carried a series of articles by University of Zagreb Professor Jovan Miric arguing that the 1974 Constitution was the source of *all* of Yugoslavia's problems and that the exaggerated decentralization had destroyed the unified market and even interfered with the market mechanism.[38] Ribicic (a Slovene), Grlickov (from Macedonia), and Hamdija Pozderac (a Bosnian Muslim) applauded Miric's series. Others, including arch-conservatives France Popit (from Slovenia), Jure Bilic (from Croatia), and Dusan Popovic (a Serb from Vojvodina), were antagonistic. Jovan Djordjevic, a coauthor of the 1974 Constitution, himself admitted that the confederal coloration assumed by the system had not been the intention of the Constitution's drafters.

Eventually, the party decided to set up a commission to review the political system and prepare recommendations for change and reform. Modeled on the Krajgher Commission for the Reform of the Economic System, this new commission was entrusted to the chairship of Tihomir

Vlaskalic, a ranking Serbian party official. The Vlaskalic Commission was asked to prepare a report for submission to the Thirteenth Party Congress.

As the Thirteenth Party Congress approached, sundry party officials broached diverse proposals aimed at reestablishing central authority. The reasoning, according to Tanjug, the official news agency, was that "the orientation of the Twelfth Congress went in the wrong direction."[39] In a strikingly pointed phrase, CC member Dusan Dragosavac told the 22nd Session of the Central Committee in November 1985 that Yugoslavia could "more easily endure a multiparty system along[side] a united League of Communists than a coalition of a number of [regional] parties within the League of Communists."[40] Strange solutions started to be proposed, such as eliminating separate status for the regional party organizations, dropping the presidents of republican central committees from ex officio membership in the LCY Presidium, suppressing local autonomy in scientific institutes, and—perhaps most surprising of all— selectively dropping the "ethnic keys" which assigned fixed quotas to specific nationality groups in sundry party and governmental bodies. In the last instance, it was argued specifically that if the LCY Central Committee was ever going to function efficiently, it would have to be reduced in size—a measure which would require some compromise with the network of ethnic, social, and age keys applied in selecting that body's membership.[41] Ultimately, the Central Committee's membership was reduced to 129 members.

In a related move, which simultaneously reflected the strains produced by Serb-Albanian frictions in Kosovo, the Constitutional Court of Serbia handed down a decision (in October 1985) annulling a number of decrees relating to cadres policy in Kosovo—decrees which had guaranteed ethnic representation in the leadership proportionate to the given group's presence in the province. These decrees had been the instrument whereby the numerically dominant Albanians had taken over the provincial party apparatus in the course of the 1970s. According to the court, however, "the application of proportional national representation . . . facilitates the suppression of the numerically smaller nations and nationalities, which is contrary to the principles of equality laid down in the constitution. Also, this principle endangers the guaranteed rights of citizens to have equal access to every job and function."[42]

What these and other proposals reflected was that the issue of recentralization vs. continued decentralism was steadily becoming the dominant subject of debate.

On the eve of the Thirteenth Party Congress, regional differences on the subject remained clear. The Slovenian Party Congress (held in April 1986), for instance, emphasized the "unacceptability" of approaches which used the economic crisis "to put forward centralist-unitarist solutions."[43] By contrast, the Montenegrin Party Congress—held a few days later—underlined the importance of "unity" in finding solutions, to the extent of seconding the earlier call for bringing scientific institutes throughout the country under central direction.[44]

But in the course of 1986, it became clear that the decentralists were becoming more isolated and less sure of themselves—with the Slovenian party remaining the only regional party organization which continued to champion the decentralized system. Centralizers were, in short, able to put together a working consensus for a partial reconstitution of central authority. The Thirteenth LCY Congress, held 25–28 June 1986, was thus replete with calls for party unity and warnings about the effects of the conversion of local party organizations by technocratic interests into agents for purely local interests. The new party statute, adopted at the Congress, transferred the right to elect members of the Central Committee from the republics to the LCY Congress, entrusted the Central Committee with the authority to oversee the work of republic and provincial party organizations and if necessary to convoke extraordinary republic and provincial congresses to halt local deviations, and—should that fail—to convoke an Extraordinary LCY Congress to rein in a headstrong republic party organization.[45] In addition, the new statute provided a more explicit affirmation of the controversial principle of democratic centralism and strengthened the ability of the party organs to discipline wayward party members.[46] In sum, as Josip Vrhovec put it, the changes were designed to reverse the processes through which the party "was beginning to lose its vanguard role."[47]

There were those who wanted to carry recentralization further yet, and a more general pressure for political change, whether in one direction or another. But as long as the party maintained its political monopoly, there were some serious constraints on political change in Yugoslavia. The first and most important factor, which I have taken pains to document, was the division of the party into eight autonomous regional organizations, gravitating toward four distinct and conflictual policy positions. A second factor—which strongly suggested that the decentralization of the 1970s could not easily be reversed, if at all—was the ethnic dimension. The sundry nationality groups had grown accustomed to governing their own republics, and—as would become clear at the end of the decade—any serious effort at recentralization could, in the circumstances, only carry grave risk.

Third, even aside from the regional elites themselves, the decentralized system threw up other vested interests, whether in the political-administrative hierarchy or in economic decision-making, interests which could be expected to fear the consequences of change in the system.

Fourth, where the "national question" was concerned, there was a more specific—if often unspoken—fear of the repercussions that curtailment of autonomy or the introduction of a "new course" would have in Croatia (the scene of a powerful nationalist movement, 1967–71) and in Kosovo (shaken by Albanian riots throughout the province in 1968 and again in 1981). A curious symptom of party caution in this area was the omission of any reference to Albanian nationalist disorders in Kosovo from the draft platform for the Thirteenth Party Congress—an omission promptly criticized by the Zagreb daily, *Vjesnik*.[48]

And fifth, there was the fact that the intelligentsia up to then had by and large accepted the premise that even the most thorough going overhaul of the system should be undertaken in partnership with actors in the regime, rather than in opposition to the regime and the system. At that time, thus, declarations that the system had failed tended to be translated into political debate, rather than into political opposition. Yet, one must register a caveat, for below the surface, the process of the defection of the intellectuals had already begun, and by 1987, various intellectuals in Belgrade, Zagreb, and Ljubljana were quietly working to overhaul, and perhaps overthrow, the system.[49] There voices, inaudible in 1985, became more and more audible, culminating in the formation of alternative political parties by some of these same intellectuals in the course of 1988–89.

CHAPTER TWO

◆

The Gathering Storm, 1987–1989

AS THE 1980s WORE ON, it became clear that the deepening economic crisis and the political inertia which characterized the system were profoundly incompatible. Rising ethnic frictions in Kosovo and, just below the surface, in Bosnia were straining the political fabric at another level too. Increasingly, there were voices calling for a "return" to some imagined pristine centralism—calls originating largely among Serbs.

In 1987, the entire political picture changed virtually overnight. A 46-year old banker-turned-politician named Slobodan Milosevic had risen to the post of chair of the Central Committee of the Serbian party in 1986, when his friend and mentor, Ivan Stambolic, assumed the post of Serbian president. Milosevic turned against his erstwhile mentor, and by September 1987, scored a major victory over him. In mid-December, Milosevic engineered Stambolic's removal from the presidency, and asserted his unilateral control of the Serbian republic.[1] Milosevic quickly abandoned the long-standing strategies of the LCY and the Serbian party organization and set out to suppress the autonomous provinces (annexing them to Serbia), to recentralize the system (at the expense of the autonomy of the other republics), and to rehabilitate the Serbian Orthodox Church, coopting it to serve as the vehicle of a revived Serbian nationalism. His policies destroyed what remained of any consensus in the system, and by late 1989, for all practical purposes (legislative, economic, cultural), Yugoslavia had ceased to exist. In its place there were four emerging national environments, which claimed the primary loyalty of their citizens. These were: Slovenia, Croatia, Serbia (including the autonomous provinces of Kosovo and Vojvodina, as well as the republic of Montenegro), and Macedonia. These four regions were increasingly self-contained and even isolated from each other, and cultural contact between them, at one time actively stimulated by the party, had become, by then, largely superficial. Serbian and Slovenian nationalism was in full blaze, while in Croatia, despite a certain passivity that could be dated to the suppression of the "Croatian spring" in December 1971, there was a marked hostility toward everything Serbian and the traditional Western orientation reasserted itself. Only in Macedonia did one still find a real sense of "Yugoslavism," although even there, there were increasing signs of grumbling about Macedonia's alleged second-rate status in the federation. And finally, multi-ethnic Bosnia-Herzegovina—43.77 percent "ethnic Muslim," 31.46 percent Serbian, and 17.34 percent Croatian (in 1991)—was internally divided and its political infrastructure shattered along ethnic lines. Bosnian officials openly described the political situation in the republic as "difficult," with some observers calling greater Serbian nationalism the greatest problem at this point and others charging that fundamentalist Islam was driving Bosnian Serbs to take flight.[2]

The Serb-Croat conflict has always been at the center of political strife, at least potentially, and in the fragile conditions associated with the rise of Slobodan Milosevic in Serbia, reemerged as the pivotal conflict in Yugoslavia. Serbian politicians spread stories of a "Vatican-Comintern conspiracy" (supposedly designed in part to benefit Croatia), and accused Croatian politicians of genocidal tendencies. Radio Mileva in Belgrade accused Croat Ante Markovic, the chair of the Federal Executive Council, of being a CIA agent, while Serbian poet Gojko Djogo's description of the Croatian communist authorities as "pro-*Ustasha*" was given publicity.[3] At the same time, Serbs talked of the Orthodox (hence "Serbian") ancestry of Croatia's Dalmatian population, revived demands for autonomy for Serbs living in Croatia, and even talked of the political rehabilitation of wartime Chetnik leader Draza Mihailovic.[4]

Croatian politicians in turn accused Serbian leader Slobodan Milosevic of "Stalinist" and "unitarist" tendencies and charged that Serbian politicians were trying to destabilize and neutralize Croatia.[5] Hence when economist Jovo Opacic attempted to organize a Serbian cultural society in Croatia in July 1989, Croatian leaders had him arrested and tried.

In quasi-confederal Yugoslavia, the six constituent republics already enjoyed vast autonomy and operated, to a considerable extent, as independent mini-states. This system had been developed in the course of the late 1960s and early 1970s in order to satisfy the desires of the distinct nationality groups for a measure of political self-determination, while at the same time preserving the communist power monopoly. The alternative route—of maintaining a unified political system but opening it up to alternative parties—had been rejected. Conscious of the relationship between pluralization and self-determination, thus, the communists substituted regional pluralization (administrative decentralization) for political pluralization (multi-party democracy), and justified the substitution by arguing that a multi-party system would only lead to fratricidal war in Yugoslav conditions. In order to maintain this fiction, Yugoslav politicians stoked the fires of inter-ethnic distrust by constant commentaries on the ethnic genocides of World War Two. Indeed, even today, it often seems that World War Two has never ended for Yugoslav politicians.

Regional pluralization quickly became a powerful force for liberalization—both because some of the leading advocates of decentralization were also liberals, and because the division of power created alternatives within the system: people who were unable to publish something in one republic, for example, might turn around and publish the same text in another republic.

This system could function reasonably smoothly as long as two conditions were present. First, it was necessary to have a final arbiter who could resolve inter-republican differences if need be. President Josip Broz Tito functioned as this arbiter until his death in May 1980; but the system he bequeathed to Yugoslavia, based on collective decision-making at all levels and the right of veto by any republic in many areas of decision-making, lacked such an arbiter.

And second, the system presumed a degree of prosperity, such as existed in the later 1970s. When the economy eroded, however, the political seams were exposed to full view and the "quasi-legitimacy" of the system disintegrated. Now, with inflation roaring at more than 1000 percent annually, and incomes sagging below minimal levels, people were becoming desperate. In some cities, people decided to live without electricity, since they could not pay the bills.[6] Crime also soared, and authorities linked the increase with economic crisis.[7] In Montenegro, 30,000 desperate citizens took to the streets in August 1989, to protest against hunger and poverty and to demand effective action.[8] And increasingly, there was talk of the need to reprivatize the economy.

In this context, Ciril Ribicic and Zdravko Tomac—the former a member of the Central Committee of the League of Communists of Slovenia, and the latter a member of the Political Science Faculty of the University of Zagreb—coauthored a book in which they argued for the "de-etatization" of the economy and the strengthening of certain features of the federation, in order to assure optimal conditions for the development of a modern market economy. As they argued, "a new economic system requires a new political system, a new economic system cannot be built within the framework of the old political system."[9]

There was a gathering consensus in Yugoslavia that the status quo could not endure much longer. In such conditions, solutions which only a year or two earlier would have sounded extreme, were now openly discussed. In summer 1989, for example, Vladimir Rabzelj, a Slovenian writer, proposed the secession of Slovenia and Croatia and their association in a new confederal state.[10] Along parallel lines, Serbian writer Antonije Isakovic, famous for his novels *Tren I* and *Tren II,* argued for the redrawing of republic boundaries and the confederalization of the system.[11]

In September 1989, in a move which would have been unthinkable only a year earlier, the Slovenian Assembly passed a series of amendments to their constitution, unilaterally granting the Slovenian republic the right of secession and the right to approve or disapprove the proclamation by federal authorities of extraordinary measures in their republic. This highly controversial move, which excited public protest meetings in Montenegro and which was immediately taken to the Federal Constitutional Court for resolution, was, thus, only symptomatic of the breakdown of the sense of community, of consensus on the rules of the game.[12]

THE MOBILIZATION OF SLOVENIA

The Slovenian amendments, which were hotly attacked in the Serbian press throughout September, were the outgrowth of the mobilization of the Slovenian public in the course of 1988 and 1989. This process can be dated to the publication by the Slovenian journal, *Nova revija* (in February 1987), of a collection of articles devoted to the "Slovenian national program," which included, *inter alia,* a protest against the second-class status of the Slovenian language in Yugoslavia.[13] But more properly, the mobilization of the Slovenian public must be traced to the trial of Janez Jansa, Ivan Borstner, David Tasic, and Franci Zavrl (the editor of *Mladina*) for publishing material about a military plan to mop up liberalism in Slovenia. The trial inflamed the Slovenian public, and the fact that the trial was conducted in Serbo-Croatian, although on Slovenian territory, only aggravated passions. There were repeated public protests, including a large demonstration by at least 40,000 people from all over Slovenia, on Ljubljana's Liberation Square, on 22 June 1988. It was the largest public gathering of Slovenes since World War Two.[14]

In response to the trial, an independent Committee for the Protection of Human Rights was formed in Ljubljana, and began issuing periodical bulletins in English.[15] More than 100,000 persons signed protest petitions drawn up by the committee, along with more than 1,000 collective organizations, including the local trade union and the Slovenian Bishops' Conference of the Catholic Church. The successful creation of this committee encouraged others, and over the course of the next few months, several embryonic political parties were launched, including the Social Democratic Alliance, the Slovenian Democratic Union, the Slovenian Christian Socialist Movement, and a "Green" Party. Meanwhile, a previously existing Slovenian Peasant Union experienced rapid growth and by September 1989, claimed some 25,000 members from all parts of Slovenia.[16]

This pluralization was tolerated by the Slovenian authorities, and this tolerance in turn encouraged both the vibrant Slovenian youth organization and the long stagnant Socialist Alliance—both nominally transmission belts for party policy—to begin plans to transform themselves into independent political parties and to field their own candidates in Slovenia's spring 1990 elections. Polls taken in August 1989 ranked the Slovenian youth organization as the most popular (potential) political party, with the Socialist Alliance in second place, and the League of Communists trailing as a distant third. Yet although the Socialist Alliance of *Slovenia* talked about functioning independently, the Socialist Alliance of *Yugoslavia* expressed no such intention; hence, the Socialist Alliance of Slovenia would in due course have to separate from the Yugoslav organization.[17] In practice, SAWPY broke up the following year, when the regional organizations in Slovenia and Croatia did indeed transform themselves into new "Socialist" parties, and when the Serbian branch merged with the League of Communists of Serbia to form a supposedly new "Socialist Party of Serbia." By the end of 1990, SAWPY no longer existed.

Meanwhile, membership in the Slovenian communist party was steadily declining for about five years. Party organizations at many factories and enterprises completely disintegrated.[18] To the extent that the party still commanded some prestige, it was in part attributable to the party's popular leader, Milan Kucan, who was easily the most popular politician in that republic (as demonstrated by his subsequent election as Slovenia's president in the free elections of spring 1990).

The Slovenes claimed that their republic, the richest and most efficient in the country, was being milked by the less efficient republics. As a result, they jealously guarded their autonomy and, at a minimum, hoped to preserve the quasi-confederal character of the system. In the wake of the trial of "the four" (Jansa et al.), the Slovenes increasingly talked about the virtues of "asymetric federation," under which they would enjoy certain special prerogatives not enjoyed by other republics. A key demand associated with this concept was for a special Slovenian military district, with all Slovenian recruits serving in Slovenian regiments, and with Slovenian as the language of command. Secession was described by essentially all Slovenes as a "last resort," if all else should fail.

Furthermore, Ciril Ribicic, in a speech to the Slovenian Central Committee on 26 September, described the new amendment sanctioning secession, as consistent with the existing federal constitution.[19]

Other republics, especially Serbia, Montenegro, and Bosnia, looked with dismay at Slovenian developments. The Yugoslav collective presidency at first demanded that the proposed Slovenian amendments be discussed at one of its sessions—but the Slovenian presidency categorically rejected the suggestion.[20] Arguments were heard in Belgrade that whatever the Slovenes might say, their proposed amendments, including the amendment concerning secession, were in fact contrary to the federal constitution. When the Slovenes remained undaunted, others talked of summoning an urgent, extraordinary session of the Federal Assembly.[21] The Slovenes went ahead undaunted, and passed their amendments.

SERBIAN NATIONAL REVIVAL AND ITS EFFECTS

The Serbian party championed a very different solution. As early as September 1981, Ivan Stambolic, a member of the Serbian Central Committee, had argued that a "unified and strong Serbia" was a prerequisite for a strong Yugoslavia;[22] the extension of vast autonomy to the autonomous provinces of Kosovo and Vojvodina, he argued, had resulted not merely in the federalization of Serbia, but in its effective disintegration.[23] By 1984, Serbia was actively pressing for the reduction of the autonomy of the provinces, as well as for an expansion of the decision-making powers of the federal organs vis-à-vis the republics. The Serbs thus were once more championing a strong center—a position often tainted with the pejorative term "unitarism" in Yugoslav parlance. Slobodan Milosevic, then only a regular member of the Serbian Central Committee, struck a defiant note. "We must free ourselves of the complex of unitarism," he said in November 1984. "Serbian communists have never been champions of unitarism. On the contrary, we have throttled every attempt at such a policy. The Serbian communists have long been saddled with a complex about unitarism, and unjustly so, and made to feel guilty for a relationship with the Serbian bourgeoisie."[24]

Despite the clarity of the Serbian position, there seemed to be little progress toward realizing Serbian objectives. Stambolic, who had served as president of the Serbian Central Committee since April 1984, was seen by many as a careerist whose commitment to the Serbian program was largely formal. Milosevic, in particular, wanted a new strategy. By summer 1987, the waxing conflict between Milosevic and Stambolic was in the open, and in autumn 1987, Stambolic was forced to resign.

In the ensuing months, Milosevic consolidated more power than any Yugoslav leader had enjoyed since Tito—although with the important reservation that Milosevic's power was limited to the republics of Serbia and Montenegro. Milosevic removed a large number of party functionaries and replaced many of the journalists at the "Politika" publishing house. He appealed to Serbian pride and Serbian nationalism—for example, by introducing more Cyrillic in a republic which had, for years, been shifting more and more to the Latin alphabet. He granted the Serbian Orthodox Church permission to build new churches and to restore old ones. And by summer 1989, the Serbian Assembly was weighing which of two traditional hymns to adopt as the official anthem of Serbia: the popular but militant song, "March to the Drina," composed by Stanislav Binicki after a Serbian military victory in 1914; or the song "Tamo daleko" [There, afar], composed in 1916 by an unknown hand, while the Serbian army was in exile on the Greek island of Korfu.[25] In Tito's time part of the text of "Tamo daleko" was banned. Above all, Milosevic replaced provincial authorities in 1988 with people loyal to him, and succeeded, in early 1989, in ramming through a series of changes to the constitutions of the Serbian republic and its autonomous provinces, which effectively reduced the provinces to shadows of their former selves.

All of these measures were enormously popular among Serbs, and Milosevic was genuinely loved by many (though not all) Serbs, as no other leader had been since Draza Mihailovic. But the very reasons which endeared him to nationalist and traditionalist elements among the Serbs made him hated and feared in Croatia and Slovenia. Milosevic was a unifying force among Serbs, but a divisive factor in Yugoslavia as a whole.

In the course of 1989, Milosevic tried to create a base of support among non-Serbs by talking about a program of "anti-bureaucratic revolution." This campaign was, however, widely viewed with a combination of distrust and cynicism outside Serbia. And Croats in particular were mindful of the fact that Serbian nationalists were raising awkward issues, among them:

- Serbs began to talk about the large-scale transfer of industry from Serbia to Croatia and Bosnia in the years 1945–1951, a transfer which Serbs now said had been intended by Tito to weaken Serbia;[26]
- Serbs talked of the "Orthodox" origin of Dalmatian Croats;
- Serbs revived a long latent claim that Montenegrins were actually Serbs, and many Montenegrins responded warmly (such a claim had been taboo as long as Tito was in power);

- Serbs attacked the entire legacy of Tito, arguing that it was above all anti-Serbian in thrust, and suggested that it was time to weed out the confederal elements introduced by Tito (such as the veto system).[27]

Slovenia, Croatia, and Macedonia responded by trying to defend Tito's legacy, and Tito personally, against Serbian attacks. In the process, Tito received support in unlikely quarters. For example, Miko Tripalo, the Croatian party secretary purged by Tito in December 1971 for "liberalism," told me in September 1989, "Croatia can, at this point, be satisfied with its position in the federation. But it is gravely threatened by Milosevic, who is trying to bring about a totalitarian revolution and achieve Greater Serbian hegemony. This threatens not only Croatia but the other republics as well. It is critical, in these circumstances, to defend Tito. He is the symbol of everything that has been achieved."[28]

Milosevic's strategy was both populist and nationalist. In endeavoring to undermine the autonomy of the autonomous provinces (successfully) and to restore the primacy of the federal government (unsuccessfully, as of this writing, in June 1991), he restored to grace many Serbian dissidents, including Milovan Djilas and the accomplished poet Gojko Djogo. He restored the *Praxis* philosophers to positions of eminence. He allowed rumors to circulate about an eventual rehabilitation of Draza Mihailovic. And, as already mentioned, he allowed the Serbian Orthodox Church to revive. Milosevic's policies in Kosovo and Vojvodina made him a national hero among Serbian nationalists. As recently as summer 1987, one could speak of real opposition currents in Serbia.[29] By the end of 1989, it was essentially impossible to speak of an opposition in Serbia: most of the opposition had gone over to Milosevic. For example, rock singer Bora Djordjevic, elected in 1989 to the Serbian Writers' Association in recognition of his prolific poetry, was writing nationalist poems about Kosovo,[30] and praised Milosevic for what he had done in the provinces. Throughout Serbia, Kosovo was in the air. Serbs gloated over their reconquest of the province. Serbian bookstores filled their shelves with books about Kosovo. Musical artists dedicated their works to Kosovo.[31] There was even a new perfume called "Miss 1389"—an allusion to the Battle of Kosovo of that year, when an invading Turkish army smashed the Serbian army, leaving the Kingdom of Serbia helpless. The Orthodox Church likewise waxed enthusiastic, and in June, published an interesting St. Vitus Day message in its newspaper, *Glas crkve*, which said, among other things: "The recent proclamation of the Republic Constitution restored to Serbia the sovereignty of the state over the whole of its territory, while retaining the existence of the two autonomies in its composition—*which can be accepted only as a temporary solution.*"[32]

The response of the Serbian opposition to Milosevic's rise had parallels in the other republics as well. It would be too much to speak of an "alliance" between regional elites and their "oppositions." But it was obvious to all concerned that there was a partial symbiosis of purpose between the Serbian political elite and the Serbian opposition, between the Slovenian political elite and the Slovenian opposition, and so on. This had consequences both for the internal politics of each republic and for the wider political climate in the country as a whole. (On the other hand, the Serbian Writers' Association boldly issued a seven-point appeal for political pluralism on 10 May, accusing Serbia's leadership of obstructing democracy.[33])

Directly related to this is the form assumed by the emergent national revival in Yugoslavia. Throughout the country there was a renewed interest in the past, especially in the national literature and national history. But in every case, this revival focused on the local nationality; in no instance did this revival assume an all-Yugoslav dimension. For example, in Serbia the revival of interest in earlier Serbian writers Njegos, Ivo Andric, and Milos Crnjanski, which began at least a decade ago, recently deepened and became politicized, with an increase of interest as well in contemporary Serbian writers Dobrica Cosic, Matija Beckovic, and Vuk Draskovic. In Slovenia, the literary revival focused on the earlier Slovenian writers Primos Trubar, France Preseren, and Ivan Cankar, with strong interest in such contemporary Slovenian writers as Andrej Hieng, Rudi Seligo, Tomas Salamun, and Drago Jancar. In both cases, the interest in the literary past was growing in direct proportion to the rise in national consciousness, and in the Slovenian case, to the growth of interest in Slovenian sovereignty.[34]

The national revival was also reflected, in part, in the growth of underground cultural groups. The cultural underground saw, in particular, the sprouting of multimedia "new art" groups in several cities: *Neue Slowenische Kunst* (New Slovenian Art) in Ljubljana, *Novi Evropski Poredak* (New European Order) in Zagreb, *Autopsija* in Ruma (near Belgrade), *Aporea* in Skopje, and *Metropolie Trans* in Osijek. These groups infused their art with political meanings, in multi-media "happenings" that featured avant garde music. *Neue Slowenische Kunst* (with its rock group "Laibach") is the best known in the West, because of its strident advocacy of totalitarianism; the group also distributed, at one point, a map showing Slovenian settlements at their greatest extent (in the 17th century)—which, given the quasi-Nazi effect of their music, suggested a kind of "Slowenien über Alles." *Aporea,* by contrast, looked to the more distant past—to the Byzantine empire—

for inspiration. The result was innovative music with strong liturgical sources and overtones. But in much the same way that *Neue Slowenische Kunst* came across as "foreign" to most Yugoslavs outside Slovenia, even more so, *Aporea* appealed strictly to a Macedonian audience, for only in Macedonia does Byzantium stir the soul. Nor is it merely a question of historical imagery; it is a question of differing national values.

At the most fundamental level, the peoples of Yugoslav lost the ability to understand each other—because they do not understand each other's values and concerns, or each other's perceptions. The president of the Serbian Writers' Union told me, for instance, that "the Albanians in Yugoslavia have more rights than minorities in any other country. They have their academy of sciences, their university, their institutes for language and culture, all the perquisites of cultural autonomy. The only thing they lack is their own national state on the territory of Serbia. The Serbs in Croatia do not enjoy as many rights as the Albanians in Kosovo."[35] To a Serb, this statement is perfectly clear and rational. To a Croat or a Slovene or a Macedonian, however, this statement is essentially unintelligible, and comes across, at best, as the emotionally charged lament of a Serbian nationalist.

Political and cultural ethnocentrism was reinforced by the tendency of Yugoslavia's nationality groups to read "their own" newspapers. Serbs read the Serbian press, Croats the Croatian press, and so on. This phenomenon extended even to Bosnia, with dramatic polarizing effects within the republic. More broadly, this signified the weakening of ties to Yugoslavia. As a prominent cultural figure told me in 1989, "the Yugoslav idea is starting to become unpopular in Yugoslavia. Nobody wants to be Yugoslav anymore. People want to be Serbian or Croatian or Slovenian. Yugoslavia doesn't mean anything anymore."[36]

Accompanying these developments, there was a revived interest in monarchy. Almost no one was seriously thinking of restoring the monarchy (although a Yugoslav opinion poll conducted in late 1988 showed that 5% of Slovenes would ideally prefer a monarchical government). But in Serbia, Croatia, and Montenegro, there were signs of a "pop" nostalgia for kings and queens. In Serbia, for example, Princess Jelena Karadjordjevic (who normally lives in Paris and in Peru) was invited by the Serbian Patriarchate to attend the 600th anniversary celebrations of the Battle of Kosovo, and received permission from Milosevic to do so. The Orthodox Church's nostalgia for the monarchy was also shown in its periodical, *Crkveni zivot,* which in 1989 featured a portrait of King Aleksandar on its front page.[37] Also in Serbia, on 10 September 1989, the remains of King Lazar were ceremoniously reinterred at the monastery of Ravanica, while local citizens hoisted a huge banner displaying the 14th century king's likeness,[38] and there was talk of transporting the last remains of King Petar II back to Yugoslavia, for burial in Oplenac.[39] Meanwhile, in Montenegro, the republic presidency agreed to receive back the remains of Montenegrin King Nikola I (a Montenegrin "green") and his family, and arrangements were made for transporting them back from San Remo.[40] And in Croatia, the decision was taken to restore the equestrian statue of Ban Josip Jelacic, the 19th century governor of Croatia, to the Square of the Republic (from which it had been removed in July 1947).[41] Jelacic, a loyal retainer of the Habsburgs, had been condemned by Marx for his role in suppressing the shortlived Hungarian Republic (1848–49), and accordingly became an important symbol for anti-communist sentiment in Croatia.

As Yugoslav unity disintegrated and nostalgia for the monarchy waxed, Crown Prince Alexander, heir to the throne of the Kingdom of Serbs, Croats, and Slovenes, offered himself as a potential king in a revived kingdom. He argued that he could provide an important symbol of unity, and that no other symbol could do the same. Despite his Serbian blood, Alexander had lived basically his entire life in England and was, for all practical purposes, a refined English gentleman first and foremost. He was not entangled in the politics of communist and post-communist Yugoslavia—a fact which encouraged some Yugoslavs to consider him a viable candidate. So removed from Yugoslavia was Alexander, in fact, that as of 1991, he was trying to learn Serbo-Croatian from a tutor. But English or not, Alexander had no power base of his own, and political discussions in the country made no reference to him. With some qualifications where Alexander is concerned (in that his popularity seemed to be greater among emigre Yugoslavs than among Yugoslavs in the country), the revival of interest in the monarchy, thus, was always nationally specific (Serbian, Croatian, Montenegrin), and thus, likewise reflected the fragmentation of the country into four environments.

POLITICAL FRAGMENTATION

It is not just culturally and economically that Yugoslavia was becoming fragmented. On the contrary, the country's fragmentation was also political, to the extent that it was necessary to speak of the emergence of different political systems in the separate republics. On the *formal* level, the political systems of the republics were still, as of autumn 1989, interchangeable: each republic had the same governmental and party structures, and—the Slovenian constitutional amendments aside— the same underlying legal-constitutional framework. On the *informal* level, however, there was a widening gap between the republics, not just in the matter of what was permitted, but also where basic procedures and operational strategies were concerned. Serbia, for example, had reverted to a traditional patrimonial system, and saw a revival of ethnic chauvinism and male chauvinism to underpin this reversion. Slobodan Milosevic was clearly the dominant figure in Serbia and people in key positions were either admirers and advocates of his, or afraid to speak out. Montenegro, run at that time by supporters of Milosevic, was, for all practical purposes, a colony of Serbia (as it remains in mid-1991). Bosnia, divided into three competing ethnic groups, was riven by intra-elite conflict and distrust, and mired by corruption. A local quip had it that Bosnia combined Austrian bureaucracy with Ottoman slowness and inefficiency—a deadly combination. Slovenia allowed opposition parties to organize, meet, and sell their newspapers on the street, and subsequently, allowed them to field candidates in the spring 1990 parliamentary elections. As in Serbia, there was a waxing rapport between the party and certain sections of the opposition, but in Slovenia, it was the opposition which was taking the initiative, not the other way around. In Croatia and Macedonia, loyalty to Tito was combined with incipient liberalism—in the former taking the form of efforts to democratize the party, while in Macedonia there were strong currents within the party in favor of moving toward a multi-party system. For example, in October 1989, Vasil Tupurkovski, the Macedonian member of the Yugoslav collective presidency, called pluralization the "top priority" on the agenda.[42] The Croatian party spoke of advocating a "Jugoslavenska sinteza" (Yugoslav synthesis), by which it meant essentially preservation of the federal system in something approximating its Titoist form; but at the same time, the Croatian party by then clearly favored a transition to a market economy and the establishment of a "semi-multiparty" system (in which "nationalist" parties would be proscribed).[43] At times, Croatian politicians seemed willing to go even further. For example, Marin Buble, a member of the Croatian Central Committee, told *Slobodna Dalmacija* in late 1989 "a multi-party system has become a necessity, indeed only a matter of time, because the development of a modern society presumes above all a modern economic market, as well as a developed democratic political system. You can't have one without the other. They are two sides of the same system."[44]

Ironically, the political fragmentation of the system was aggravated by Milosevic's attempt to consolidate a strong center. In the case of Macedonia, for example, which in 1988 was gravitating toward Milosevic's camp, the Serbs alienated Macedonians by trying to pass a measure that would have allowed Serbs who had land titles from the interwar period to reclaim their land. Although aimed at Kosovo, the measure would have had consequences in Macedonia too. The two republics fell out. Later, in October 1989, the Serbian leadership insensitively backed a proposal to declare 1 December—the day on which Yugoslavia was first united in 1918—a national holiday. This move again inflamed the Macedonians, who recalled that in its first incarnation, Yugoslavia was known as the "Kingdom of the Serbs, Croats, and Slovenes"—the Macedonians, then called "south Serbs," were excluded.[45] Almost at the same time, evidence surfaced that the Serbian security service had been operating in Bosnia without the knowledge or approval of Bosnian authorities; Ivan Cvitkovic, secretary of the Bosnian party presidency, denounced Serbia's actions as "an attack on the sovereignty of Bosnia-Herzegovia."[46]

Milosevic's championing of "an effective, modern state" also won him enemies. The reaction to Milosevic recapitulated, in some ways, the reaction sparked by 18th century Habsburg Emperor Josef II, who sought to consolidate a strong center, spoke in terms of political "modernization," championed a certain kind of liberalism, and ultimately inflamed insecurity among the non-German peoples of his empire by promoting German as the single language of administration. A central demand in Milosevic's program was for a reform of the Federal Assembly. Under the system bequeathed by Tito, both houses of the bicameral legislature apportioned equal numbers of delegates to each constituent republic. Milosevic argued that this was inconsistent with the democratic principle of "one human, one vote." He demanded that *one* of the two chambers—specifically, the Federal Chamber—be reorganized so that the delegates to that chamber would represent equal numbers of citizens. In effect, his proposal would have closely followed the American model. The Slovenes, however, angrily rejected this proposal as a device to undermine their sovereignty, and both Slovenes and Croats worried that the proposal might be designed to give the Serbs political hegemony within the system. The fact that Serbs were enthusiastic about the proposal only seemed to confirm Slovenian and Croatian fears.

ISSUES ON THE AGENDA

There were four pivotal issues on the Yugoslav political agenda in the late 1980s: the federal question, the economy, pluralization, and the breakdown of the sense of community.

The federal question. There were four alternative scenarios available, that attempted to preserve the Yugoslav state: confederalization (championed by a few Slovenian intellectuals, along with Serbian novelist Antonije Isakovic, and others), asymmetric federation (championed by the Slovenian party), consolidation of a strong center (championed by the Serbian party and most Serbian intellectuals), and continuation of the status quo (not really championed by anyone, although Macedonia was clearly wary of any of the alternatives being proposed). Beginning in 1988, both communists and non-communists tended, on the whole to discuss the first two scenarios within the framework of the continuation of the post-Titoist system of regional state monopolies, that is to say, with local republic elites making the key decisions affecting economic development and political life within their republics. Taken in isolation, thus, the federal question accentuated the nationalities question, even as it distorted it. Indeed, the federal question dominated discussion and marginalized all other questions—which was dangerous insofar as all four issues were serious.

The economy. There was a broad consensus among both economists and laymen in Yugoslavia that radical economic reform was needed. In the more developed republics, the tendency was to talk in terms of reprivatization and the establishment of a true market economy. In the less developed republics, chiefly Macedonia and Bosnia, there were those who feared that such a change would only benefit the more developed regions, and that they would be net losers. More fundamentally, reprivatizing the economy was a political question. Dismantling nationalized enterprises meant that republic elites, state-appointed directors, and the self-managing interest communities would all lose power. Inevitably, there were those who resisted reprivatization.

Pluralization. There were about a dozen independent political parties in Yugoslavia as of late 1989—some legally registered, some awaiting registration, and some denied registration and thus technically illegal. Most of these were based in Ljubljana or Zagreb. There were also between one and two dozen independent social and political interest groups, devoted variously to feminist, ecological, gay rights, pacifist, cultural, or other concerns. Most of these were based in Belgrade, Ljubljana, and Zagreb, although some were to be found in other cities. Many of them were issuing bulletins or other periodicals; some of them (particularly in Slovenia) were protected through registration as an activity of the local youth organization (a legal fiction).

Political pluralization in Yugoslavia was a symptom of societal mobilization and reflected, at the same time, the breakdown of the old political order. At the same time, the question of pluralization was organically tied to the federal question, since it lay within the jurisdiction of republic, not federal, authorities to grant or withhold the registration of political associations.

Breakdown of the sense of community. The foregoing issues were well understood in Yugoslavia and were being intelligently, albeit sometimes polemically, debated. Surprisingly, the breakdown of the sense of community, which was intuitively clear, received almost no explicit attention in the press, and there have been no serious proposals to deal with this issue—i.e., unless secession of one or another republic is counted as a "solution."

And yet this fourth dilemma threatened the stability of the Yugoslav political order. The breakdown of communication across republic borders and nationality groups is the key to the disintegration of inter-ethnic relations in Yugoslavia in the late 1980s—a process which can be traced, on one level, to the Kosovo riots of April 1981,[47] and, on another level, to the very foundation of the state. So far advanced was this process by 1989 that people spoke openly of impending civil war, and compared Yugoslavia to Lebanon.

Reprivatization and political pluralization might have defused the crisis, had they been carried out at the end of the 1970s, or even by 1984 or 1985. But the longer the delay, the more economic deterioration aggravated the entire political climate and contributed, in particular, to the worsening of inter-ethnic relations.

Some Yugoslavs took to citing the Helsinki Act, which barred any change in European borders, as an impediment to Slovenian secession or to the breakup of Yugoslavia. The citation was folly. Western powers were, to be sure, ready to provide Yugoslavia with much needed credits, at least until Milosevic's unconstitutional moves in spring 1991, but it was scarcely to be believed that the signatories of the Helsinki Act would use armed force to hold Yugoslavia together.

CHAPTER THREE

◆

Brotherhood and Unity, 1989–1991

ON 25 JUNE 1991, Slovenia and Croatia unilaterally declared their independence, making good on their threat to take matters into their own hands if interrepublican negotiations remained deadlocked.[1] The following day, the Serb-dominated Yugoslav National Army (JNA) sent tanks and helicopters crashing across the Croatian-Slovenian border into Slovenia. Hundreds of Slovenian civilians were killed or wounded, alongside casualties among both JNA units and units of the Slovenian Territorial Militia. The JNA strafed civilian trucks, bombed private homes and farms, and shot and killed civilians sitting at cafes, working in their fields, and engaging in other peaceful pursuits. The army also wrought considerable damage to Slovenia's economic infrastructure, including roads and bridges. The army, which in late 1990, had formed a special political party linked to Slobodan Milosevic and pledged to restoring hardline communism throughout the country, was clearly demonstrating *its* understanding of the meaning of the old Titoist phrase, "brotherhood and unity."

After two days of fighting, the JNA controlled the Ljubljana airport and all major access roads to Italy, Austria, and Hungary. The sides agreed on a truce. The European community signalled their refusal to recognize Slovenian or Croatian independence, and sent a delegation to pressure the combatants to find a peaceful solution, while US Secretary of State James Baker advised Slovenes to negotiate—a recommendation that amounted to advising the Slovenes to capitulate to Serbian hegemony and the prospect of re-communization. Do Slovenes and Croats enjoy the right of national self-determination? Slobodan Milosevic, the JNA, the European community, and the US Department of State all joined in giving a resounding "no" to this question. That is unlikely to be the end of the story, however.

SOURCES OF DISCORD

The country has, of course, been beset with problems from the time of its establishment in 1918, and one may quite accurately say that no sooner was the multi-ethnic state constituted than it started to fall apart. Over the course of its 70-year history, Yugoslavia lurched from crisis to crisis, abandoning one unstable formula for another. Finally, in the course of 1989–91, the unifying infrastructure of the country largely dissolved. Slovenia and Croatia first declared that their local laws took priority over federal laws. The republics subsequently withheld budgetary contributions to the federal government, throwing the federal budget into crisis. Three republics (Slovenia, Croatia, and Bosnia) issued declarations of sovereignty (in 1990) and threatened to secede (albeit under rather different conditions). A fourth republic—Macedonia—has also, at this writing, been considering issuance of a similar declaration of sovereignty. Economic, cultural, and social relations between the republics were largely frozen, if not cut off altogether. For all practical purposes, Yugoslavia had already broken up, even before the crises of 1991. The question was whether its squabbling politicians could manage to piece this Humpty Dumpty together again. To do so, they would have needed to find a radically new formula.

Yet, any peaceful dismantling of the union would have required some meeting of minds, some willingness on the part of all concerned to recognize that the status quo was untenable and that the problem could not be resolved by force. But, as an anonymous Slovene wit put it recently, Yugoslavia is in such a mess that it can not even disintegrate properly. Serious nationality-based conflicts and disagreements have marred Yugoslav politics from the beginning, and the intractability of differences has often encouraged extremist solutions, which predictably have crashed on the shoals of opposition.

The years 1918–1945 saw a series of experiments with pseudo-democratic Serbian hegemony, royal dictatorship, Serb-Croat settlement with other groups neglected, and fascism. None of these formulas worked.

Josip Broz Tito's partisans started out as run-of-the-mill Stalinists. But their expulsion from the Cominform by Stalin in June 1948 forced them to find their own formula, and in the process, gave them a new image. Tito became the new David, to Stalin's Goliath, and was seen as a hero in the West. And in the 1960s and 1970s, it even appeared that Yugoslavia had finally found the key to solving its most important problems. The constitution of 1974 seemed to provide political stability (using cautiously crafted practices of ethnic quotas, strict rotation of cadres, and the universal enjoyment by constituent republics of the right to veto federal legislation). The economy was enjoying a boom. And then there was Tito—who played a crucial role as arbiter in the system, pulling it back from deadlock when all else failed. Even the nationality question seemed—in the years 1971–1981—to have been laid to rest.

But between 1979 and 1982, several things changed, causing Yugoslavia's leaders to reach the point, by 1983, of openly admitting, for the first time since 1948 expulsion, that the country was in crisis. First, the economy began to deteriorate—largely as a result of internal dynamics; the process was sharpened and quickened by the steep increase in oil prices after 1973. Second, the deaths of Vice President Edvard Kardelj in 1979 and President Tito in 1980 deprived the country not only of unifying symbols, but more importantly, of strong leaders capable of imposing unity. A third factor contributing to the disintegration of the old order was the outbreak, in April 1981, of widespread anti-Serbian rioting among the Albanian population of the then-autonomous province of Kosovo. These riots proved to be the clarion call of a new phase in which underground groups of Albanian nationalists proliferated and in which Serb-Albanian frictions intensified. And fourth, there was the disastrous prime ministership of Branko Mikulic, whose mismanagement contributed to a general plummeting of public confidence in government officials and whose term of office was blemished, in particular, by the damaging Agrokomerc financial scandal of summer 1987.

Yet for all that, it required a catalyst to take Yugoslavia from "mere" crisis to the brink of civil war. That catalyst was Slobodan Milosevic. As already noted, Milosevic ended the policy of balance identified with his predecessor, Ivan Stambolic, and adopted a program of bare-faced Serbian nationalism. Milosevic took politics to the streets, mobilizing large crowds of angry peasants (mostly middle-aged males) in a move to topple the local governments of the Republic Montenegro and the provinces of Vojvodina and Kosovo. Sweeping his rivals out of power in these federal units, he installed his own supporters. Meanwhile, in a series of measures, he dismantled the autonomy of the provinces, subordinated them to the Serbian legislature and court system, shut down the provincial assembly in Kosovo (an illegal move on his part), ordered the arrest of the duly-elected members of the now-banned Kosovo Assembly, and, finally, suppressed Kosovo's major Albanian-language daily newspaper, *Rilindja*.[2]

After dealing with Montenegro, Vojvodina, and Kosovo, Milosevic turned his eyes to Bosnia and Macedonia, as outlined in the preceding chapter. Even Slovenia and Croatia came to fear that Milosevic aspired to be a new Tito, and watched with horror as he promoted his "reform" plan, which aimed at reducing the powers of the republics and strengthening a central government which he, obviously, planned to control. Earlier allies in 1970–1971, Slovenia and Croatia had become politically estranged in the early and mid-1980s, at a time when party liberals prevailed in Slovenia, while party conservatives held sway in Croatia. Now, sharing a common apprehension of Serbia's nationalist regime, Slovenia and Croatia forged a new alliance, which gave rise to talk of the formation of a Slovenian-Croatian confederation (if the joint talks with the other republics should fail).

SERBS AND NON-SERBS

Yugoslavia did not arise on the basis of self-determination. It was created by Serbian bayonets, which installed the Serbian king as King of Yugoslavia. To force unity, Serbian armies had to put down armed resistance in several parts of the country, including in Montenegro and Kosovo.[3] The interwar regime was a Serbian regime to which Croats never assented, and in which Albanians, Muslims, and Macedonians were deprived of their national rights. Macedonians were treated as "south Serbs," and offered education in the Serbian language. Albanians were expelled wholesale to Albania; the Belgrade regime confiscated their land, some 154,287 acres, turning much of it over to Serbian settlers.[4] The government propagated a theory of the "tri-named people," which held that everyone in the kingdom, aside from the Albanians, was "really" a Serb, even if some people might not agree. Croats, for example, were viewed as "Catholic Serbs," while Slovenes were considered "alpine Serbs." The Slovenes' distinctive language was declared to be "poor Serbian."

All of this created problems which culminated in the splintering of the country in World War Two, and the installation of a fascist regime in Croatia. Large numbers of people of all nationalities died in Yugoslavia during the war. But when the war ended, instead of subsiding, inter-ethnic hatreds hardened, feeding on bitter recollections of the interwar kingdom and the war. Shortsighted party leaders stoked these hatreds, by dwelling endlessly on the atrocities of the war, and by blaming many of them (in Croatia) on the Catholic Church and its functionaries.

The past has never been laid to rest in Yugoslavia. By contrast with the United States, where historical memory is quite short, peoples in Yugoslavia talk about events in 1389, 1459, 1921, 1941, 1948, 1970–1971, as if they were fresh. The wounds of the past have never healed. In a recent illustration of the way the past haunts the present, tens of thousands of anti-communist demonstrators assembled on 27 March to mark the 50th anniversary of the military coup that overthrew a pro-

Nazi Serbian government and to draw a parallel to the present Serbian regime, which many accuse of "fascism." Or again, the Party of Democratic Action of Kosovo included, in its program, a demand for autonomy for the Sandzak of Novi Pazar, on the argument that the Sandzak was a part of Bosnia in 1459.[5]

The past has also figured actively in the lively polemics between the pro-Milosevic and anti-Milosevic camps, most especially in the arsenal of anti-Croatian rhetoric spewed out by Serbia's controlled press. For Yugoslavs, World War Two seems never to have ended. Serbs continue to assail the Catholic Church for alleged complicity in wartime atrocities—provoking the Church, at one point, into publishing a wartime Vatican decree in which the Holy See had explicitly forbidden its clergy to collaborate in any way with the Croatian fascist authorities (the *Ustasha*). Croatian historian and political activist Franjo Tudjman devoted his 1989 *Absurdities of Historical Reality,* to debunking Serbian myths about the past.[6]

Of course, different nationalities remember the past in different ways. The Serbs remember the Tito era as an anti-Serbian era, and cite Tito's transfer of large numbers of industrial plants from Serbia to Croatia and Slovenia in the late 1940s, which Serbs say was motivated by the desire to weaken and despoil Serbia. Serbs have also complained that the creation of the republics of Montenegro and Bosnia was artificial and that those territories, along with the territories established as autonomous provinces, should have been placed under strict Serbian control. Croats and Albanians, by contrast, are apt to remember Tito's many concessions to the Serbs, in particular in the first 20 years of communism. The 1946 trial of Croatian archbishop Alojzije Stepinac, on trumped-up charges of collaboration with the *Ustasha,* was, in Croatian eyes, a concession to Serbian hatred (especially among Orthodox clergy and believers) of Catholics and Croats alike. Likewise, Croats, Macedonians, Albanians, and ethnic Muslims alike remember that until July 1966, Tito worked closely with Aleksandar Rankovic, head of the secret police, in pursuing a centralist policy injurious to the interests of non-Serbs.

These different memories, set atop unhealed wounds, provide the seedbed for deep bitterness, resentments, and recurrent desires for revenge.

The Tito era need not have ended as it did. In the late 1960s and the dawn of the seventies, Tito allowed liberals in Slovenia, Croatia, Macedonia, and Serbia to chart a new course. The result was the growth among people of a sense of control over their own destiny. In particular, Croats vested great hope in the Croatian republic's leaders at that time—Miko Tripalo and Savka Dabcevic-Kucar—who came to be seen as legitimate leaders. Tripalo told me in 1989, that as a result of the loosening up of power structures, "there developed a rather broad democratic popular movement, which started to publish a large number of its own newspapers and magazines, thus creating forums in which people could speak freely. And the whole political life which had been closed to the public, now opened up and people started to speak their minds, both about the way things were then and about how things had been in the past."[7]

In December 1971, Tito removed Tripalo and Dabcevic-Kucar from power. He subsequently also fired liberals in the other republics. As a result, these liberals were mythologized in the public consciousness and even gained in stature as late Titoism cracked and crumbled. By late 1990, Tripalo and Dabcevic-Kucar had emerged from a kind of internal exile and were once again taking part in political discourse. In Macedonia, Kiro Gligorov, one of the liberals of the 1970–1971 era, returned to politics as president of Macedonia. In Slovenia, the memoirs of the late Stane Kavcic, the leading liberal of the early seventies, were published and widely read. In Slovenia, Croatia, Bosnia, and Macedonia, it was the dissidents of yesteryear who took hold of the reins of power in 1990. The current presidents of Croatia and Bosnia, in fact—Franjo Tudjman and Alija Izetbegovic—both spent time in prison in the early 1980s after being tried on charges, respectively, of Croatian nationalism and Islamic fundamentalism.

THE SPREAD OF CIVIL TURMOIL

During the years 1989–91, civil turmoil, which had overtly afflicted Kosovo since 1981, spread through much of the country, giving rise to serious fears of impending civil war. Civil turmoil often figures as a preliminary phase which ultimately gives rise to civil war. Yugoslavia was clearly in a state of civil turmoil by summer 1989. The question was, could it avert the final descent to civil war? As of the end of June 1991, however, a peaceful *and harmonious* (and hence, stable) solution appeared to be utterly impossible. Despite the erosion of interrepublican ties, beginning with the Slovenian-Serbian relationship, Yugoslav-minded politicians in the squabbling republics were not yet prepared to give up on the "Yugoslav idea." Throughout much of 1990, they pinned their hopes on democratization, privatization of the economy, and, in particular, on Ante Markovic's program of economic stringency, which, it was hoped, would finally restabilize the Yugoslav economy. Ultimately, they were disappointed. The introduction of multi-party elections proved insufficient because, despite the election of non-communist liberals in Slovenia, Croatia, Bosnia, and Macedonia, Slobodan Milosevic clung to power in Serbia and continued to advocate a policy aimed at maximizing Serbian hegemony, talking even of Serbia's desire to annex Montenegro, as well as large portions of Croatia and Bosnia.

Neither the destabilization of Kosovo nor the alienation of Slovenia was sufficient to push the Yugoslav drama to what now appears to be its final act. The heart of the Yugoslav national question has always been the Serb-Croat relationship, since these two long-standing rivals together constituted about 56 per cent of the country's population. Accordingly, the turning point came in the form of an uprising by Croatia's small Serbian minority (12 per cent of Croatia's total population). This uprising was adumbrated in summer 1989, when Dr. Jovo Opacic, a 45-year old Serbian economist, attempted to establish a cultural society for Croatia's Serbs (to build up special theaters, newspapers, radio stations, and other cultural and media infrastructure in the Serbian variant of the language). Croatia's then-communist authorities balked and put Opacic in prison. Developments took a dangerous turn in July 1990, when Croatian Serbs set up a Serbian National Council. Since this council was organized in defiance of the Croatian authorities and since its chief purpose was to work for Serbian autonomy within, or secession from, Croatia, it was, in fact, a potentially revolutionary body. During August and September 1990, the council conducted an illegal referendum among Croatia's 531,502 Serbs; some 756,549 Serbs voted for Serbian autonomy[8]—betraying the fact that many Serbs from Serbia had crossed over the border in order to influence the vote. But the Serbian uprising only turned violent in October, when local Serbs raided gun shops and police stations, arming themselves, set up barricades, and mined sections of railway lines leading into the districts of greatest Serbian concentration. Soon, arms shipments, supposedly earmarked for the Yugoslav National Army, were "inexplicably" routed through the Croatian town of Knin (center of the Serbian rebellion), where local Serbs unloaded the arms.[9]

With Slovenia already threatening secession, Croatia promised to secede if Slovenia did so, and Bosnian President Alija Izetbegovic underlined, on several occasions, that Bosnia would not remain associated with a truncated Yugoslavia ruled by Milosevic, and that if Croatia seceded, so too would Bosnia.[10] Serbian president Milosevic, in turn, declared that if the federation broke up, Serbia would seek to annex Serbian-inhabited portions of Croatia and Bosnia—which is geopolitical nonsense, since the populations, especially in Bosnia, are dispersed in such a way that it would be utterly impossible to draw a clear border dividing ethnic groups. In March 1991, Serbia organized Serbian defense units, not under federal command,[11] following similar moves by Slovenia and Croatia. Meanwhile, angry Serbs, spurred on by

Milosevic, formed "citizens' militias" in Croatia and Herzegovina; these militias are, of course, beholden to Milosevic, not to the local governments of the republics in which they operate.

The Serbian-dominated army, meanwhile, grew apprehensive of Slovenian and Croatian moves to slash their contributions to the military budget, and in November, formed a revived communist party, with Slobodan Milosevic's wife, Mirjana, among the leading figures of the party. In December, General Veljko Kadijevic, federal Minister of Defense, told a *Danas* reporter that the army would not permit Yugoslavia to become another "Lebanon,"[12] and the following month, the army came close to invading Croatia. An eleventh hour inter-republican agreement averted immediate danger, but the threat prompted Slovenia and Croatia to conclude an agreement to coordinate in the spheres of security and defense. A subsequent "assurance" from the army (in March) that it would not interfere in the political negotiations which continued among the heads of the six republics was not particularly assuring, in that the generals' communique clearly left open the possibility of military intervention to suppress Slovenian self-determination and quash the conflict between Serbs and Croats[13]—moves which would self-evidently be directed at Slovenia's and Croatia's expense and that many, including the present writer, suspected could can only contribute to intensifying inter-ethnic hatreds and igniting civil war. Rumors circulated in early 1991 to the effect that Admiral Branko Mamula, a former Defense Minister, supposedly intended to launch a coup, declare military rule, and set himself up as dictator.[14] But neither Kadijevic nor Mamula was in a position, in this multi-ethnic country, to play Jaruzelski. And even Jaruzelski, it will be recalled, ultimately failed and was forced to scuttle his own regime.

THE DISINTEGRATION OF THE ECONOMY

The Yugoslav economy has, for all practical purposes, disintegrated. With unemployment standing at more than 15 per cent, an annual inflation rate of 127 per cent (as of March 1991), a foreign debt of $22 billion, and a 1990 trade deficit of $2.7 billion, the economic infrastructure itself is becoming unravelled, holding the promise of continued deterioration. All six republics experienced economic decline in 1990. The worst off was Montenegro, where industrial production fell 15.8 per cent in the first nine months of 1990. During the same period, industrial production declined 13.5 per cent in Serbia, 10.8 per cent in Croatia, 10.6 per cent in Slovenia and Macedonia, and 6.2 per cent in Bosnia-Herzegovina.[15]

Markovic's widely touted program of economic reform, which was introduced in the beginning of 1990, froze wages and prices, and brought inflation down from a rate of 2,000 per cent annually to about 4 per cent, virtually overnight. But soon inflation once again crept upwards. Markovic's reform itself included pegging the dinar to the German mark, thus making the Yugoslav currency convertible. Unfortunately, the fixed exchange rate gave the dinar artificial strength, and the immediate result was a surge in imports, and the bankruptcy of many once-healthy exporters.[16] Foreign currency reserves plunged from $6.5 billion to $3.6 billion with a year,[17] forcing the Markovic government to abandon convertibility and devalue the dinar.

Reprivatization came too late to avert economic catastrophe. Although the private sector has been measurably more efficient that the social sector,[18] Yugoslavia's 16,490 private firms (as of February 1991) accounted for only 2.4 per cent of the overall income of the Yugoslav economy—too little to make a difference. Meanwhile, foreign investors were once again scared off. Political instability and the talk of civil war and military coup were bad enough. But add to that the severe difficulties in doing business across republic lines and the fact that local courts no longer recognized the validity of other republics' laws, and you have the makings of an especially undesirable investment prospect. Nationalism played a role in this too, as the republics took actions injurious to the economic interests of companies based in other republics. In Serbia, for example, the Croatian-based INA petrochemical company was forced to pay a 150 per cent surcharge on all gasoline sales, even though Serbian petrochemical companies paid no such tax; as a result, INA decided, early 1991, to curtail its operations in Serbia.

The Yugoslav government approached the West, hat in hand, with a request for yet another economic bailout, this time to the tune of $4 billion. Meanwhile, the Swiss newspaper, *Neue Zürcher Zeitung*, questioned whether it was realistic to pin any hopes on yet another infusion of money into this economically inefficient country, underlining that for all practical purposes, the productive sector in Yugoslavia had collapsed.[19] Even in relatively more prosperous Slovenia, even before the JNA wreaked severe damage on the republic's economic infrastructure in June 1991, local authorities expected the economy to decline for at least another two years, before any revival could begin.

THE FEDERAL BUDGET

All of this provided the backdrop for serious damage to the federal budget. Already in November 1990, Slovenia, Serbia, and Vojvodina announced that they would make no further tax payments to the federation.[20] After the Milosevic government stole some $1.8 billion from the federal treasury in December—essentially distributed among Serbs in the form of wage increases, in order to "buy" the election for Milosevic—the Slovenian and Croatian governments announced that they would recognize no further debts incurred by the federal government. As a result of these pressures, in December, the federal government was operating at a level 15 per cent below its basic budgetary needs, and had had to lay off some 2,700 federal officials, thus reducing the ability of the central government to function.[21] The federal government was unable, in turn, to meet its commitments to the republics (in the form of subsidies to the three less developed republics, funds for stimulating exports, war veterans' pension supplements, and other funds), and in March, the government of Bosnia announced that, unless the federal government settled its debts with Bosnia "within a week," Bosnia would cease all payments to the federal budget.[22] The governments of Montenegro and Macedonia also complained about the federal government's failure to honor financial commitments.[23] The republics, most especially Serbia, Croatia, and Slovenia, also slowed their contributions to the military budget. More particularly, the Slovenian government declared that it would not pay off its obligations to the army so long as there was a threat of the introduction of emergency measures, and that it was unilaterally reducing its contribution to the 1991 military budget from 15 billion dinars to about 3 billion dinars.[24] As a result, the army was not able to pay its bills, and some food suppliers refused to send any more provisions to the army, because they had not been paid in two months. To address this situation, the Federal Executive Council redirected some funds earmarked for other purposes to the army and, in February, took out a loan with the National Bank of Yugoslavia, in order to permit the army to continue to function.[25]

In a word, both the federal government and the army ended up in serious financial straits, and their ability to continue to function under given conditions became open to serious question. This consideration alone points to some proximate change in the political equilibrium in the country, regardless of the military clashes of June 1991 and their immediate results.

THE REPUBLICS AWAKEN

Enough has been said already to make it clear that the will to remain in union has seriously atrophied. As of late 1990, some 88 per cent of Slovenes considered secession their best option. In May 1991, 94.3 per cent of Croats likewise voted for independence; a sizeable majority of Albanians and a growing number of Macedonians also favored this solution for their own regions.[26] The figures for Slovenes and Croats would be close to 100 per cent as of mid-1991. The governments of Slovenia and Croatia became openly secessionist. Pro-secessionist movements emerged among the Muslims of Novi Pazar, the Albanians of Kosovo, and the Macedonians, alongside Serbian secessionist groups operating in parts of Croatia, Montenegro, and Bosnia, seeking annexation to Serbia.[27]

Kosovo occupied the top of the agenda for almost a decade after the spring 1981 riots.[28] Today Kosovo is already in a state of siege. The provincial assembly was shut down by Milosevic in July 1990, the major Albanian-language daily was suppressed on orders from Milosevic, even the local youth organization "no longer exists."[29] At the same time, while the Serbian government continued to fire Albanian employees in Kosovo indiscriminately, local Albanians and Serbs organized antagonistic "self-defense units," arming themselves for a showdown.[30] In January, the Skopje-based Albanian-language paper, *Flaka e Vellazerimit,* reported that Serbian authorities were confiscating arms possessed by Albanians, even those for which they had proper licenses, while Serbs went unharrassed and were allowed to retain unlicensed arms, with no questions asked.[31]

As for the idea that the army could play a tranquilizing role in Kosovo, note should be taken of the latest rash of reports of the murder of Albanian recruits by Serbian conscripts in the Yugoslav National Army.[32] A survey conducted by the popular Albanian-language newspaper, *Zeri i Rinise,* in early 1991 found that more than half of Kosovar Albanians surveyed hoped for annexation by Albania, while 31 per cent were in favor of an armed struggle against Serbia, and only 7 per cent saw any point in attempting to enter into dialogue with the Serbs.[33]

Croatia and Bosnia likewise became dangerous flashpoints. The proclamation of secession from Croatia, by Serbs of the so-called Krajina, was one of the more dangerous developments of early 1991, the gravity of which was amply demonstrated in the armed incursion by Serbs, on 31 March, into the Plitvice National Park, which some Serbs evidently wanted to annex. In Bosnia, Alija Izetbegovic, now president of Bosnia, declared in late October that "if the republics of Slovenia and Croatia secede from Yugoslavia, the Republic of Bosnia-Herzegovina will immediately proclaim its independence."[34] Two weeks later, Radovan Karadzic, leader of the Serbian Democratic Party for Bosnia-Herzegovina, promised that if Bosnia seceded from Yugoslavia, the Serbs of Bosnia, who do not, it will be recalled, inhabit a compact area, would secede from Bosnia, in effect plunging Bosnia into serious chaos.[35]

In Montenegro—long divided between pro-Serbian Montenegrins and anti-Serbian Montenegrins—the biggest change in the months between

September 1990 and June 1991 was an increase in pressure on Montenegro by Milosevic supporters, to submit to annexation by Serbia. A Movement for the Unification of Serbia and Montenegro was organized and, on 6 November, submitted an appeal, signed by 10,000 citizens of Montenegro and Serbia, to the Serbian and Montenegrin assemblies, for a referendum on the unification of the two republics. The Montenegrin government resisted such pressures, even as pro-Serbian and anti-Serbian groups proliferated in the republic.

Even Macedonia saw a sudden rise in national consciousness among all the nationality groups living there: Macedonians, Albanians, Serbs, Gypsies, and others. There were at least two active nationalist organizations in Macedonia, both of which demanded immediate secession from Yugoslavia: the Movement for All-Macedonian Action, and the Internal Macedonian Revolutionary Organization-Democratic Party for Macedonian National Unity.[36] The latter urged that the Yugoslav National Army be withdrawn from Macedonia. In that organization's view, "only the Territorial Defense of Macedonia can stand as the legitimate defender of Macedonia . . ."[37] Not surprisingly, the Bulgarian government expressed its opinion about Macedonian statehood. But, in a complete reversal of the irredentist policy of the Zhivkov era, the Bulgarian Foreign Ministry declared its full support for an independent Macedonian state and affirmed that it no longer nurtured any territorial pretensions vis-a-vis Macedonia.[38] This Bulgarian declaration was probably designed to further weaken Milosevic's position in the south.

There was even new wind for the sails of regional autonomist movements. Aside from the aforementioned movements of Muslims in the Sandzak of Novi Pazar and of Serbs in Croatia and Bosnia-Herzegovina, there were also signs in 1990–91 of waxing autonomism in Istria,[39] Dalmatia,[40] and Vojvodina, as well as a sharp anti-Hungarian backlash among some of Vojvodina's Serbs.[41]

In October 1990, Slovenia and Croatia had issued a joint proposal for transforming the Yugoslav state into a confederation.[42] This proposal was immediately rejected by Serbia and Montenegro. During the early months of 1991, Slovenia, Croatia, and Macedonia argued for confederalization, Bosnia was willing to go along with confederalization, and Serbia and Montenegro remained opposed. Of the six republics, the four pro-confederal republics viewed their borders as state borders not subject to administrative change by Belgrade; only Serbia and Montenegro held to the view that the borders separating the republics were administrative in character and subject to revision. Slovenia, Croatia, and Bosnia wanted to depoliticize the army—a move opposed by Serbia and Montenegro—while Macedonia had not yet worked out a clear policy in this area.[43]

Throughout the early months of 1991, the six republics conducted a series of summit talks, to avert civil war and find a path to inter-republican agreement. But none of these meetings produced any progress. And it was unclear, as long as Milosevic remained in power in Serbia, how any progress might be reached. In this context, the massive anti-Milosevic demonstrations in Belgrade for several days in March seemed a hopeful sign; they certainly indicated a new confidence among his local opposition. Predictably, the Milosevic government responded with bans, tear gas, and arrests. Helsinki Watch commented,

> The actions of the Serbian government, and particularly the Serbian police force, violated Principle VII of the Helsinki Final Act which calls on participating states to "respect human rights and fundamental freedoms." Also, the use of excessive force by the Serbian police . . . violates Article 6 of the International Covenant on Civil and Political Rights (ICCPR) . . . The Serbian government's actions on March 9 and 10 also violated Article 2 (1) of the ICCPR, which states that parties to the Covenant will undertake "to respect and ensure" the rights recognized in the Covenant. The Serbian government's interference with the demonstrations on March 9 and 10 also infringed the right of peaceful assembly and association, as guaranteed in Articles 21 and 22 of the ICCPR. Moreover, the arrests of some demonstrators on March 9 violated Article 9 of the ICCPR, which claims that: "No one shall be subjected to arbitrary arrest or detention."[44]

Ultimately, the demonstrations won a few concessions in the media, and compelled the resignation of Serbian interior minister Radmilo Bogdanovic the following month.[45] But Milosevic remained in power, and his policy remained unchanged.

In the absence of an inter-republican agreement, the republics increasingly simply by-passed the federal government. Milan Kucan, the President of Slovenia, put the issue very succinctly, in an address to the Slovenian Assembly on 20 February:

> We [have] proceeded from the fact that Yugoslavia, as a joint federal state, has politically and economically disintegrated. The federal state and its entities have been functioning with an increasing number of difficulties, and now are doing so under the conditions of a financial blockade on the part of the republics. The republics have built up or are building up their autonomous, constitutional-political, legal, and economic systems and, on that basis—despite the fact that they do not admit it—they behave very much as independent subjects from a constitutional and legal aspect.[46]

ON THE BRINK

By April 1991, Bosnia and Macedonia had converted to the confederalist cause already being advocated by Slovenia and Croatia.[47] Slovenia, Croatia, and Bosnia had already declared the sovereignty of their respective republics, and Slovenia and Croatia were by then making preparations for independence. On 7 April, the Internal Macedonian Revolutionary Organization—Democratic Party for Macedonian National Unity—followed in their footsteps and approved a statute advocating the "comprehensive political, economic, and spiritual independence of the Macedonian state."[48]

The interrepublican summit meetings remained deadlocked, with Serbia and Montenegro unwilling to turn back from their hegemonist course. Meanwhile, the country continued to unravel. Slavonian Serbs—including many who had come to the region from Serbia and other parts in the 1970s in search of jobs[49]—declared their intention to secede from Croatia and to join Vojvodina, thus coming under Milosevic's rule.[50] The self-proclaimed Krajina, declared by Croatia's Serbs, announced its plan to seek annexation to Serbia. Meanwhile, Croats living in the Krajina region took steps to register their opposition to this move and to proclaim their intention to remain part of Croatia.[51] After the seizure of Croatia's Plitvice National Park by Serbian armed militias in late March, the JNA sent its tanks to occupy the park.[52] In fact, the JNA repeatedly intervened in Serb-Croat conflicts during the early months of 1991, without authorization from either the collective presidency or the Republic of Croatia.

In mid-May, Borisav Jovic (a Serb) was to step down as president of the collective presidency. He was supposed to be succeeded in office by Stipe Mesic, the noncommunist representative from Croatia. But Mesic naively announced, in advance, that upon his succession, he intended to fire the entire Chief of Staff of the JNA, because it had been acting without the constitutionally required authorization of the collective presidency.[53] When it came time for Mesic to assume office, Milosevic used the four votes he controlled in that body (Serbia, Montenegro, Kosovo, and Vojvodina) to block Mesic's succession, thus disrupting the work of that body. The Croatian Republic appeared unprepared for this development, but, all the same, Franjo Tudjman agreed to meet Slobodan Milosevic and concluded what he (Tudjman) thought of as a "special agreement" between the two.

As this was going on, acting JNA commander General Adzic declared himself in favor of a prophylactic "extermination of tens of thousands of Croats [which] would provoke some grumbling around the world but [which] would be soon forgotten."[54] The army clashed with Croatian workers in Slavonski Brod, when the latter tried to prevent the army from removing 100 new tanks from an arms factory.[55] Army tanks and troops were also deployed against Croats in Listica (a Croatian town in Bosnia). In several instances, there were reports that Serbian forces were making use of former members of Romania's secret police, the Securitate, who had fled Romania after the ouster of Romanian President Nicolae Ceausescu in December 1989. Croatian police, in fact, intercepted some radio transmissions among Serbian forces; they were in Romanian.[56] In Borovo Selo, a Croatian town whose largely Serbian population were among those who had entered Slavonia in the 1970s in search of work, shooting erupted in early May, resulting in 16 deaths and an unspecified number of wounded. When Croatian authorities dispatched police to the region, the Serbs agreed to give the police safe passage under a white flag. But when the Croatian police entered the village, white flags in hand, the Serbs opened fire on them, killing 13 police and wounding 21. Some Croatian police were mutilated by Serbs: their eyes were gouged out, their throats slit, and their genitals cut off.[57] Once again, the army sent in troops, as they had done in previous weeks in Kijevo, Sibenik, and other towns in Croatia.

In mid-May, the pro-communist chiefs of staff of the Yugoslav army, navy, and air force met in Belgrade, behind closed doors, to plan the disposition of forces in the coming action. "Duties were determined for the army commmands, units and institutions of the Yugoslav People's Army," said a Defense Ministry statement after the meeting.[58] The army amassed large concentrations of forces in the northern part of Bosnia-Herzegovina,[59] sent troops to Maribor the night of 26 May to arrest Colonel Vladimir Milosevic, the commander of Slovenia's eastern territorial defense district,[60] and drew up plans for seizing control of Slovenia's borders and airport at Ljubljana.[61] Meanwhile, the JNA continued to demand the complete disarmament and disbanding of the Slovenian and Croatian defense militias—moves that would have left those republics defenseless and that were accordingly resisted. Slovenia and Croatia turned to private arms merchants in Western Europe and the United States, in search of heavy artillery and other weaponry.[62]

But Slovenia and Croatia faced a serious obstacle. In spite of early expressions of sympathy from the German, Austrian, and Italian governments, the states of Western Europe held back from offering diplomatic recognition or support to these two republics. Their withholding of recognition was, at least in part, a reflection of uncertainty. US President George Bush believed that Yugoslav "brotherhood and unity" should be maintained at all costs, that it was in America's interest to abandon the pro-Western elites in Slovenia and Croatia and to buttress the hate-mongering (and anti-Western) Milosevic, even as his actions resulted in the deaths of hundreds of civilians, and that the moderate, pro-Western, democratic forces in Slovenia and Croatia could safely be sacrificed on the altar of "brotherhood and unity" without deepening Slovenian and Croatian resentment and driving their populations in extremist directions, including in the direction of fascism. Bush also was said to believe that ostracizing democratic Slovenia and Croatia, while supporting communist Serbia, would send the "correct" message to Soviet President Gorbachev: presumably that message was that the US would not undertake *any* measures to assist Lithuania, Georgia, or any other independence-minded Soviet republics, regardless of the extent of force that Moscow might apply in order to attempt to destroy the independence movements. The result was that the US applied pressure on the European community to ostracize Slovenia and Croatia, made IMF loans contingent upon Yugoslav unity, and sent Secretary of State James Baker to Yugoslavia in June 1991 to declare publicly that the republics should "negotiate." The only form of "negotiation" compatible with the preservation of Yugoslav unity, as Bush and Baker should have known, would have been the complete surrender of the Slovenian and Croatian governments to Serbian *diktat,* resulting in the removal of local democratic forces, whether by Milosevic or by local discontents.

The Slovenian government had previously announced that it would secede from Yugoslavia by 26 June, if no progress had been made by then toward resolving the crisis. When Slovenia followed through on this threat, JNA units stationed in Croatia crossed into Slovenia and seized control of the border and the airport, according to plan. Slovenian forces put up resistance and inflicted losses on the JNA. The loss of life and infrastructure damage caused by the JNA were already noted at the outset of this chapter. The US responded to this assault, by urging the Slovenian government to withdraw its declaration of independence and to "negotiate" with Serbia.

The JNA has (as of June 1991) 138,000 troops on active duty and 400,000 troops in the reserves. It has 1,850 battle tanks (mostly old Soviet T-54 and T-55 tanks, but also some Yugoslav T-72s). It has some 2,000 towed artillery pieces, 500 armoured personnel carriers, and other Soviet-made weaponry. The navy commands 10,000 troops, with four frigates, 59 patrol and coastal craft, and five small submarines at its disposal. The 32,000-strong air force has 455 combat aircraft, including MiG-29s, and 198 helicopters.[63]

Slovenia has 200,000 troops at its disposal (as of June 1991),[64] while Croatia claimed to be able to mobilize also about 200,000 troops on short order.[65] Slovenia and Croatia also possessed an unspecified number of tanks, anti-tank weapons, and other weaponry, most of it allegedly imported from Germany and Hungary.

Slovenia had, to some extent, relied on a defense agreement, which it had concluded with Croatia, to present a solid front against Serbia. But in May 1991, Croatian President Tudjman allowed himself to be persuaded to abandon his Slovenian ally in exchange for Serbian promises of goodwill. Hence, when JNA tanks were sent rolling out of Croatia into Slovenia, Tudjman made no move to hinder their advance. Tudjman did not believe that these same tanks might be used against Croatia, once Slovenia was subjugated.

The chances of reviving Yugoslavia had died long before the JNA's brutal assault on Slovenia in late June 1991. But the assault, undertaken in the name of "unity," was a logical capstone to the program pursued by Milosevic since 1987 and a fulfillment of long-standing fears among Yugoslavs that this multi-ethnic country was heading toward civil war. The delayed confirmation of Stipe Mesic as president of the collective presidency on 30 June could not dispel the tensions created by the resort to military force and came too late to constitute a very hopeful sign.

PART TWO

Culture

CHAPTER FOUR

◆

The Press

IN THE YEARS SINCE TITO died (that is, since May 1980), the Yugoslav press has figured as a fairly precise barometer of the broader institutional and political context. Like Yugoslavia itself, the press has been dramatically decentralized, and all efforts to achieve a "unified information system" have proved unavailing. Like Yugoslavia itself, the press experienced a period of "release" after the death of Tito; during this period, in the absence of the helmsman, the press shared in the new, general exploration of new paths, in particular in launching the general discussion of the Goli Otok prison camp.[1] As in the case of the Yugoslav system more broadly, subsequent attempts (1983-1985) to rein in the press by and large failed[2]—and, indeed, throughout much of the 1980s the press continued to report the dissatisfaction of responsible agencies with its work. And like Yugoslavia itself, the press reflected the more general chaos which afflicted Yugoslavia on both the *inter*-republican and *intra*-republican level and which resulted in a measure of at first unintended liberalization. As journalists repeatedly discovered in communist Yugoslavia, if it proved impossible to publish something in one periodical outlet, regardless of the reason, it might be a simple matter to get it published in a different periodical: the youth press has often provided this kind of service as an "alternative" outlet; other times it has been a matter of crossing inter-republican borders and taking one's story to a periodical based in another federal unit.

In 1962, there were some 1,949 newspapers and magazines being published in Yugoslavia. This figure rose to 2,080 in 1975 and reached 3,020 in 1981. In 1987, there were 3,063 newspapers and magazines being published in Yugoslavia, of which 27 were daily newspapers. Their total circulation came to about 2,700,000 copies.[3] The Yugoslav National Army accounted for 22 of these periodicals,[4] while religious organizations published some 200 newspapers and other periodicals of a religious nature.[5] In 1962, there were some 3,300 professional journalists working in Yugoslavia. This figure rose to 4,700 in 1975 and 11,000 in 1981. As of 1987, there were some 202 radio stations in Yugoslavia, and television centers in all the republics and provinces.

THE PURPOSE OF THE PRESS
AND THE APPLICATION OF CENSORSHIP

The Titoists, like communists elsewhere, conceived of the press explicitly in terms of underpinning the system. "The purpose of the social system of information," said a 1987 source, "is to supply data and information indispensable for self-management and delegate decision-making at all levels . . ."[6] Objectivity was explicitly scorned as a "bourgeois" notion. Journalists, rather, were instructed to serve as "a meaningful subject force in society" and to be "decisive" in the struggle "against exploitative consciousness and counterrevolutionary ideology."[7] The Titoist system of controlling editorial appointments and of weeding out journalists who became too independent in their thinking reflected this assigned purpose.

It is often said that Yugoslavia, unlike the other communist countries of Eastern Europe, did not have a censorship *office*. Strictly speaking, this was true—at least formally. But there have been various levels and ways in which censorship *activity* was carried on, and in which political authorities attempted to assure that the general contents of publications accorded with what they considered acceptable. To an outside observer this may seem incomprehensible in view of the intense polemics which frequently have raged in the Yugoslav press, in view of the repeatedly demonstrated ability of the Catholic weekly, *Glas koncila,* to defend itself against mudslinging throughout the communist era, and in view of the "alternative outlet" syndrome. The explanation of this complexity is to be sought in three sources: first, as previously mentioned, the press has lain within the jurisdiction of republican authorities, and hence, the evolution of Yugoslavia after 1963 into a set of eight often warring republican/provincial power centers has been accompanied, necessarily, by a republicanization of the press; second, even within a single republic, the authorities always appreciated that the press had to be diverse if it was to operate effectively, and hence that the youth press, the women's press, even the pornographic press, had to have sphere-specific areas of leeway if they were to reach their audiences and function effectively; and third, the communist authorities simply did not have the resources or the will to assert bloc-style control (and indeed, the supervisors of the youth press were often sympathetic to the coverage of that press).

During the era of communism (roughly speaking, to the end of 1989), every publisher was required by law to send copies of the galley proofs to the Office of the State Prosecutor, before a given issue of a periodical was actually published. This requirement applied to every periodical published in Yugoslavia regardless of its sponsorship, content, or intended audience.[8] The Prosecutor's Office was, however, understaffed and read comparatively little of the voluminous material which crossed its desk: amateur radio magazines, fashion magazines, sports magazines, and so forth were apt to be ignored, for instance, with greater attention paid to the mainline secular press (*Borba, Politika, Vjesnik,* etc.) and secondarily to the religious press. Partly for that reason there have been few stories of pre-publication censorship in Yugoslavia.[9] More typically, if the authorities found something amiss, the issue in question had not only been printed but also distributed—and the article in question would no doubt have been read by many. The authorities then had to reckon with the fact that suppression of the issue would inevitably heighten public interest in the issue. One informant recounted his experiences with the authorities:

> Our newspaper has been banned three times in all, three times over a span of 20 years. But the bad thing when they ban an issue is that they come to your office and they demand the addresses of all the subscribers and you must give all the addresses, and then they go to the churches and confiscate the unsold issues. And then, if they want to do so, they go to the subscribers and demand to have the issue surrendered. It's dreadful. The previous editor told me they received letters from old people saying please don't send the newspaper to us any more because the police came late in the night and said, "You received an 'enemy' newspaper. Give it to us." So in a way it is better if an issue is banned before distribution.[10]

A ban could be issued by either federal or republican authorities, the latter exercising this prerogative more rarely than the former. A republican ban applied only within the borders of the republic, so that, for instance, if Croatian authorities were to ban an issue of *Mladost,* the very same issue could be freely and openly sold in Serbia, Bosnia, and elsewhere in Yugoslavia. Both the federal and republican bans could be challenged in court, and from time to time this resulted in a ban being overturned.

The State Prosecutor's Office was concerned with the day-to-day routine, and had its eyes fixed, as it were, on the trees rather than on the forest. Other review agencies were responsible for monitoring the overall performance of the press, viz., the Commission for Ideological Work and the Commission for Political-Propaganda Activity in Information, both attached to the Central Committee of the League of

Communists of Yugoslavia (LCY), the Section for Information and Public Opinion of the Socialist Alliance of Working People of Yugoslavia (SAWPY), the Committee for Press, Radio and Television of the CC SAWPY, and republican branches of these bodies. These bodies were required to issue annual reports on the functioning of the press.[11] These reports, judging from reports in the press itself, tended to dwell on perceived shortcomings and problems.[12] In addition, the Association of Journalists of each given federal unit periodically reviewed the performance of its members.[13]

The State Secretariat for Information was the body authorized to announce news bans, but in practice, news bans have been announced by others as well. In February 1986, for instance, the president of the Federal Assembly told the 60 Yugoslav journalists accredited to cover the assembly's deliberations that they were not to write about what irate Serbs from Kosovo were saying that day in the assembly. But since this ban was illegal and since it affected one of the most burning issues of the day, viz., Serb-Albanian tensions in the province of Kosovo, journalists protested, some wrote sharp commentaries about the news "embargo," and within a few days, several publications printed the substance of the meeting, the embargo notwithstanding.[14] Journalist Mihailo Rasic voiced the sentiment of many in the media in describing that ban as a "semi-private action" imposed without proper authority.[15]

Other matters have also been subject to news bans in recent years. Perhaps the most controversial was the abortive attempt to limit news coverage of the April 1981 riots in Kosovo to official communiques prepared by the government.[16] In another instance of an unsuccessful ban, authorities at first tried to prevent reportage of the March 10, 1986 session of the CC of the Croatian party, at which Milka Planinc and Jure Bilic failed to be nominated to represent Croatia in the Presidium of the CC LCY. Similarly, in October 1985, Yugoslav newspapers were not allowed to report that Palestinian terrorist Abu Abbas was in Belgrade,[17] while the Yugoslav press became much more reticent in the late 1980s than it had been earlier in discussing Yugoslavia's foreign debt. Writing in the pages of the party weekly, *Komunist,* Zdravko Lekovic complained in June 1987 that one could legitimately speak of "a censorship of information in a broad sense," adding that information about events in Kosovo was still being blocked and that the press had been unable to obtain basic statistics about many investments even though they were *not* secret.[18] There were other sundry specific proscriptions, as well as limits in the spheres of foreign policy, national mythology, religious policy, and nationalities policy,[19] though these limits changed somewhat over time and were, in any case, periodically tested by daring editors.

In addition to the political authorities themselves, the army also has occasionally expressed its opinion about coverage of its activities in the press. In March 1985, for instance, the Ljubljana Army District Command prepared an analysis of the public information media in Slovenia and, while generally satisfied with the treatment it had been accorded in the press, found several articles in the Slovenian youth press "unacceptable and extremely harmful . . . because they present a distorted picture of life and work in the Yugoslav National Army. The publishing of such texts," the statement continued, "cannot be permitted any longer."[20]

In general, when one abstracts the situation to a "global" level, authorities tended to believe that the press's basic assignment was to strengthen the values of socialist self-management and to support the policies of the LCY, assisting the politicians in finding and implementing "necessary solutions."[21] As recently as September 1985, *Komunist,* the organ of the LCY, described itself as aspiring "to be the class weapon of the League of Communists [and] to contribute . . . to the strengthening of the unity in action and thought of the League of Communists."[22] Accordingly, in the communist era, Yugoslav newspapers were apt to be criticized for failing to support (or even for being at variance with) party policy, for confronting the public with differing analyses, for "confusing" the public, for overemphasis of negative phenomena in society, for loss of "seriousness," even for "neutrality" in the treatment of burning social issues.[23] Yugoslavia's 11,000 journalists—90 per cent of whom were party members as of 1987[24]—were expected, during the communist era, to take their cues from the party. When they displayed too much independence, they were apt to be criticized for setting themselves up as independent judges of society or as "some kind of arbiter or conscience of society."[25] This, however, led to some strange dilemmas with circumspection and uncertainty leading to a situation where, as one Yugoslav journalist put it, "many journalists, and the younger ones in particular, find it difficult to decide what their position is due to the fact that the LC is often late in taking necessary actions."[26]

NATIONALISM AND THE
REPUBLICANIZATION OF THE PRESS

The federalization of the Yugoslav political system was intended to defuse nationalism by granting nationality-based federal units wide-ranging autonomy. Instead of defusing nationalism, however, federalization transformed the nationalities factor by shifting the center of gravity from the federal government to the republican governments and by arming those governments with the powers to seek "national" objectives (e.g., Serbian and Montenegrin interest in the construction of the now-completed Belgrade-Bar railway).

In the years since Tito died, it became increasingly evident that the nationalities factor was far from being solved. In the initial months after the April 1981 riots, the Albanian-language press in Kosovo was subjected to stiff criticism, and some editors were replaced. Already in mid-June 1981, an extraordinary session of the Association of Kosovo Journalists was convened, in order to identify shortcomings which needed to be corrected. Yet, two years later, the Provincial Committee for Information found that reportage in the province's Albanian-language daily, *Rilindja,* differed rather substantially from what was offered in the local Serbo-Croatian daily, *Jedinstvo.* Subsequently, a session of the Information Commission of the LCY noted, in November 1987, that while *Jedinstvo* reported evidence of discrimination against Serbo-Croatian, reported that the emigration of Slavs from the province was rising, and adhered to the official line, *Rilindja* discounted any discrimination, reported that out-migration was declining, and talked of "unacceptable" demands from Serbs and Montenegrins.[27] In late 1985, Kosovo's journalists were still being told to counter "counterrevolutionary ideologies and action" and to find ways to discourage the emigration of Serbs and Montenegrins from the province.[28] Later, in August 1986, *Rilindja* was still said to be marred by "superficiality, one-sidedness, lack of commitment, and . . . an excessive insistence on national elements that very often leads to the very brink of nationalism."[29] *Jedinstvo* was simultaneously charged with having engaged in "masquerades" designed to obscure the position of the journalist and the paper.[30]

The sector for public information of the Republic Committee for Information of SR Serbia carried out an analysis of the provincial press of Kosovo and Vojvodina, covering the period September 14, 1987 to January 20, 1988, and examining the following papers: *Dnevnik, Magyar Szo,* and *Stav* from Vojvodina, and *Jedinstvo* and *Rilindja* from Kosovo. The study found that the Hungarian-language *Magyar Szo* devoted more space than did the Serbo-Croatian language *Dnevnik,* to commentary on the proposed constitutional changes, especially where measures affecting the position of the Hungarian minority were concerned. Of the three Vojvodinan papers, *Stav,* the organ of the provincial youth organization, was the most openly and explicitly critical of the proposed changes. In Kosovo, there were more fundamental differences in coverage: the Albanian-language daily, *Rilindja,* fiercely criticized the proposed changes, whereas the Serbo-Croatian daily, *Jedinstvo,* assumed a non-committal posture.[31] Later, however, *Rilindja's* staff switched to the offensive and criticized the press from other republics for "one-sidedness" in their treatment of Kosovo.[32]

The chief culprit among these "other republics" was surely Serbia, whose press was criticized for "petit-bourgeois liberalism and nationalism" during a session of the Presidium of the CC LC Serbia in February 1983. Momcilo Baljak, who presented the opening report at that session, seemed particularly upset that "no editorial office is willing to criticize the texts to be found in the book, *Stvarno i moguce* [The Real and the Possible], by Dobrica Cosic, which has just been published by Otokar Kersovani, the Rijeka publishing house. These texts are permeated with anxiety for the Serbian people, and in essence they reflect the socio-socialist and unitarist concept of our society."[33] Two months later, Dragoljub Trailovic resigned his post as chief editor of the influential Belgrade daily, *Politika,* amid charges of Serbian nationalism and complaints that he had failed to respond appropriately to the staging of a play inspired by Greater Serbian nationalist concepts.[34]

This did not settle matters, however, and the same issue came up for discussion in September 1987, when Ivan Stojanovic, director of the "Politika" Publishing House, and Zivana Olbina, a member of *Politika*'s editorial staff, created a stir by accusing the newspaper of indulging in a nationalist obsession with Kosovo, and of sensationalizing nationalist causes.[35] At the end of a stormy session at which the staff by and large rejected her charge that *Politika* was sliding into "anticommunism," Olbina resigned from the council. The following month Stojanovic was himself forced to resign, amid charges that he had failed to exercise proper control over the periodicals being published by "Politika" Publishers. The result, as his critics pointed out, was that the periodicals being published by "Politika" frequently disagreed among themselves about facts or the interpretations of facts, even at times to the point of conducting polemics with each other.[36]

In late 1987, after seizing power in Serbia, Milosevic moved to assert his control of the Serbian press. He replaced the editors of publications at Belgrade's "Politika" publishing house and a number of good writers were sent off to glorious exile as foreign correspondents. In this way, Milosevic assured himself of the subservience and unanimity of viewpoint on the part of the Serbian press. Interestingly enough, the editor-in-chief of *Politika* had never been a political appointee until Milosevic's arrival.[37] Belgrade's "Borba" publishing house, by contrast, which publishes the daily papers, *Borba* and *Vecernje novosti,* remained independent, because all the Yugoslav republics enjoyed influence in its operation.

Slovenia similarly produced controversy in this area. In February 1987 the cultural monthly, *Nova revija,* brought out its issue no. 57, devoted entirely to the Slovenian national question. The contributors to this issue, who included some of the leading Slovenian intellectuals, suggested that Slovenia had suffered by its incorporation into Yugoslavia, described the so-called National Liberation Struggle as a civil war punctuated by a struggle for power, and argued that the communist-controlled Anti-Fascist Council of 1943 had no legitimate basis for behaving as a government.[38] One of the contributors—Tine Hribar, in his article, "Slovenian statehood"—called the Socialist Republic of Slovenia an inadequate reflection of Slovenian sovereignty, while another writer—Alenka Goljevsek—outlined a program of virtual independence for Slovenia, in which the Slovenian government would dispose of its own armed forces.[39]

Joze Smole, president of the Republic Conference of SAWP Slovenia, called the views expressed in that issue "unacceptable."[40] The editor of *Nova revija* was quickly fired. And various party bodies throughout Slovenia issued sharp condemnations of the journal.[41] The original 3,500 copies of the issue quickly sold out, but *Knjizevne novine* in Belgrade soon put out a special issue, setting forth all the essentials of the controversial issue, only now in Serbo-Croatian translation. The issue became a *cause celebre.* Politicians and other public figures throughout Yugoslavia spoke out against *Nova revija,* and there was talk of banning the issue. In March 1987, the executive council of the journal met and lent its full support to the editorial board of *Nova revija,* while the journal's new editor underlined that he endorsed the controversial issue and intended to assert continuity in editorial policy. Ultimately, the Slovenian public prosecutor engaged in polemics with the federal prosecutor over the issue, and the journal found enough backers within the Slovenian leadership to ride out the storm.[42]

Slovenia, Serbia, and Kosovo were the areas where nationalism in the press became the most controversial. But they were not the only ones. In October 1986, for instance, the Macedonian party CC expressed discontent with its local press, finding that certain papers were giving undue attention to local troubles. CC member Metodi Petrovski mentioned, in particular, excessive coverage by Macedonian media of a brawl between Albanian and Macedonian youth. He urged more even reporting of news from other Yugoslav republics.[43]

Despite the old Titoist formula according to which party spokespersons should restrict themselves to criticizing nationalist phenomena in their own republics, the very opposite became the case and the various newspapers preferred to criticize nationalist excesses of *other* nationality groups.[44]

Explicit nationalism was not the only symptom of the republicanization of the press, however. There was a kind of implicit nationalism, better described as *localism,* which some papers have been trying hard to steer clear of. *Borba* has long taken particular pains to assure the "all-Yugoslav" character of its coverage,[45] and it may well be the only genuine *Yugoslav* newspaper among the major dailies. In the late 1980s, *Vjesnik* started looking beyond its Croatian horizons and, for a time, aspired to a country-wide audience.[46] More recently, however, it has given up this aspiration. *Politika,* of course, looks back with pride to its long tradition as an independent paper and, at least until Milosevic's seizure of power and subjugation of the "Politika" publishing house, liked to think of itself as a paper for all Yugoslavia; realistically speaking, its readership has always been limited to Serbs and Montenegrins, however, since most Croats do not bother to learn the Cyrillic alphabet.[47]

A NEW LAW ON THE PRESS

Yugoslavs began talking about a new law concerning the press and public information in early 1979,[48] but due to the amount of controversy generated, it was not until May 1985 that the law was finally adopted. The chief purpose of the new legislation, as tirelessly pointed out in the press itself, was to produce greater uniformity in the press across republican boundaries. Beyond that, the law was also intended to strengthen the founding agencies' control over their organs, whether the agency concerned was one of SAWPY's branches, the LCY, or a socio-cultural organization.[49] Shortly after the passage of the new law, *Komunist* spoke optimistically of "the fact that with this law a unified regime for public information for all of Yugoslavia has been introduced."[50] This optimism proved illusory. Even where *Komunist* itself was concerned, there was not much unity among its various local editions. Indeed, *Mladost,* the magazine published by the Socialist Youth Federation, pointed out that nothing had changed almost a year and a half later. On the contrary, as *Mladost* observed, "In the eight editions of *Komunist,* whose mastheads differ only in reflecting the republic or provincial names, the Yugoslav portion has been melting away more and more, and has almost disappeared, because republic and provincial editorial boards have been carrying more and more articles in accordance with their republic and provincial top leaders' attitudes."[51] And again, if the law had really succeeded in creating a "unified information system," it should have been possible to avoid the dispute of December 1986. On that occasion, the Slovenian SAWP organization criticized the Croatian SAWP organization for allowing *Vjesnik* to publish a commentary which was alleged to be injurious to the interests of the Slovene minority community in Italy as well as to wider Slovenian interests.[52]

Despite the shortcomings of the new law, its passage gave rise to talk of "the importance of coordinating the republican and provincial information media laws with the federal ones."[53] Going one step further, and in harmony with more general aspirations in S. R. Serbia to erode some of the autonomy enjoyed by the autonomous provinces of Kosovo and Vojvodina (both administratively parts of S. R. Serbia), the Serbian Assembly proposed in 1987 that the two provinces agree to the passage of a unified republican law on public information. In effect, the proposal asked the provinces to decline to pass their own information laws and merely to accept the extension of the Serbian law into the areas of their jurisdiction. A few months later the Serbian League of Journalists proposed to revise the statute of the Yugoslav League of Journalists to give the provincial associations lesser representation in the presiding council of the Yugoslav organization. Not surprisingly, both provinces rejected these initiatives, and polemics ensued.[54]

By 1988–89, there was growing consensus among Yugoslav journalists that the 1985 Law on Press and Information was already obsolete. For one thing, Yugoslav appeals courts were repeatedly overturning the temporary ban of specific papers. In March 1988, for example, a court ruled that there was no cause to ban an issue of *Mladina*, the youth paper of Slovenia. The issue in question had included an article to the effect that Yugoslavia's leaders were responsible for leading the country into "hopeless crisis." The court, however, ruled that the article in question "contained no untrue information which could disturb the public."[55] Later, in August 1988, a decision by the Split public prosecutor to ban an issue of *Omladinska Iskra*, for having published the text of a speech by Milovan Djilas at a meeting in Maribor, was overturned by the Supreme Court of Croatia.[56] And that same month, the Split District Court overturned a ban of the August 28 issue of *Nedjeljna Dalmacija*, which the public prosecutor had claimed had "hostile" content.[57]

Yugoslav journalists were bridling at the rein. Already in October 1988, at its annual conference, the Union of Yugoslav Journalists "called for an end to the 'informal marriage' of political structures and mass media and demanded a greater measure of independence for their profession."[58] "The existing press law is obsolete and needs to be revised completely," a prominent Slovenian journalist told me in 1989. "According to the letter of the law, we could be charged with infringements every day. But we just go ahead and publish what we want, and take our chances."[59] In particular, federal law included an article (no. 139) relating to high treason, formulated so vaguely that people could be—and in the past, were—prosecuted for bad intentions. Another grievance had to do with the appointment of editors. Many prominent Yugoslav papers were, until recently, the organs of the Socialist Alliance of Working People—including *Borba, Vjesnik,* and *Delo*—which meant that the editor-in-chief, the managing editor, and the director were all appointed by the Alliance, rather than being selected by the journalists themselves (as the journalists preferred).

THE YOUTH PRESS

Various bits of evidence suggest that in certain concrete ways (e.g., coverage of the rock group Laibach), the party gave the youth press more latitude than was enjoyed by the mainline daily press. At the same time, the recurrent testing of the limits by the youth press and the recurrent impulses, on the part of the authorities, to ban specific issues, suggest that part of this relatively greater latitude should be attributed to the greater daring and even recklessness of some journalists and editors in publications intended for young people.[60]

The most visible youth periodicals in Yugoslavia recently have been *Mladina* and *Katedra* from Slovenia, *Mladost* and *Studentski list* from Croatia, *NON, Student,* and *Vidik* from Serbia, and *Nasi dani* and *Valter* from Bosnia. Of these *Mladina* has probably been the most controversial in recent years. I propose to throw some light on the youth press by examining the case of *Mladina* in some detail.

Mladina was long officially the organ of the Socialist Youth Organization of Slovenia, which, in theory, picked the editor. In practice, the editorial board has chosen the editor for quite some time, subject (until very recently) to the approval of the now defunct youth organization. The editorial staff clashed with the authorities over editorial policy throughout the 1970s, but even when the authorities intervened more directly in the selection of the editor, *Mladina* remained defiantly independent. In fact, *Mladina* and Ljubljana's Radio Student played an important role in opening up the discussion of previously taboo subjects (like political prisoners) in the early 1980s.[61] A staff member of *Mladina* recalls that period: "The first reaction of the authorities was to ban specific issues of *Mladina.* Then they would call the people of Radio Student to party headquarters and they told us that what we were doing was not right. They threatened to kick us out of the party. But the party organization in Radio Student stood up for its people and defended us."[62] Democratic centralism, thus, had proven fictitious.

In late 1984 the Yugoslav authorities decided to put half a dozen Serbian intellectuals on trial for "dissent." *Mladina*[63] defended them, resulting in a boom for *Mladina*'s circulation, which rose from 10,000 when the trial began to 18,000 by the time the trial was over, climbing subsequently to 28,000 by mid-1987. In October 1985, *Mladina* published a long interview with Vladimir Seks, a lawyer from Osijek. Before taking up duties as a lawyer, Seks had been a public prosecutor, and in this capacity he had found out (in 1981) that the security police were routinely opening all foreign correspondence coming into Osijek. He decided to take the police to court, but, as a result, immediately lost his job and was himself taken to court on charges of Croatian nationalism. Seks did not serve any time then, but after serving as the defense lawyer for the six Serbian intellectuals in 1984, the earlier sentence was revived and Seks went to prison for six months.[64] His interview with *Mladina* was conducted shortly after his release from prison.

Slovenian authorities were dismayed and banned the issue. But the *Mladina* staff took the case to the Supreme Court of Slovenia, which overturned the ban, allowed *Mladina* to re-release the issue, certain that the abortive ban could only have excited wide interest in the issue. This stimulated a certain self-confidence among the staff of *Mladina,* who took to describing the incident as the "last" time the magazine was banned. In late July 1987, however, the public prosecutor in Ljubljana imposed a temporary ban on a double-issue scheduled for release by *Mladina.*[65]

Mladina started to play tricks on the authorities. Well aware that the galley proofs would be checked "higher up," the staff on one occasion prepared a dirty poem about Tito without intending to publish it. When the magazine came out, the police were ready with an order to ban it, but the poem was not in the magazine.

1986 brought new confrontations. In February, *Mladina* was preparing to publish an article criticizing Prime Minister Branko Mikulic for political trials in his native Bosnia. The article suggested that his record disqualified him as prime minister. The editorial staff was abruptly summoned before the Central Committee of the Slovenian party and threatened with imprisonment unless the article was withdrawn. The staff caved in, but the page on which the article had been scheduled to appear was left blank. Later, the article was published in the youth newspaper from Maribor, *Katedra.*[66]

The following month, *Mladina* featured an article about the elections, speculating that the communist party would "probably" win and describing them as "elections of the delegates of delegates of delegates of delegates." Other satirical articles followed. By late summer, Pavlo Car, the Slovenian public prosecutor, was openly complaining of

a mass sowing of bitterness, pessimism, carping, and political insinuations, that has been perpetrated by the press, radio and television, publishing houses, various tribunes, and round-table conferences . . . that "craftily walk on the brink of the criminal zones." . . . In Car's words, the specific culprits include three Slovenian newspapers, *Mladina, Nova revija,* and *Katedra,* and in addition to them the Commission for the Protection of Thought and Writing of the Writers Association of Slovenia.[67]

The editors of *Mladina, Katedra,* and *Nova revija* joined the chairman of the Slovenian Commission for the Protection of Thought and Writing and the president of the Slovenian Writers' Association in signing a letter protesting Car's statements.[68] But Car refused to retract anything.[69]

Katedra, the organ of the students of the University of Maribor, has been increasingly visible since the mid-1980s, and has shown itself repeatedly ready to take risks. In January 1987, for instance, the newspaper published an interview with Serbian intellectual Kosta Cavoski, co-author of an important study of the Yugoslav communist party's consolidation of its power monopoly in the late 1940s.[70] In March the paper published an interview with Yugoslav dissident Milovan Djilas: the interview had originally been scheduled to appear in *Mladina,* but when authorities prevented *Mladina* from publishing it, the text was passed on to *Katedra.* It was the first time Djilas had been heard in his own country since his disgrace in 1954.[71] When *Katedra* returned less than three months later with an open letter from Serbian nationalist Vojislav Seselj, said to "insult the representatives of the socio-political life of our country," authorities banned the issue.[72] Yet when *Mladina* criticized Defense Minister Branko Mamula in February 1988 for his involvement in an arms sale to Ethiopia and for assigning a group of soldiers (among them Slovenes) to help build a villa for his use in Opatija, the federal prosecutor instructed the Slovenian prosecutor to initiate legal proceedings against *Mladina*'s editor, Franci Zavrl. Among other things, *Mladina* had called Mamula a "merchant of death." But the Slovenian prosecutor decided to arraign Zavrl not on the charge suggested by Belgrade—of "offending the honor of Yugoslavia and of its army"—but on the minor charge of personal defamation, which carried a maximum penalty of three months in prison or a fine.[73]

Two months later, *Mladina* published materials showing that the army was preparing a plan to arrest politically "undesirable" figures (including journalists) in Slovenia and quash the movement for democratization. A Slovenian human rights publication records that, "At the meeting of the [Yugoslav] Military Council, the Commander of Ljubljana Army Region is given the duty to come to an agreement with the Slovene Ministry for Internal Affairs, concerning security measures in Slovenia on the basis of the opinions of the Military Council, [to] begin criminal prosecution of the writers of some of the army about the army, and [to] order imprisonments . . . if, as a result, there was public unrest."[74] Orders were sent to stop publication of the offending issue, and three journalists and one enlisted man were put on trial. The trial electrified the Slovenian public and directly contributed to the proliferation of independent committees and parties in Slovenia.[75]

Mladina remained in the forefront of the movement for democratization, publishing the results of a poll in December 1988, showing that 64 per cent of Slovenes considered it necessary to introduce a multi-party system, and that in free elections, the communists would obtain only 7.3 per cent of the vote (as compared with 26.9 per cent for the social democrats, 18.7 per cent for the Christian Democrats, and 14.2 per cent for the Greens).[76]

Among other youth publications, the Serbian youth-oriented publications *Student* and *Vidik* have likewise repeatedly come under critical scrutiny, have sometimes been chastened for lapsing into "anti-Marxist" views,[77] and from time to time have had their wrists slapped—for example, in late September 1987, when the deputy editor and five members of the editorial staff of *Student* were forced to resign.[78] There were also complaints in 1986 about "bourgeois" orientations in Croatia's youth press,[79] while the Albanian-language organ of the Kosovo Socialist Youth Federation, *Zeri i Rinise,* was criticized that same year for failing to take a forceful line against Albanian nationalism and irredentism.[80]

Finally, a brief mention of the Sarajevo weekly magazine, *Nasi dani,* is warranted. Already by 1988, *Nasi dani* was being praised as the vanguard of a movement to liberalize the Bosnian press.[81] This magazine made a decisive contribution to the history of Yugoslav journalism with its 3 March 1989 issue, in which it ran an article headlined "Journalism is a dangerous profession." In particular, the article outlined the persecutions suffered by courageous journalists, such as Belgrade journalist Milovan Brkic (arrested and charged some 200 times) and Sisak journalist Ratko Dmitrovic (jailed for three months because he dared to write an article critical of a local party baron).[82] Needless to say, this issue of *Nasi dani,* like others before and after, was quickly banned.

LIFE OF A JOURNALIST

A journalist's life, in Yugoslavia, is difficult—or as Austrians are supposed to be fond of saying, "hopeless but not serious." The "average" Yugoslav journalist is male, 40 years old (as of 1989) and has less than 20 years to live—(54 per cent of Yugoslav journalists die before reaching retirement age). He has one child but is either divorced or about to be divorced. He smokes 40 cheap cigarettes a day, drinks brandy, suffers from recurrent stomach aches, rents his apartment, and does not own his own car. Eighty-one per cent of journalists surveyed in 1989 were members of the League of Communists, and 65 per cent had a university degree.[83] The average journalist's monthly salary is about $150–200. In Montenegro, 60 per cent of journalists in Radio-Television Titograd and 50 per cent of the journalists writing for *Pobjeda* did not own their own apartments in 1983.[84] In Slovenia, journalists have been complaining that their incomes are low and their living standards in decline.[85] Stress is a constant occupational hazard.[86]

Journalists were cautioned to write "responsibly." If they were thought to have failed in this task, they could be subject to prosecution. But where journalists have been fired not through their own fault, they have been assured financial sustenance from the official "solidarity fund" of the journalists' association. In the course of 1986, a group of Serbian journalists took the initiative in setting up an independent solidarity fund—the implication being that they could not rely on the official fund. Authorities quickly declared that the independent fund was "unnecessary" and that its real purpose was to organize a forum for political opposition. At least two journalists were expelled from the (Vojvodina) Journalists' Federation because of their affiliation with the independent solidarity fund.[87] But before the end of the year, a similar solidarity fund was set up in Slovenia.

About the same time, Slovenian journalists took an initiative which betrayed their desire for ideological latitude. Specifically, in October 1986, the Slovenian Journalists' Association unanimously adopted a resolution to drop from its statutes a clause requiring members to be "consciously loyal to the ideas of Marxism-Leninism" and promised to seek "even more extensive changes to the Yugoslav journalists' charter."[88] *Delo,* the Slovenian daily, carried an article defending the proposal that the affirmation of loyalty to Marxism-Leninism be dropped from the Yugoslav Journalists' Charter, while the Bosnian daily, *Oslobodjenje,* criticized the proposal. The latter, in its unattributed commentary, was certainly hostile to the Slovene proposal and argued that "what is obviously offered and wished [for] is that our press should de jure open itself to all possible ideological and political orientations and in fact legalize the breakthrough of authors of largely rightist or falsely leftist positions, a breakthrough that has been virtually realized in some newspapers."[89] The subject was also taken up in *Politika.* But eventually, with the disintegration of Yugoslavia the entire question became moot.

A CRITICAL PRESS

The Yugoslav press is famous for being critical. But, of course, it is critical in different ways. One may, perhaps, distinguish between criticism which is directed "inward" and criticism which is directed "outward." By the former, I mean criticism of the government (in the communist era) or the party, or of communist party policies, or of persons in the political establishment, or investigative reporting which probes issues of the day. By the latter, I shall mean criticism directed specifically against non-party sectors of society, such as rock musicians, dissidents, and religious institutions.

Inward criticism has always been, of course, the more problematical from the authorities' point of view. The communists, in particular, were well aware that a critical/investigative approach contributed to making a publication interesting, and that in the absence of such an approach, a publication could adhere to party formulae and end up being boring and ineffective. The party organ *Komunist,* as was repeatedly admitted, suffered from this problem and its influence as of 1987 was correspondingly described as "minimal."[90] In 1989, publication of *Komunist* was terminated. Still, it is understandable that those being criticized take umbrage at the fact: Tomislav Bardin, a delegate to the Serbian Assembly, objected when *Duga* published an article critical of that body's discussion of language equality in Kosovo[91]; the veterans' organization in Zagreb raised a small clamor about how it was being portrayed in *Danas, Polet, NIN,* and *Politika*[92]; even where the 1987 Agrokomerc scandal is concerned, there were polemics about press coverage.[93]

NIN was in the forefront of investigative journalism in the early 1980s. Later, the biweekly Belgrade feature magazine, *Duga,* with its feisty interviews, became a magazine to watch. Illustrative of *Duga*'s bold journalism was an interview with Miso Pavicevic, a member of the Council of the Federation, published in October 1985. In this interview, Pavicevic spoke of the older (partisan) generation "losing its way" and noted that the present crisis in Yugoslavia could only be described as the result of "a process which has been going on for over a decade and a half." By this he meant above all the process of decentralization which had contributed to satisfying the autonomist aspirations among Yugoslavia's diverse nationality groups. The result, for Pavicevic, was that Yugoslav policy-making was frequently deadlocked or strangled, and in his view, little time remained for Yugoslavia to find a solution, before it would be threatened with serious disintegration.[94] *Duga* was also prepared to probe scandals and to allow public figures to vent their frustrations. At times, *Duga* allowed itself to get carried away by its enthusiasm for "exposing" the "truth." The pages of *Duga* started to recall the muckraking tradition of turn-of-the-century America. And eventually, *Duga,* along with *Reporter* (a now-defunct semi-pornographic magazine), and *Ilustrovana politika,* would find itself accused of sensationalistic and tendentious reporting.[95] After 1987, *Duga* became simply another mouthpiece for Milosevic.

In September 1986, the Republican Conference of SAWP Serbia reviewed *Duga*'s performance and concluded that the magazine had "published a number of articles whose content and message is, from an ideological and political standpoint, unacceptable. This relates, in particular, to certain interviews, letters, and features that, in a sensationalist way, sow distrust, stimulate nationalist sentiment, and provoke disputes." The Conference also complained of "articles containing historical lies and that wrote in an unacceptable way about LCY cadres."[96] The following year *Duga*'s editor (along with the editors of *NIN, Intervju,* and *Svet*) was replaced, but even so, Serbian party chairman Slobodan Milosevic declared, "The situation in *Duga* will not change until there are broader changes in the editorial staff of *Duga*."[97]

Then there is the case of Ranka Cicak, an enterprising journalist, who, after uncovering a scam operation involving pig farmers and local politicians, was charged with having insulted Tito in a private conversation and with having justified both Croatian separatism and Albanian irredentism, imprisoned for six months, and later injured in a mysterious traffic accident.[98]

Again, when party authorities banned a professional meeting of the Philosophical Society of Serbia, which was to have discussed "the possibilities of reform in socialist countries," *Knjizevne novine* provided a forum in which the Society's president could register his protest.[99]

The communist authorities said they wanted criticism but such criticism had to be "progressive" and "in line with self-management," and not contrary to LCY policy.[100] In a micro-example of this kind of thinking, the traditionally conservative *Borba,* upon canceling publication of a pre-announced interview with drama director Ljubisa Ristic in 1984, wrote, "The editors of this paper are not in agreement with some of Ristic's views and he did not consent to having them excluded. So, as a result, we are publishing another . . . discussion [instead]."[101]

And finally, there is *outward* criticism, in the sense in which I have defined it. Outward criticism is not a feature in the entire secular press. The youth press contains very little, if any, outward criticism, at least not at the party's bid. Magazines like *Duga, Start,* and *Reporter* likewise have engaged in little outward criticism, and for that matter, *Danas* and *NIN* also do not make much space for criticizing persons outside the party. The daily press on the other hand, was, in communist times—and in Milosevic's Serbia, still is—a routine vehicle for outward criticism.

The churches were (until the late 1980s) one target of *outward criticism.* Where the Catholic Church is concerned, such criticism ranged from complaints about Cardinal Kuharic's annual defense of

Cardinal Stepinac (d. 1960), who was convicted, in a rather dubious trial in 1946, of collaboration with the fascists during World War Two,[102] to charges that unnamed church circles were calling on believers "to settle accounts with the communists, emphasizing that the communists [were] on the top of the list for liquidation, if another government [took] over,"[103] to insinuations that Pope John Paul II went to Chile to endorse the Pinochet regime when in fact the very opposite was the case,[104] to claims that the Church organ *Glas koncila* called communism one of the "most reactionary ideologies of the century."[105] In September 1986, the Novi Sad daily, *Dnevnik,* published an article adorned with a caricature of a man in an Ustasha uniform, standing in front of a barbed wire fence and waving a copy of *Glas koncila*[106]: the clear implcation was that the paper—the official organ of the Zagreb archdiocese—was advocating fascistic ideas. Usually *Glas koncila* contented itself with expostulations on its editorial page. On this occasion, however, the editor took *Dnevnik* to court. The district court refused to consider the case; so *Glas koncila* took the case to the Higher Court in Novi Sad.[107] The court ultimately handed down a judgment in *Dnevnik*'s favor. The decision, signed by President of the Court Mirjana Caric, explained that "the connection of part of the Catholic clergy in Croatia . . . with the Ustasha movement and its activity during the National Liberation War, *as well as later,* is not new or unknown, but falls into [the category of] historically established fact.[108] Hence *Glas koncila,* which was established only in the mid-1960s, could be "legitimately" portrayed as pro-Ustasha. But *Dnevnik* and Belgrade's *Vecernje novosti* were, for some time, the most hostile toward the Catholic Church, while other papers increasingly adopted a more balanced approach.

The Serbian Orthodox Church likewise found that its treatment at the hands of the secular media was uneven (until the end of 1987). Misleading and disparaging reports surfaced most frequently in *Oslobodjenje,* the Bosnian daily, although these reports were sometimes reprinted in other newspapers.[109]

Outward criticism—whether of religious leaders or dissident intellectuals or rock stars or other persons—would sometimes portray the persons concerned as engaged in illegal activity (though, usually, no one would be arrested or brought to trial) or as morally degenerate or politically disloyal or as disseminating disinformation (which, typically, would be challenged only in a polemical or sarcastic way). Outward criticism, thus, unlike inward criticism, has had more to do with trying to cast a pall over the reputations of certain people and with signalling to the readership that these people were, at least for party members, "off limits," than with any serious effort to raise and discuss issues. Outward criticism was a political tool of sectors of the political establishment; inward criticism was more usually a vehicle for persons (whether inside or outside the establishment) who were critical of the regime.

THE STRUGGLE FOR THE PRESS

After March 1988 and the entire *Mladina* affair, there was a subtle change in the attitudes and confidence of journalists vis-à-vis the authorities. Specific issues of prominent publications such as *Knjizevne novine, Start,* and *Nedjeljna Dalmacija* were banned—the first-named for publishing material "that could cause public concern"[110]— and in summer 1988, the influential weekly magazine, *NIN,* was subjected to a "house-cleaning," as various members of the editorial staff were fired and punished.[111] Meanwhile, Belgrade's "Politika" publishing house (of which *NIN* was, for that matter, a part) became the craven instrument of Slobodan Milosevic, and its newspapers started publishing a string of mendacious stories—falsely alleging that Albanian locals in Kosovo had fired mortars and bazookas at Serbian police,[112] falsely alleging that Croatian President Tudjman was receiving "instructions" from the Vatican and West Germany, and so forth.

By 1989, there were clear signs of revolt among journalists. As early as September 1989, the Society of Journalists of Croatia registered a strong protest against the policy of using the press as a "transmission belt" for the party line.[113] In Montenegro, when local party authorities sought to replace the editor of *Pobjeda* for political reasons, six of the paper's journalists called foul.[114] In Vojvodina, journalists protested editorial appointments and demanded the right to select their own editors.[115] And in Serbia, journalists of *Politika,* together with staff writers of Belgrade Television, joined in criticizing the political control of editorial policy and in demanding a relaxation of control.[116]

Pluralist-minded journalists scored an early victory in September 1989, with the disbanding of the *Komunist* party organization and the cessation of its work. *Komunist* had been one of the least credible and least read papers, despite its enormous print run (500,000 copies weekly in 1983). In Slovenia and Croatia, pluralization was achieved incrementally, so that one can scarcely find a date on which to pin the label "watershed." In Serbia, by contrast, breakthrough clearly came in March 1991, when Milosevic was forced to surrender his absolute control of the press. In Novi Sad, political appointee Svetozar Gavric was forced to step down as editor only four hours after his appointment, because journalists of *Dnevnik* were no longer willing to accept the old practice of political appointments.[117] In Belgrade, more than 100 journalists of the "Politika" publishing house demanded the resignation of the editors of *Politika, Politika ekspres, NIN, Intervju,* and *TV Politika,* and their replacement by professionals respected by the journalists. These developments were closely followed, on 18 March, by *Politika* journalists' call for journalistic independence.[118]

In essence, the journalists themselves abolished the old party monopoly of the press. The Federal Assembly adopted a new press law in November 1990, legalizing the free press, abolishing the censorship (which *Borba* explicitly referred to as such), and allowing foreign investors to own up to 49 per cent of the stock in any periodical.[119] The Serbian Assembly followed on 28 March 1991—within two weeks of the aforementioned protests—and likewise proclaimed an end to censorship and political control of the press. On the following day, *NIN* proclaimed its independence, with a commentary headlined "Fall of the Bastille."[120] In the same issue, *NIN* called on the Milosevic government to step down.

Meanwhile, a string of new, privately-owned periodicals began appearing, including: *Vreme* (Belgrade), *Bastina* (Belgrade), *RI Telefax* (Rijeka), and *Novi tjednik* (Rijeka).

CONCLUSION

The republicanization of the press has been a basic fact of Yugoslav public life and has been one of a number of factors which have pushed in the direction of the disintegration of the country. People in Bosnia commonly say that local Muslims read the Bosnian republic press (*Oslobodjenje, AS*), local Croats read the Croatian republic press (chiefly *Vjesnik* and *Vecernji list*), and Bosnian Serbs read the Serbian republic press (chiefly *Politika* but also *Politika ekspres*). In October 1989, the Belgrade daily, *Borba,* published the results of a public opinion poll in which 120 persons (20 per republic) were asked which papers they considered the most influential in the country, which they most respected, which they least respected, and which they read the most frequently. While the results for Slovenia and Macedonia are clearly affected by the fact that these republics speak different languages, it is clear that for all republics there is a close correlation between republic of residence and orientations toward the press (see Tables 4.1 and 4.2).

Only Macedonians (8 per cent), for example, cited the Skopje daily, *Nova Makedonija,* as one of the most influential papers in the country, and only Slovenes cited Slovenian periodicals (*Delo* 18 per cent, *Mladina* 11 per cent, and *Vecer* 7 per cent) among the most influential. Fifty-

TABLE 4.1   Which Periodical Do You Respect the Most? (120 people, 1989) (percentage)

	Bosnia	Croatia	Macedonia	Montenegro	Serbia	Slovenia
Serbian Papers						
Politika	25		27	27	31	
NIN			13	7	5	
Duga					9	
TV Revija				7		
Croatian Papers						
Vjesnik	4	10				
Start		14			14	
Slobodna Dalmacija		19				
Vecernji list	7	5				
Slovenian Papers						
Delo						23
Vecer						14
Mladina						9
Other Papers						
Borba			10			
Vecernje novosti				10		
Nova Makedonija			6			
Oslobodjenje	11					
Pobjeda				10		
Women's magazines						23
None			19			9

Source: Borba, October 2, 1989, p. 7, translated in Foreign Broadcast Information Service, Daily Report (Eastern Europe), October 23, 1989, pp. 58–59.

four per cent of Serbs mentioned *Politika,* but only 8 per cent of Croats did so. Only Croats and Bosnians cited the Croatian press.[121]

Asked what periodicals they respected most, 54 per cent of Serbs cited a Serbian periodical, 58 per cent of Croats cited a Croatian periodical, and 58 per cent of Montenegrins cited either a Montenegrin or a Serbian publication. Results in the other republics were more mixed.

And in terms of readership, 56 per cent of Macedonians rely chiefly on Macedonian periodicals, 42 per cent of Serbs rely chiefly on Serbian or Vojvodinan (*Dnevnik*) periodicals, 79 per cent of Croats rely chiefly on Croatian periodicals, 72 per cent of Slovenes on Slovenian periodicals, 68 per cent of Montenegrins on Montenegrin or Serbian periodicals, but only 26 per cent of Bosnians on Bosnian publications. Only in Bosnia did a large number of respondents (17 per cent) cite women's magazines as their major source of news and information.

Naturally, the influence any newspaper enjoys fluctuates over time. *Borba* and *Slobodna Dalmacija* were marginal papers ten years ago;

TABLE 4.2 Which Periodical Do You Read the Most Frequently? (120 people, 1989) (percentage)

	Bosnia	Croatia	Macedonia	Montenegro	Serbia	Slovenia
Serbian Papers						
Politika	9		12	18	30	
NIN			8	7	6	
Croatian Papers						
Vjesnik		15				
Start		7			6	
Slobodna Dalmacija		26				
Vecernji list	9	19				
Danas					6	
Slovenian Papers						
Delo						24
Vecer						10
Mladina						5
Ljubljanski Dnevnik						10
Revija						20
Macedonian Papers						
Nova Makedonija			33			
Politikin zabavnik			17			
Vecer			6			
Other						
Vecernje novosti	11	12	6	10	6	
Oslobodjenje	20					
Pobjeda				35		
Women's magazines	17					

Source: Borba, October 2, 1989, p. 7, translated in Foreign Broadcast Information Service, *Daily Report* (Eastern Europe), October 23, 1989, pp. 59–60.

by 1989, they were, together with *Delo,* arguably the most widely respected papers in the country. But neither *Slobodna Dalmacija* nor *Delo* can claim a wide readership outside their respective republics. Leaving aside ethnically mixed Bosnia, only the Serbian periodicals *Politika* and *NIN,* the Croatian weekly magazine *Danas* and fortnightly *Start,* and the Belgrade publications *Borba* and *Vecernje novosti* can claim a wide readership that extends beyond the boundaries of the republic in which they are published.[122]

The highest circulations are enjoyed by the evening tabloids *(Vecernje novosti, Vecernji list,* and *Politika ekspres),* although *Politika* and *Slobodna Dalmacija* also have circulations over 100,000 (see Table 4.3). Among Church publications, only the Catholic papers, *Druzina* and *Glas koncila,* have circulations in excess of 100,000.

I began this essay by noting that the press reflects the more general chaos which characterizes Yugoslavia. I shall close by noting that this

TABLE 4.3 Yugoslav Newspapers with Circulations Larger than 10,000 in Rank Order (1990)

	1990 sales (no. of copies)	1983 sales (no. of copies)
Vecernie novosti (Belgrade)	222,282	339,859
Vecernji list (Zagreb)	221,942	309,839
Politika ekspres (Belgrade)	198,790	249,758
Politikz (Belgrade)	184,551	243,826
Slobodna Dalmacija (Split)	107,483	71,571
Druzina (Ljubljana, Catholic)	100,000[a]	n/a
Glas koncila (Zagreb, Catholic)	100,000[a]	n/a
Delo (Ljubljana)	94,280	99,840
Ognjisce Koper, Catholic)	n/a	80,000[b]
Vjesnik (Zagreb)	74,563	73,030
Sportske novosti (Zagreb)	70,597	141,247
Vecernje novine (Sarajevo)	66,911	35,049
Novi list—Glas Istre (Rijeka)	56,586	71,274
Vecer (Maribor)	54,561	55,476
Mali koncil (Zagreb, Catholic)	n/a	50,000[d]
Oslobodjenje (Sarajevo)	47,690	71,557
Sport (Belgrade)	45,670	106,781
Sportski zurnal	42,142	n/a
Dnevnik (Novi Sad)	39,677	34,158
Borba (Belgrade)	31,408	30,976
Preporod (Sarajevo, Islamic)	n/a	30,000[d]
Nova Makedonija (Skopje)	23,404	25,089
Vecer (Skopje)	22,948	31,959
Pravoslavlje (Belgrade Orthodox)	n/a	22,000[c]
Magyar Szo (Novi Sad)	20,708	26,485
Pobjeda (Titograd)	19,570	20,073
Glas Slavonije	12,349	26,485

[a]1987.
[b]1973.
[c]1982.
[d]Number printed.

Sources: Nasa stampa (July-August 1983), pp. 9–10; *Nasa stampa* (February 1984), p. 9; AKSA (May 20, 1983); *NIN* (May 22, 1983), trans. in Foreign Broadcast Information Service, *Daily Report* (Eastern Europe), June 1, 1983; interviews, Belgrade and Zagreb, July 1982; and interviews, Zagreb and Ljubljana, June-July 1987; and *Slobodna Dalmacija* (Split), March 21, 1991, p. 23, trans. in FBIS, *Daily Report* (Eastern Europe), April 9, 1991, p. 42.

chaos—both at the systemic level and within the sphere of journalism specifically—was in part the deliberate design of the Tito era and served certain functions, in part the product of the partially successful struggle of certain editorial staffs (especially of *Start, Duga, NIN,* and the youth press) to broaden their latitude, in part the by-product of federalization, republicanization and devolution, and in part, a by-product of the gathering crisis and weakening of authority at the center. Ultimately, the republicanization of the press played a role in buttressing pressures for pluralization.

CHAPTER FIVE

◆

Rock Music

Yugoslavia, on your feet, and sing!
Whoever doesn't listen to this song,
Will hear a storm!

—Goran Bregovic and Bijelo dugme,
in "Pljuni i zapjevaj, moja Jugoslavijo" (1987)

WHEN GORAN BREGOVIC AND his group White Button (Bijelo dugme) began singing their song, "Spit and sing, my Yugoslavia," their fans would rise to their feet, tens of thousands of them, and sing along. The mood of the song was defiant. It was, Bregovic maintains, "a song which can frighten the politicians."[1] Later, in spring and summer 1988, when supporters of Serbian leader Slobodan Milosevic took to the streets in tens of thousands, to protest against the governments of Vojvodina and Montenegro and to show support, in Serbia, for Milosevic, they sang this song. It was, it turned out, a song of insurrection. The governments of Vojvodina and Montenegro fell, and were replaced with supporters of Milosevic.

This story is unusual only in degree, not in essence. Yugoslav rock music has long been deeply colored by political messages and political allusions. In this respect, Yugoslav rock music has been more typical of the East than of the West, where rock had reverted, by the 1970s, to its original cast as entertainment, and is less likely to engage in political communication. In the communist world, by contrast, including Yugoslavia, rock was very much attuned to political messages.

Many Yugoslav rock musicians are quite conscious of their role as bards or social critics, and many of their songs are topical, reflecting broader public moods and concerns. As Goran Bregovic put it, "We can't have any alternative parties or any alternative political programs. So there are not too many places where you can gather large groups of people and communicate ideas which are not official. Rock 'n' roll is one of the most important vehicles for helping people in communist countries to think in a different way."[2]

Rock music in a culturally diverse, politically decentralized environment such as Yugoslavia inevitably develops differently from the way it develops in an ethnically homogeneous, politically centralized system—let alone in a pluralist Western system. To begin with, the composite nationality groups of Yugoslavia have diverse musical culturess and psychological frameworks, so that musical devices which strike a resonant chord in, let us say, Macedonia, may seem arcane and very foreign in Slovenia or Croatia. Second, in conditions of republic "etatism" (as the Yugoslavs call their version of federalized state ownership), the market is fragmented and divided, with clear barriers. For rock musicians, the absence of a unified market means that there have long been in essence five independent rock networks in Yugoslavia: in Slovenia, Croatia, Bosnia, Vojvodina, and Serbia, and a star may hit it big in one republic and be ignored elsewhere.[3] There is an "intermittent" rock scene in Macedonia, centered in Skopje, but both because of tighter financial constraints in that republic and because of the language (which restricts the market), there is no record company in Macedonia. As a result, many Macedonian rock groups are unable to make albums and therefore, in the absence of publicity, wither away.[4]

THE EARLY YEARS

The pre-history of rock music in Yugoslavia was not propitious for the free development of the new genre. World War Two was scarcely over when Milovan Djilas, then head of propaganda of the CPY, set the tone for the regime's cultural policy in the early years. "America," said Djilas in 1947, "is our sworn enemy, and jazz, likewise, as the product of [the American system]."[5] Tito himself told his biographic, Vladimir Dedijer, at that time, "I like our folk music, but not stylized, as people start to do nowadays . . . Jazz, in my opinion, is not music. It is racket!"[6] Shortly after the war, therefore, Marshal Tito summoned some of Yugoslavia's top composers to his palace and told them that pop music and jazz cheated people of their money and spoiled young people.

With Tito's expulsion from the Cominform on 28 June 1948, music became potentially dangerous, as many unfortunate Yugoslavs discovered. Singing the wrong song could mean prison or penal labor. Russian songs—in political vogue for the three years immediately prior—were now definitely *out*. American tunes were, however, just as risky, as rival groups struggled to prove their communist "purity." Even Yugoslav folk songs risked accusations of bourgeois nationalism (even if Tito did like that genre). Some music had served several masters—a traditional

Croatian football song from earlier in the century had later been adapted, with new words, to serve as a patriotic song for the fascist regime. In the postwar period, the communists wrote new words. Other songs, innocent in their incarnation, might have become pernicious through later association, and unless the singer was certain, it was better not to sing indigenous music. These factors contributed, thus, to the sudden popularity of Mexican folk songs among the public, above all because they were ideologically and political safe.

But 1948 ultimately set Yugoslavia on a different course from the Soviet bloc states. Tito's decision, after his break with Stalin in 1948, to open Yugoslavia to contacts with the West was fateful for the development of rock 'n' roll, because it meant that Western rock would penetrate Yugoslavia more quickly and more easily than other countries in Eastern Europe. It meant, in consequence, that Yugoslav rock music would develop much more rapidly than rock music in, let us say, Hungary or Czechoslovakia, let alone Romania or Bulgaria.

As early as 1953, thus, Yugoslav jazz musicians were able—despite the authorities' dislike of the genre—to establish a musicians' association. By 1957, Predrag Ivanovic and his Orchestra were at the height of their popularity; their fare—American pop music of the day. And by the latter years of the fifties, rock 'n' roll was making its first inroads in the Balkans.

The early years of rock music in Yugoslavia were very much under the shadow of the West. Indeed, at its inception, the only interesting rock music came from either the United States or Great Britain. Bill Haley and the Comets, Chuck Berry, Buddy Holly, Jerry Lee Lewis, and Little Richard were among the artists whose music was heard in Yugoslavia before the end of the 1950s. Interest among Yugoslav young people in rock music took a leap at the beginning of the 1960s, when they started listening to the British groups Johnny and the Hurricanes, and the Shadows. Then the Zagreb record company "Jugoton" signed a deal with RCA to release some of Elvis Presley's records in Yugoslavia, and later brought out a domestic pressing of Chubby Checker's "Let's Twist Again." The Belgrade record company PGP RTB (a spin-off company from Radio-Television Belgrade) released a pressing of Johnny Hallyday's "Twist" also at this time.[7]

One of Yugoslavia's earliest rock stars was Karlo Metikos, who, in 1964, launched his recording career with a PGP RTB record, "Matt Collins sings R&R." Singing under a pseudonym, Metikos was the first Yugoslav artist to record covers of some of the original rock classics.[8]

In the years 1960–61, it was still relatively difficult for Yugoslavs to travel. But local rock musicians, who at that time were largely copying British and American songs, were determined to keep up with the latest releases. They would listen to Radio Luxemburg every night, and at 2 a.m., Radio Luxemburg would play the top ten songs of the day. At that time, the Shadows were the most influential group for Yugoslav rockers; hence, because the Shadows had three guitars and one percussionist, every Yugoslav group at that time had three guitars and one percussionist.[9]

In 1961, Josip Kovac, a composer from Subotica (Vojvodina), came up with the idea of organizing a festival of popular music by young talent. The first festival was so successful that it was repeated a year later; the result was an annual pop festival in which, over time, the rock component became ever more important. Some of Yugoslavia's biggest rock stars have performed at the Subotica Festival at one time or another. The 30th annual festival in Subotica was held 24–27 May 1990.[10]

The Beatles were scarcely noticed in Yugoslavia until 1964 or 1965, but then they arrived in force. The Rolling Stones briefly eclipsed the Beatles in popularity in Yugoslavia, after the release of their album, "Satisfaction." But the Beatles soon recaptured the limelight. The June 25, 1967 satellite emission of "All You Need is Love" was seen by an estimated 150 million people around the world, including many young people in Yugoslavia. By October of that year, Jugoton released a domestic pressing of "Sgt. Pepper's Lonely Hearts Club Band." And by then, there were also Yugoslav pressings of "A Collection of Beatles Oldies," the Beach Boys' "Greatest Hits," Jimi Hendrix's "Are You Experienced?," and singles by various other artists, including the Walker Brothers, the Spencer Davies Group, and Arthur Brown.[11]

At that time, Yugoslav groups were exclusively oriented toward the American and British repertoire. Groups such as White Arrows (Bijele strijele), Red Corals (Crveni koralji), the Golden Boys (Zlatni decaci), Indexes (Indeksi), Chameleons (Kameleoni), Silhouettes (Siluete), Robots (Roboti), Elipse, the Boyfriends (Rdecki decki), the Five Flames (Plamenih pet), and Dreamers (Sanjalice) were characteristic of this trend. Some of these groups, in particular Elipse (from Belgrade), Hurricanes (Uragani, from Rijeka), Robots (from Zagreb), and We (Mi, from Sibenik) became interested in black music, in particular the music of Aretha Franklin, Wilson Pickett, and Otis Redding. Later, some of these groups started to write their own soul music, in Croatian, though on the whole, without success.[12]

About this time, Drago Mlinarec put together a band he called Group 220. The group played original music, modeled on American rock of the time, but showed some versatility, e.g., by doing a rock version of a traditional *Schlager* hit, "Vecer na Robleku."

The most important rock groups in Sarajevo in the late 1960s were Cicak and Codex (Kodeksi). While groups in Belgrade and Zagreb were playing soul music, these Sarajevo bands tuned in to progressive rock currents. Codex, in particular—led by Zeljko Bebek—showed an affinity for the musical styles of Cream and Jimi Hendrix.

One of the most often mentioned groups from the 1960s is Korni Group, named for its leader, Kornell Kovach, a classically trained pianist who would later devote himself to composing and producing records. Korni Group was formed in 1968 in Belgrade and played for six years. The group constantly tested the limits of the market, composing rock "symphonies" and showing a clear preference for longer pieces, rather than short commercially-oriented songs. Korni Group created a small scandal at a Zagreb concert in 1969 by playing a 20-minute song; audiences at that time were not accustomed to such things. Korni Group was also the first Yugoslav band to put out an LP on the international market, with an album produced by Carlo Alberto Rossi in Milan.[13]

REBELLION OR CONFORMITY

Deliberations about rock 'n' roll took place at the highest level, and Tito and Kardelj are said to have personally decided against the repressive approach favored in Moscow, Prague, Bucharest, and Tirana, for example. They believed that a policy of toleration within carefully controlled limits could produce better results. The result, according to journalist Dusan Vesic, is that "from the middle of the sixties until only a few years ago, [Yugoslav] rockers were the greatest servants of the Tito regime!"[14]

Hence, although, almost from the beginning, the party's cultural commissars were sensitive to rock's potential for stirring rebellious sentiments, they opted for cooptation rather than repression. Astutely, they made it worthwhile for rock musicians to cooperate. The result was a pronounced sycophantic streak in Yugoslav rock, beginning at an early stage.

The group Indeksi, for example—prominent in the mid-1960s—penned a song, "Yugoslavia" which included the lines,

> We knew that the sun was smiling on us,
> because we have Tito for our marshal!

Much later, Indeksi veteran Davorin Popovic produced an album, *Mostar Rain: Our Name is Tito,* which was released shortly after Tito's death in May 1980. It included a song titled, "After Tito, Tito" (lyrics by J. Sliska, based on a text by Misa Maric):

While he lived, he was
with us and with the world
While he lived, he was
the sun above the planet.

While he lived, he was
a wild hero in a tale
While he lived, he was
such, that we were proud of him.

And what now, southern land?
If anyone should ask us,
we shall say, again Tito:
After Tito, Tito.

We shall say, again Tito.
Tito lives with us
Tito was just one man,
but we are also Tito![15]

Kornell Kovach, who retired from performing in 1974 in order to devote himself to composing, has been described, unflatteringly, by *Pop Rock* magazine as having been "the greatest patriot of Yugoslav rock 'n' roll."[16] His early song, "People's Government," celebrated Tito's smashing of "the traitorous clique."

Even Bora Djordjevic, who donned the mantle of rock rebel in the 1980s, was circumspect in the Tito era. In 1977, for example, he sang a panegyric song, "The World of Tito," in duet with Gorica Popovic, on the album, *Brigadier songs*. Zeljko Bebek (at one time, a close associate of Goran Bregovic's) and pop singer Djordje Balasevic are other performers who were willing to "carry the torch" for Tito. Not all rock musicians played "panegyric rock," but many did. Their presence and subsequent success provide clues as to the nature of the Tito and post-Tito regimes.

YUGOSLAV ROCK COMES OF AGE

As Ljuba Trifunovic points out, 1974, the year in which Korni Group folded, was also the year in which Goran Bregovic created White Button. Bregovic's new group drew unabashedly on ethnic melodies and succeeded, in the process, in giving a "Yugoslav" stamp to rock music. White Button quickly established itself as one of the most popular groups in the country—a position it has never lost. Already in the late

1970s, White Button concerts were rousing young fans (especially of the opposite sex) to paroxysms of "Buttonmania."[17]

By 1976, members of the establishment began to notice that the rock scene was growing. University of Belgrade Professor Sergij Lukac wrote a series of hard-hitting articles for *NIN*, which blasted White Button. Similarly, Sladjana Aleksandra Milosevic, a soft rock vocalist from Belgrade, was subjected to regular press attacks at this time; the articles typically criticized her Western-style attire and attacked her for "erotic aggressiveness."[18] Other rock performers were also given rude, even vicious treatment in the press, but, for the most part, these had no practical significance for the rock scene and no party forum has ever undertaken to campaign against rock or to obstruct the holding of large rock concerts.[19]

The 1970s were in fact the years of the big "Boom" rock festivals in Yugoslavia, drawing thousands of fans to Woodstock-style events in Ljubljana, Novi Sad, and eventually Belgrade. The "Boom" festivals were eventually stopped—for commercial reasons[20]—but smaller festivals have continued to this day, in Skopje, Zemun, Novi Sad, Avala, and elsewhere.

By the 1970s, Yugoslav rock groups, which at first had felt (like rock groups throughout the world) that rock could only be sung in English, were composing and singing in their own languages—Serbo-Croatian, Slovenian, and in much smaller numbers, Macedonian.

The major rock groups of the late 1970s were White Button, Azra (now defunct), Index (the first Yugoslav group to play its own material), Bora Djordjevic's Fish Soup (Riblja corba) from Belgrade, and the Macedonian group, Bread and Salt (Leb i sol). The last two bands were established only in 1978.[21]

Belgrade and Sarajevo were the clear centers for rock 'n' roll in the 1970s, with Zagreb and Ljubljana close behind, and, for commercial reasons, Serbo-Croatian was the language of rock. Bread and Salt aspired to a national audience and therefore sang most of its songs in Serbo-Croatian, not Macedonian. Similarly, the Slovenian group Bulldozer (Buldozer), seeking a national audience, sang in Serbo-Croatian, rather than in Slovenian.

Bulldozer became, in fact, one of the legends of the 1970s. A kind of Yugoslav equivalent of the Mothers of Invention, Bulldozer took up political themes at a time when most Yugoslav rock groups still avoided politics. In their song, "Good morning Madame Jovanovic," for example, they seemed to satirize both Jovanka Tito and the Yugoslav National Army at the same time—daring in any era.[22]

Yugoslavia has shared in *all* the major American and world trends in rock music. When punk developed in Britain, for instance, it quickly spread to Yugoslavia, where groups like the Bastards (Pankrti, from Ljubljana), Electric Orgasm (Elektricni orgazam, from Belgrade), and Dirty Theater (Prljavo kazaliste, from Zagreb) got their start playing punk. Ljubljana became a center for punk and even punk-Nazi music, with groups such as Epidemic, the Trash of Civilization, and the "4-R" (Fourth Reich). Now, in the post-punk era, Ljubljana is still a haven for underground music, as served up, for example, by the bands Demolition Group and Del Masochistas. Some of these groups—Bastards, Dirty Theater, and Electric Orgasm, in particular—later evolved away from punk.

New wave (*novi talas*) came to Yugoslavia at the end of the 1970s. Rock-a-billy, heavy metal, trash metal, speed metal, death metal, and assorted other currents have also won adherents in the country. By 1986, heavy metal had built up sufficient presence to make it possible to hold what proved to be only the first in a series of annual heavy metal concerts in Sarajevo. Groups such as Storm Cloud (Storm klaud), Bombarder, Earthquake (Zemljotres), Formula 4, Dr. Steel (from Rijeka), and Legion (Legija, from Zagreb) took part in the first such festival, attended by some 2,000 fans. By 1988, the festival had become a two-day event, and the list of participating bands had grown, to include Atomic Shelter (Atomsko skloniste), Kerber, the Eighth Traveler (Osmi putnik, from Split), Heavy Company, and Fiery Kiss (Vatreni poljubac, from Sarajevo).[23]

The most important rock groups in Yugoslavia today are: the *Belgrade* groups Fish Soup, Bajaga and the Instructors (formed in 1984), and Yu-Group; *Sarajevo*'s White Button; *Ljubljana*'s Laibach (formed in 1980) and Falcons (formed in summer 1989); and *Skopje*'s Bread and Salt. Other groups which have attracted attention in the last two to three years include two *Zagreb* bands—Dee Dee Mellow (formed in 1988 and discussed below) and Modesty (formed from the wreckage of two demo bands)—and the Belgrade band, Department Store (Robna kuca), formed at the medical faculty of the University of Belgrade in April 1988 and enjoying considerable popularity in Belgrade by 1990. Zagreb's Dirty Theater (Prljavo kazaliste) slowly built its reputation as a solid band, and was widely considered Croatia's most popular rock band in 1990 and 1991. Also strong are the band Electric Orgasm (Elektricni orgazam) from Belgrade, though it has not performed in public since about 1988, and the riotous and ever-popular Party Breakers (Partibrejkers) also from Belgrade. These latter two groups probably do not, however, enjoy quite the influence that most of the aforementioned bands mentioned above do. Some all-female acts also deserve mention, specifically Cacadou Look (established in the mid-1980s in Opatija and singing largely in English) and Boja (a Vojvodina band).

The Rijeka group Flight 3 (Let 3) features females on guitar and bass guitar, while their male lead singer has performed in lingerie.[24]

Yugoslavia's top female solo vocalist, since the mid-1980s, is Snezana Miskovic Viktorija, voted top female vocalist by *Pop Rock* readers in a 1988 survey.[25] Other women to make their mark in the late 1980s include Marina Perezic (a member of a duo, Denis and Denis, which made two records before she left the duo and went solo), Neda Ukraden (a pop singer from Sarajevo), Josipa Lisac (who got her start in the late 1970s in Zagreb), and Baby Doll (alias Dragana Saric, from Belgrade, who recorded one album and a few singles, spinning exotic songs built on Arabic themes, after spending six months in Cairo).[26] A special mention should also be made of YU-Madonna (alias, Andrea Makoter of Maribor), who performed at a number of festivals in summer 1988, mimicking *the* Madonna in singing style, attire, mannerisms, etc.[27] Among the top male vocalists one may mention Oliver Mandic (a Belgrade singer who created a small storm in the mid-1980s by performing in drag), Rambo Amadeus (whom I like to think of as the PDQ Bach of rock music, because of a piece he once staged for 12 vacuum cleaners),[28] and Tonny Montano (an ever-changing, ever-present entertainer, who has evolved from punk to rockabilly to parody with a "beat" look). Aside from these, one may make a special mention of Djordje Balasevic, a bard singer with wide influence, performing message-songs. In Russia, Balasevic would be counted as a "rock" performer, because of his lyrics; in Yugoslavia he is considered, as he would be in the West, a pop singer, because of his music.

THE ETHNIC IMPULSE

When rock first came to Yugoslavia, musical adepts approached it in much the way that one would learn a new language. They studied the existing patterns and techniques and worked to master them and replicate them. There was little thought given, at first, to innovation. But as young Yugoslav musicians mastered the new "language" and matured musically, they became increasingly willing to innovate and to look to autochthonous sources of musical inspiration. Inevitably, some of them turned to the folk heritage of Yugoslavia.

The first group to do so was White Button, and the Sarajevo group continues to draw upon folk idioms for inspiration. Bregovic himself argues that ethnic and folk music is the richest source for material, and that it is the most promising future for rock music (and not just in Yugoslavia).

But White Button has not been alone in this. Fiery Kiss, for example, during the 10 years of its existence (1977–1987), incorporated a lot of folk elements into their melodies, and some of their songs used a syncopation which is native to Balkan folk music, not to rock. The group adapted Bosnian folk music, with its blend of Turkish and Arabian elements, and played it on traditional rock instruments. The symbiosis of folk and rock in the performance art of Fiery Kiss was reflected in the fact that a lot of their songs were picked up by the popular folk singer Hanka Paldum and marketed as "folk" songs. In a fitting close to this story, the group's leader, Milic Vukasinovic, eventually became dissatisifed with the modest earnings as a rock musician and made the switch to folk.[29]

Another Sarajevo band, Blue Orchestra (Plavi Orkestar), which enjoys considerable popularity among teenagers, did something similar in its record, "Death to Fascism!" (Smrt fasizmu!—the old partisan greeting from World War Two). Released in 1987, the album blended folk musical motifs with partisan themes, singing about the war, the liberation of Belgrade, and Jovanka Tito, the late president's widow. In one song, the group sang the refrain, "Fa-fa-fascist! Don't be a fascist!" The album was celebrated as a species of "new patriotism," and inevitably provoked controversy. Some people suggested (ludicrously) that their lyrics had been written by the Central Committee; others attacked them as "state enemy no. 1."[30] They found themselves cast as the "new partisans" of Yugoslav rock music. Sasa Losic, the leader of the Blue Orchestra, went into deep depression, and when he emerged out of this depression in 1989, with the release of a new album, he was preaching a new musical philosophy: "Rock 'n' roll has reached its limit, the end of its possibilities. We keep going back to the fifties, the sixties, the seventies. Punk was, in reality, a primal energy for rock 'n' roll. Then there were the new romantics of sympho-rock in the 1970s. Now we are returning to the trends of the seventies."[31]

Ethnic music figures in an entirely different way in the music of the Zagreb group, Dee Dee Mellow. Instead of drawing on indigenous sources, the group has looked beyond European frontiers, for inspiration, and their first album included, among other things, a rendition of a Peruvian Indian song ("Adios Pueblo de Ayacucho"), and an adaptation of an American Indian song, sung in the Sioux language ("Sitting Bull Song").[32] Put together largely by former members of the then dormant group Haustor—specifically Jura Nolosevic, Srdjan 'Gul' Gulic, and Igor Pavlitza—Dee Dee Mellow continues Haustor's tradition of social commentary, but with a new twist. Instead of brooding about the gravity of the situation, the new group responds with silliness (the next stage after despair). Hence, in one song, written at a time when newspapers already cost 3000 dinars and by which time literally everybody had become a "millionaire" in inflated dinars, they sing,

What am I going to do
with all of this money?
Wine yoghurt,
and a half a loaf of bread.

Other bands have also drawn upon ethnic music. For example, YU-Group, at the end of the 1970s, did a song ("Kosovo Flower") using traditional Albanian rythms.

And finally, there are regionally specific trends in Vojvodina and Macedonia which reflect the synthesis of folk elements and rock music. The Hungarian inhabitants of Vojvodina share in a musical phenomenon common also to Hungary and the Hungarian population of Transylvania. Known as *sogor* rock (brother-in-law rock), the genre uses the rythms of Hungarian folk music and even some of the traditional folk instruments, but plays them in a rock format. The performers themselves are generally attired rather more in the tradition of folk performers than like rock musicians, and their music has no resonance beyond the Hungarian population. *Sogor* rock started in hotels and bars in the late 1970s, but the first *sogor* records were released only in 1987.

Macedonia is far more interesting, in this regard, having given birth to a new tendency, which, for lack of a better term, one may call "Byzantine rock." To a considerable extent, this is the brainchild of Goran Trajkovski, now the leading musical figure in the independent multimedia cultural group *Aporea* (*Apo*krifna *rea*lnost, Apocryphal Reality). Trajkovski explains his thinking in these terms: "Everything in Macedonia is connected with Orthodoxy, and Orthodoxy is very much the legacy of Byzantium. The Church was the chief civilizing force here for hundreds of years. So our religion always connects us with our past. As a result, the sense of history is very different here from what it is in Slovenia, for example. Our ideas in Aporea, our work, our music, are all derived from Orthodoxy."[33]

In 1984, Trajkovski created the Fall of Byzantium (Padat na Vizantija), and began to work with Orthodox liturgical music in a rock format. The effect was to preserve the spirit of the traditional music but to transform it into patterns which are intelligible to the modern listener. The Fall of Byzantium folded in 1985, but its work was continued, in a multi-media format, by Aporea (although it would be hard to call Aporea's music "rock").

Existing alongside Aporea is the rock group Mizar, which was created in 1981 as a kind of post-punk band. At first it seemed oriented toward something akin to Pink Floyd,[34] but even so, from the very beginning, Mizar drew upon traditional Macedonian music and culture for inspiration.[35] Later Mizar likewise began to look to Orthodox music for material, but with a difference. Whereas Aporea glorifies Byzantine culture, Mizar, according to Trajkovski, "rejected Byzantium, and Byzantine culture." For almost two years (1985–87), Mizar was cooperating closely with Aporea, but in 1987, there was a rift and Mizar went its own way. Like the Fall of Byzantium, Mizar sings largely in Macedonian (a point which distinguishes it from the better known band, Bread and Salt), although Mizar has also sung some songs in Old Church Slavonic (the language preferred by Aporea).

POLITICIANS AND ROCK

There is something intrinsically "oppositionist" about rock music: that is completely obvious to everyone. Rock is, in its very soul, about freedom, about individual self-determination, about self-expression. That is why any effort to harness rock music to a role supportive of official policy—as was made in the USSR in the case of the official group Happy Guys in the pre-Gorbachev era—is bound to end up looking ridiculous. That is also one reason, though not the only reason, why the first generation of rockers invariably confronted distrust, fear, and even hostility from political authorities—not just in Yugoslavia, but throughout the world, including in the United States, even, to some extent, if they were willing to serve the authorities.[36]

The Sarajevo band Smoking Forbidden (Zabranjeno pusenje) had an experience that may illustrate the point. During a concert in Rijeka in November 1984, one of the loudspeakers (brand name "Marshal") suddenly stopped functioning. Disgusted with this unforeseen inconvenience, band leader Nele Karajlic exclaimed, "The marshal has broken down." Everyone at the concert knew that he was talking about the amplifier. But a month later, unknown persons hostile to the group decided to create trouble, and a series of sharp attacks appeared in *Vjesnik, Politika, Borba,* and elsewhere, asking why Karajlic had not said, instead, "The Marshal *is dead.*" The papers then insinuated that Karajlic had deliberately shown disrespect.[37] The band suffered. Previously scheduled concerts were abruptly canceled, and new bookings could not be obtained. Finally, in early 1985, Karajlic wrote an open letter to *Politika,* explaining the situation and making it clear that no disrespect to Marshal Tito had been intended. The letter was published, and in February 1985, the group staged a "comeback" concert in Belgrade, attended by some 10,000 fans. The atmosphere was nervous, and the first two rows were taken by police.[38]

Fish Soup's Bora Djordjevic was taken to court twice—in 1987[39] and in 1989—but was acquitted both times. In both cases, his lyrics got him into trouble. But that did not prevent him from publishing four books of poetry and being elected to the Serbian Association of Writers.

White Button's Goran Bregovic was *threatened* with court action after the group performed a song in which the traditional national hymns of the Serbs and Croats were played back to back, but nothing came of it.

On the whole, however, it is rare that the political authorities take the trouble to discuss the political merits or demerits of a particular ensemble. The most striking examples when such discussions took place come from Slovenia. In the first instance, after the punk-Nazi group "4-R" displayed swastikas at a concert and performed in Nazi-style uniforms, the School of Political Science of Ljubljana University organized a roundtable discussion about punk-Naziism, attended by the Slovenian Republic Secretary for Internal Affairs and representatives from the Ljubljana City Secretariat for Internal Affairs and the Supreme Court of Slovenia. But "4-R" was a minor band, and as such, it could provoke only a low level of response.

Authorities paid much more attention, by far, to the art rock group Laibach, which likewise performed in Nazi regalia, but which was far more sophisticated and far more influential than "4-R." Laibach introduced itself as the Musical Division of a totalitarian movement calling itself *Neue Slowenische Kunst* (New Slovenian Art). German was the preferred language for this movement, because it is historically identified with Naziism. A member of *Neue Slowenische Kunst* told me in 1987, "The very fact that Naziism is always tarred as the blackest evil is a way of not dealing with its social content and meaning." Another NSK member told me in 1989, "We want a great totalitarian leader. God is a totalitarian being. Totalitarianism, for us, is a positive phenomenon. We admire leaders like Alexander the Great, Caesar, Napoleon. As for Hitler, his mistake was to confuse the general with the particular." And yet, Laibach is clearly fixated on Hitler: he is the central inspiration for their artistry, in both form and substance. Their record covers feature swastikas, they sing militant, Nazi-sounding "rock" in German; and when the group decided to do a cover on the Beatles' album "Let it Be" in 1988, they pointedly left out the title song and replaced it with a militant rendition of "Auf der Lüeburger Heide." The effect is right out of a Nazi propaganda film.

Earlier, in 1987, the group released an album significantly titled "Opus Dei"—the Work of God. Taking a song, "Life is life," which had originally been performed by a German group, Opus, as an innocent, soft rock number, Laibach recast it as a militant, eerily totalitarian march. They sing,

When we all give the power
We give our best,
All that we can, our fullest efforts,
With no thought to rest.

And we all get the power
We all get the best
When everyone gives everything
Then everyone will get everything.
Life is life!

Life is life.
When we all feel the power,
Life is life.
When we all feel the pain,

Life is life.
It's the feeling of the people,
Life is life.
It's the feeling of the land.

Laibach clearly benefitted from the relatively more liberal atmosphere prevailing in Slovenia. In other parts of Yugoslavia, the group might have been banned altogether. But even in Slovenia, authorities would not allow anything to be published in the republic about Laibach, until 1983 or 1984, except in the youth magazine, *Mladina*.[40] Elsewhere, Laibach experienced first hand the significance of decentralization in a federalized system. Laibach was prevented from performing in many cities in Yugoslavia.[41] For example, until 1986, Laibach was banned from appearing in Bosnia-Herzegovina altogether, and the group did not actually play in that republic until 7 April 1989, when it performed at Sarajevo's Center for the Social Activities of Youth. When the manager of that Center first scheduled them to perform, there was tremendous pressure on him from the authorities to cancel the concert, including threatening phone calls to his unlisted home phone. He did not sleep for two nights before the concert, but he refused to cave in, and the concert went ahead as planned. Predictably, after the concert, the authorities bragged about what good democrats they were to have authorized the concert.

Created in September 1980, Laibach has released about a dozen albums overseas, although the albums can be purchased, as imports, in Slovenia. They have succeeded, unlike any other Yugoslav rock group, in building a worldwide following, and in 1989, for example, did an American concert tour, performing in New York, Washington DC, Boston, and Los Angeles.

CENSORSHIP—NOW YOU SEE IT, NOW YOU DON'T

Tito did not establish a separate Office of Censorship per se, and there certainly has not been any government office entrusted with the task of listening to rock demos and determining what may and may not be pressed. Yet all the same, the communist system was set up in such a way that censorship resulted. In any recording company, the responsible editor was always a party member, and was required to review all rock songs before a disc would be pressed. And even while they might be sympathetic to the rock musicians, record producers, studio directors, and concert managers frequently feared what *might* happen to them if they allowed certain things to be performed. Hence, rather than take a chance, they tended to play it safe. The result was that rock musicians have had to change their costumes, change their record jackets, delete certain songs from certain albums, adjust their repertoire at certain concerts, and even rewrite their lyrics. Talking to rock musicians in Yugoslavia, I heard numerous stories of intervention by nervous record producers and so forth. The intention was sometimes not primarily to suppress anything, but simply to save their own skins. The result was a form of censorship.

For example, Smoking Forbidden made a rock video with the title, "Maniac," about a politician, a family man, who has an illicit romantic adventure, literally going mad in the process. In the video, the mad politician uses "Tops" crackers as bait to lure the girl of his dreams. The video was made in March 1987, a few months before the Agrokomerc corruption scandal broke. But as it turned out, "Tops" crackers were made by Agrokomerc. Nobody would believe that the video had been made *before* Agrokomerc made the headlines. That was a contributing factor to keeping the video off TV.

Goran Bregovic's White Button likewise had its share of problems. In 1976, for example, Bregovic wanted to title his album *Hey! I Want to be Stupid*. He had to be happy with the bland *Hey! I Want*. Nor were the authorities happy when Bregovic took on religion, and in 1979, he had trouble with the line, "and Christ was a bastard and a worry [to his mother]," intended for a song for the album, *Batanga and the Princess*. Even in 1986, Bregovic ran into trouble when he wanted to engage Vice Vukov to sing a song on his album, *Spit and Sing, my Yugoslavia!* Vukov had been viewed as a kind of bard of Croatian nationalism back in 1970–71 and now, 15 years later, the Chief of Police of the Republic of Bosnia took part in discussions about

Bregovic's desire to involve Vukov in one song.[42] Vukov finally made his comeback in 1989, with a record of Neapolitan songs.

Bora Djordjevic has had similar problems with his songs and poems. In 1970, for example, he was prevented from singing the line, "Yet another scabby day"—lest this pessimism be taken as directed against the system.[43] In 1982, after the release of the latest Fish Soup album, the Veterans Association of Macedonia became upset because some of the old partisans felt that one of the songs included lines insulting to veterans of the national liberation struggle. Some hotheads in the Veterans Association said the album should be banned; others wanted to ban Fish Soup altogether. A few even talked about getting rock music banned altogether in Yugoslavia—as it was, at the time, in Albania. But Bora had contacts in high places, including a close relative, and eventually an unnamed high official contacted Kosta Nadj (the head of the Veterans Association of Yugoslavia) and told him to call off the hounds.[44]

Again, in 1984, Bora was preparing his album, *Tonight, Drunk Musicians Play for You,* for release by Jugoton, when the recording company's chief editor, Dubravko Majnaric, rejected Bora's song, "Sudba, Udba, Ozna,"[45] with the rhetorical question, "Young man, what do you know about UDBa and OZNA?"[46] The song "Power of the Opposition" could not be included on his 1987 album "The Truth" (Istina) for political reasons, but was released on videocassette a year or two later.[47] Various texts originally intended for his second book (published in spring 1987, while Ivan Stambolic was still the party boss in Serbia),[48] were prohibited at that time, only to be passed for publication in his subsequent book,[49] by which time Slobodan Milosevic had replaced Stambolic as the party boss in Serbia. Among the poems originally banned are several nationalist poems about Kosovo, for example:

Eenie meenie minie mo,
I'm a little rabbit
I eat little chickens
I have a big stomach
I eat little Serbs.

No one could mistake the fact that the poem was about Kosovo's Albanians. Or again:

I don't buy that pure shit
that they come to Sumadija,
but if they come to Sumadija,
I prefer to kick the bucket.

I don't need that Balkan city,
I need the Patriachate of Pec.
I need a little change
in surnames in Prizren.

And never will there be any peace
between me and the "Illyrian."
Is it possible that some Shiptar
will seize the Serbian crown and scepter?

These poems, out of favor in Stambolic's day, came very much into favor with the political authorities once Milosevic took charge in Serbia. Similarly, Bora Djordjevic's original criticisms of Tito were courageous when Stambolic was in charge. Now Milosevic himself criticizes the man he prefers to call "Josip Broz."

But there is more to Bora than just nationalism; he is, above all, quintessentially anti-establishment. In another once banned poem, he writes,

Oh God, give me a black Mercedes,
with a little registration,
so that I can finally view myself
as an official fool.

Oh God, give me a black Mercedes
with at least six doors
so that I can tap my havana
into a gold ashtray.

Oh God, give me a black Mercedes
because it is a miracle above all miracles.
It is beautiful to drive unpenalized
over flowers and people.[50]

Sometimes, record producers have approved an album but pressured the group to make alterations. The Bastards, for example, were compelled to change an album cover in 1982, because the producer was nervous about the original design.[51] Or again, Goran Bregovic's White Button had to put up with having sections of their songs literally spliced out, after being recorded, because the words were considered "potentially offensive." Needless to say, this left some telltale signs in their early albums.

It is symptomatic of the nature of a watched society that people fear to get involved in others' troubles. The result, as Vesic dolefully noted in 1990, was a lack of solidarity among Yugoslav rock musicians. When White Button was under fire in 1976, not a single band came to its defense. When the Veterans Association of Macedonia attacked Bora's Fish Soup in 1982, again not a single rock musician or rock band raised a voice in protest, and Bora had to rely on his own resources.[52] Rock musicians who tried to play the gadfly, found it impossible, thus, to ignite anything like a protest movement. Or, to put it analogically, in Tito's Yugoslavia, the system did not allow enough freedom for anyone to be able to play a role anything like Joan Baez or Bob Dylan did in the late 1960s in the US.

Editorial interventions of a political nature were thus commonplace, but one should not exaggerate their frequency either. There are many groups who have never had any problems with "intervention," especially commercial bands with no social awareness. The problems begin when a band becomes socially aware.

To be socially aware is not necessarily to be politically controversial or critical, however. Rock groups have addressed issues of social isolation, growing up, ethnic feuding, and other issues which are not necessarily troubling to the authorities. The late President Tito (elected "without termination of mandate") likewise remains a favorite theme for Yugoslav rock groups. For example, the Elvis J. Kurtovic Band of Sarajevo released an album in 1988 with the tongue-in-cheek title, "The Wonderful World of Private Business." It includes a song nominally about Emperor Haile Selassie of Ethiopia:

When I was young
the teacher took us to the main street
to see his Majesty Haile Selassie
drive past in a black limousine.
We were all so happy,
and the street was packed with people
all to see our friend from nonaligned Ethiopia.

He was an amazing man,
loved by the masses,
wise like Gandhi,
and as handsome as Nasser.
Of all our friends,
he was the best.
He led his people
to wealth and happiness.

Set to rock rhythms, it was perfectly clear that the lyrics were not intended to be taken solemnly. Thus, even though the song appeared on the album, the group was not allowed to perform it on television.[53]

Another Sarajevo group, Smoking Forbidden (Zabranjeno pusenje), tried to capture people's mood when Tito died—the sense of loss, the sense of greatness past. The song works allegorically, talking about the great soccer player Hase's last match:

The people go into the stadium
and it was hushed.
People said,
Today is Hase's last game . . .
They spoke of his past glories,
Of what a great player he had been.
They talked of how he beat the Germans
and the Russians
and the British.
And then the referee blew the whistle,
With the game tied at 1-to-1.
The people leave in silence,
nobody is talking.
Sunday stops in its tracks,
but May goes on.
Some fans chant,
"Go team, charge.
There is only one Hase."[54]

NEW PRIMITIVISM

When Elvis J. Kurtovic, "Dr." Nele Karajlic, and a few other rock musicians in Sarajevo decided to satirize the cultural and political backwardness of some of their fellow citizens, they gave their "movement" a name—"new primitivism." The idea took shape at a cafe in the Bascarsija district of Sarajevo, over a copy of the local newspaper, *Oslobodjenje*. It was 1981, and *Oslobodjenje* was reflecting on a new film, "Quadrophenia," which dealt with Teddy-boys and Mods in Great Britain. *Oslobodjenje* launched into a long jeremiad about "long-haired punks and hippies" whom "local good youths" would "devour." Kurtovic, Karajlic, and friends knew, of course, that punks don't have long hair like hippies. But the text inspired them. They decided to satirize these "local good youth" by dressing and acting like them, and singing about them; they adopted the name "new primitives." "We started to dress without any taste, quite deliberately," Kurtovic recalls. "We looked like those *Gastarbeiter* in the film, *Montenegro*. Our music combined American rock ideologies, Japanese technology, and local domestic primitivism."[55] Their satire was not appreciated by the "old primitives," however, who understood that they were the butt of "new primitive" humor. But the "new primitives" made a serious point. In Karajlic's words, "The basic problem in Yugoslavia is not politics, but culture. There is no great culture here—no great classical composers, only a few important writers, a handful of great sculptors. If you don't have great culture, you can't have great ideas. And if you are behind in ideas, everything else follows."[56] Or in Kurtovic's words, "The problem of this country is primitivism. We can change the whole system and adopt capitalism, but we won't be like West Germany, we'll be like Turkey—primitive."

A classic product of "new primitivism" was the song, "Anarchy all over Bascarsija," which dealt with the reflections of a typical "old primitive." He feels good about having beaten up a young hippie, gets nervous when he sees the letter "A" scrawled on a wall in the Bascarsija district, and broods about the West, because it is changing the way young people dress.[57]

New primitivism was, of course, never a movement as such. But this satirical treatment won the Elvis J. Kurtovic Band and Karajlic's Smoking Forbidden a loyal following among Yugoslav young people, and won them the respect of intellectuals in the country.

THE SUPPORT SYSTEM

Rock music is a product which must be managed, promoted, advertised, and sold. The "support system" is, thus, a critical factor in the Yugoslav rock scene.

There are 11 record and cassette companies in Yugoslav which produce at least some rock (as of 1987). The major companies are Jugoton of Zagreb, which issues about 30 new rock albums each year, and PGP RTB of Belgrade, which issues about 45–50 new rock albums each year. Together these two companies thus account for 75–80 per cent of all new albums marketed in Yugoslavia.[58] The chief recording outlets for Slovenian groups are the Ljubljana companies Helidon and RTV Ljubljana. Relatively few records are reissued after the initial pressings are sold out, and many groups which are popular in their own republics (e.g., the Bastards in Slovenia, and the Nis group Galija in Serbia) receive little or no organized promotion outside their own republics. 100,000 in sales is widely viewed as the barrier to be broken, but experimental bands generally have to be happy with sales of 2,000–

5,000. Several people told me that while the companies put a lot of money into promoting folk music, they make no serious efforts to promote rock music, and that there are, for example, practically no commercials for rock records at all. Even so, some rock records sell 500,000 copies or more.

The key person in the life of a rock 'n' roll band is its manager. Some managers work exclusively with one band (e.g., Bajaga's Sasa Dragic), others work with two or more groups at once (e.g., Goran "Fox" Lisica, who works as manager for the Slovenian group Videosex and the Macedonian group Mizar, and more recently has been managing and promoting rock groups in Rijeka and Opatija), still others work within an agency or as the musical director of a Student Cultural Center or House of Youth (such as Skopje's Pande Dimovski), and still others operate as "free-lance managers," working as intermediaries between student cultural centers and the individual groups (such as Belgrade's Ilija Stankovic). Managers face various problems in their trade, including the low motivation of directors in subsidized clubs (some clubs, such as Sarajevo's Center for the Social Activities of Youth, are *not* subsidized), and the low prices charged for tickets in economically strapped Kosovo and Macedonia—making it difficult to cover expenses in those regions, and hence to schedule concerts by visiting groups there, except as large gala events. In Kosovo, the most successful rock concerts have been produced in Pristina's Bora i Ramiz Hall—the largest hall in town—which has a capacity of 10,000.[59] Because the support system is relatively underdeveloped, the group manager sometimes finds himself having to engage in relatively mundane tasks such as chauffering, delivering mail, distributing posters, and so forth.[60]

The media are also a crucial part of the support system. The "super" channel on television carries a lot of rock videos, from both Yugoslavia and abroad, and this is an important medium for promotion. There are also various television and radio programs which feature individual artists and groups, such as the weekly interview show "U sred srede" (In the Middle of Wednesday), featured on Belgrade Television, and a weekly radio rock interview show carried on Belgrade's Radio Studio B. "U sred srede," directed by Tanja Petrovic, has the distinction of being the only long program on Belgrade television (three hours weekly) to play strictly Yugoslav rock.[61]

And finally, the printed media play an important role. There are at least five magazines oriented exclusively toward the rock scene. These are Pero Lovsin's *Gram* (Ljubljana, in Slovenian), *Heroina* (Zagreb, in Croatian), *Ritam* (Belgrade, in Serbo-Croatian), *Disko selektor* (Skopje, in Macedonian), and *Cao* (Belgrade, Serbo-Croatian, focusing on foreign rock). Petar Popovic's *Rock* magazine (later *Pop Rock*) was the most influential rock magazine in the late 1980s, but folded abruptly in 1990. In its heyday, *Pop Rock* had come under fire, from time to time, for favoring Belgrade groups in its coverage, but *Pop Rock* in fact carried articles about all the major groups, including those based in other cities and republics. Aside from these, there are a large number of newspapers and magazines that have regular or semi-regular columns devoted to rock, including *Mladina* (Ljubljana), *Polet* (Zagreb), *Valter* (Sarajevo), *Iskra* (Split), *Mlad Borec* (Skopje), and *Politika ekspres* (Belgrade).

YUGOSLAVIA'S ROCK SCENE TODAY

Yugoslav rock made international news in May 1989 when Boardwalk (Riva), a hitherto little-known soft-rock band from Zadar, took first prize at the 34th Eurovision Music Festival at Lausanne, with their song, "Rock Me."[62] The fact that the group came from the small coastal town of Zadar was significant, in that it showed that rock 'n' roll in Yugoslavia is by no means the monopoly of the big cities. Later that same year—in September—Novi Sad was host to the Seventh Festival of the European Radio Diffusion Union, a mammoth international event that drew entertainers from such countries as Britain, Ireland, the Soviet Union, Finland, the Netherlands, Hungary, and Sweden.[63] Yugoslavia has, at one time or another, hosted many world-class rock performers, including Alice Cooper,[64] Tina Turner,[65] Black Sabbath,[66] David Bowie,[67] Jerry Lee Lewis,[68] Sisters of Mercy,[69] and others.

The rock scene in Yugoslavia is highly diverse, replicating most, if not all, trends worldwide, including rap rock, techno-pop, and—as the Slovenian group Borghesia epitomizes—industrial rock containing sado-masochistic overtones.[70] Improvisational rock also has its practitioners—for example, the Zagreb underground band, Voodoobuddah. In 1988, Yugoslavia produced its first rock operetta, Vladimir Milacic's "Creators and Creatures" (Kreatori i kreature), and in 1989, its first rock movie, "The Fall of Rock 'n' Roll," featuring original compositions by Vlada Divljan, Srdjan 'Gele' Gojkovic, and Dusan 'Koja' Kojic. In the film, Kojic—otherwise the leader of the Belgrade group, Discipline of the Spine (Disciplina kicme)—plays the role of a "mini"-superhero, who wants to ride on public transport without a ticket and whose big enemy is, thus, the ticket inspector.

Rock music is seen by many of its purveyors as transnational, as a force that can bring people together and create ties of mutual acceptance. Symptomatically, some of the leading figures in the rock scene emphasize that they are "Yugoslavs," rather than Serbs or Croats. But as the general political situation in Yugoslavia worsens, bands are increasingly identified with their respective republics. Bands which used to be able to play in Slovenia, for example (such as White Button and Electric Orgasm), have, more recently, found it impossible to book concerts there. Other bands, like the Serbian group Fish Soup, have found that attendance at their concerts in other parts of the country (specifically Croatia, in the case of Fish Soup) has dropped since about 1987, when nationalism started to rise. Jasenko Houra, lead singer of Dirty Theater, told the Croatian weekly, *Danas,* in 1989, that among Zagreb rock groups, only Psychomodo Pop was still welcome in Belgrade.[71] Like everything else in Yugoslavia, rock music, too, is affected by "the national question." This is not hard and fast, of course. At the Avala Rock Festival in Belgrade (mid-August 1990)—to take an example of inter-republican exchange—groups came from many parts of the country including Sarajevo (Blue Orchestra), Rijeka (Fit), Split (Devils), Zagreb (a revived Haustor), and elsewhere. Nesa (of the Nis rock group, Galija) has talked of wanting to play all over the country, and to serve as a kind of cultural bridge.[72] But many groups have no ambitions beyond their own republican borders. Zagreb's Dirty Theater, for example, has no interest in playing outside Croatia,[73] while the Skopje group, Memory, which produced the first Macedonian-language rock LP in Yugoslavia in 1990 (Mizar having produced only cassettes), is expressly geared to Macedonian national identity and culture.[74]

The partial pluralization of 1988–91 has inevitably had effects on the rock scene. In most republics, to begin with, rock groups enjoy greater freedom than hitherto (though Slobodan Milosevic has kept a tight reign on culture in Serbia). There have also been more directly political reflections affecting rock musicians. In Belgrade, for example, a political party calling itself the Big Rock n' Roll Party (Velika Rokenrol Partija) was officially registered with the Serbian Secretariat for Justice in October 1990.[75] The party was the brainchild of Bora Djordjevic. In Bosnia, to take another example, several political parties tried to recruit Goran Bregovic to run as a candidate for parliament. He declined all overtures.[76] In Croatia, on the other hand, Bruno Langer of Atomic Shelter ran unsuccessfully for election to the Croatian *Sabor,* in 1990, as an unaffiliated (independent) candidate.[77]

The Yugoslav economy as of 1990–91 has essentially bottomed out. This has dramatically curtailed the purchasing power of rock fans, and concert attendance, generally, has declined.[78] Hopelessness has a way of breaking through as rejectionism, even nihilism, and some of this may also be detected in the rock scene today. The Satan Panonski band from the village of Ceric, near Vinkovci (Slavonia), equates *nation* with *punk*. Its 1990 album, *Nuclear Olympic Games,* included the song, "Hard Blood Shock" (sung in English):

auto-destruction is eruption
it will destroy all my enemies
my victory is toxicant peace
this is not punk
this is not rock
this is this is
hard blood shock.[79]

Rock music in Yugoslavia is no longer in its infancy. On the contrary, Yugoslav rock has reached considerable maturity in terms of both musical composition and lyrics, and can be said to be developing autonomously, though not, of course, in a vacuum. Rock musicians have to struggle with various problems known to rock musicians in the US and Britain. But some of the problems they confront on a daily basis set Yugoslavia apart from the US, such as the economic crisis, which constricts the market for rock records, the national question, which has been a contributing factor to a rising aggressiveness among rock audiences and which has created some booking problems for rock groups, the continued paranoia (or circumspection, if one prefers) of various record producers and studio directors, the civil war (since June 1991), and a certain cultural conservatism that still sometimes affects politicians, journalists, and even potential audiences, albeit in different ways and to different degrees.[80]

CHAPTER SIX

◆

Women and Men

CULTURE MAY BE VIEWED as a web of values, norms, and social mores, which predetermine modal attitudes and affect behaviors. Culture, in that sense, is reducible to a series of constituent parts, which will include ethnic culture (of a specific group, including recollection and an interpretation of the group's history), religious culture (based in one or another religious organization), aesthetic culture (determining the dominant modes of entertainment and artistic expression, and the comparative values attached to different genres), and gender culture, among others. All of these cultures tend to perpetrate an illusion of continuity, presenting themselves, at any given time, as the rock of tradition, inherited unchanged over the ages—regardless of the recency of the "tradition" or how many changes have in fact occurred. Sexual conservatives of the late twentieth century, for example, imagine that they are trying to preserve and maintain a way of life which has been unchanged and unchallenged until the generation of the 1960s. They forget the ancient world, the Renaissance, the ribald fifteenth and sixteenth centuries, and other eras, when the pendulum swang toward liberality, promiscuity, diversity, and tolerance.

Gender culture, specifically, defines how women and men must behave in order to be viewed as socially integrated or "normal" (conforming to a set of norms imposed from outside). It provides the basis for claims of precedence, dictates how the relationship between love and sex is viewed (markedly differently in past cultures of Japan, the Middle East, Italy, and America, for example), and even prescribes norms for relations between the parents of each sex and their offspring.

Aside from a general gender culture, we may also speak of specific cultures for women and men. Women are raised to know and understand female culture, and men to know and understand male culture. And except in unusual cases (e.g., transsexuals), the boundary is rarely crossed: men, thus, tend to find it impossible to understand female culture (although women are often quite adept at understanding male culture). The existence of this cultural boundary and consequent male difficulty in understanding female culture constitute important sources of communications breakdowns between the sexes generally and of the persistence—despite all logic—of male chauvinism more specifically.

Gender cultures are themselves linked with and affected by their associated cultures. And in particular, the Muslim and Orthodox religious cultures in Yugoslavia bolster values and attitudes less tolerant of women than, by contrast, the Protestant and Catholic cultures in this same country. These religious cultures have regional concentrations (Muslims in Bosnia and Kosovo, Orthodox in Serbia, Macedonia, and Montenegro, Catholics in Slovenia and Croatia, and pockets of Protestants in Vojvodina, as well as in the larger cities of Slovenia and Croatia). As a consequence, gender cultures in Yugoslavia differ quite considerably from republic to republic, north to south.

Gender culture is also affected by the presence or absence of institutional alternatives to the dominant Church. This is at least one reason why there are such strong differences, in all countries, between urban culture and rural culture. And again, because traditional culture in Yugoslavia is patriarchal (differing in degree from region to region), urban culture, insofar as it provides some attenuation of traditional culture, is more conducive to the advancement of women than is rural culture.

And finally, to complete the picture, social class must be calculated as a factor in gender relations. Generally, families in which both partners are educated and hold more prestigious jobs tend to be more egalitarian than families where the marital partners are less well educated and working in unskilled jobs or in agriculture. Or to put it simply, a female lawyer has a better chance of being treated with genuine respect and as an equal by men, than a peasant woman or a florist.

Certainly, other factors influence gender relations in the family, such as alcoholism, insanity, loss of one's job, sickness, and personality quirks, to mention only a few. But these factors cannot be determinative of larger social patterns, and can at most mediate those larger culturally determined patterns at the level of the specific family.

This interwoven cultural bedrock makes it difficult for feminists to change behaviors, because in order to do so, they must modify attitudes at a number of levels and challenge the target audience to rethink norms that have tended to be taken for granted. If, among rural Albanians of Kosovo, women have tended, for as long as they can remember, to feed the men, letting them eat by themselves, before sitting down only after the men have finished, to eat the leftovers, how do you go about convincing Kosovo's women and men that they should eat together and treat each other with dignity? Bette Denich recorded, in 1974, that similar customs were characteristic also of traditional rural Serbs as well as other South Slav peoples:

> In Serbia ceremonial seating arrangements are by ranks, with males from elders through adolescents seated at the head of the table, with all women—beginning with the eldest—lined up below the lowest-ranking males. Within the household stylized behaviors also reiterate the theme of female subordination. In some South Slavic pastoral regions custom requires that a new daughter-in-law show respect by kissing the hands of all males in the household—including the children. In Serbia, women's subsidiary status is reenacted whenever there are guests: men serve as hosts, sitting and drinking with the guests, while the women prepare food and carry it to the table but do not sit with the guests. Sarakatsani men and women always eat separately, the men first eating their fill, [and] the women taking the leftovers. Albanian men are served by women, who then eat separately in the kitchen with the children. In many Yugoslav regions, women's degradation ceremonies include washing the feet of their husbands and fathers-in-law.[1]

Such behaviors are reinforced by normative structures shared by both the female and male cultures in the society.

There are distinct female and male cultures. They must necessarily complement each other. When one of them—whether female or male culture—changes, the result is change in the compatibility of the cultures, producing stress. This stress can be relieved only by changing the partner culture in some compatible direction or by repressing the change in the original culture. For example, a culture of female subservience is compatible with a culture of male domination. Feminism changes the former, producing tension. This, in a word, is the dynamic of feminism, and it encapsulates an important aspect of gender relations in Ljubljana, Zagreb, Belgrade, and other urban environments in Yugoslavia.

Viewed in this way, patriarchal society is not just discriminatory against women as individuals with specific genitalia and reproductive functions; on the contrary, it is the systematic effort to assert the primacy (rather than equality) of male culture over female culture. It discriminates against a culture. Male culture is declared, under patriarchy, to be the norm, and female culture is ghettoized.[2]

SERBIAN PASTORALISM
AND THE MALE COMPLEX

Slovenia, on the one hand, and Serbia and Kosovo, on the other, figure as extremes along a continuum defining female status in multi-cultural

Yugoslavia. In Slovenia, women enjoy a status equivalent to Austrian or Czech women, and their essential equality and participation in public life are taken for granted, even if some social inequality prevails here too. Slovenian women enjoy much greater independence and status than the women of Serbia and Kosovo. In the latter regions, by contrast, women are pointedly made to feel inferior. In Serbia, this is aptly symbolized by the common male practice of frequent expectoration on public streets and sidewalks—a practice which affirms the spitter's claim to some ill-defined "superiority" over his environment. Serbian women, by contrast, do not spit in public places.

Differences in religious faith, I suggested above, may have something to do with the regional differences in the status of women in Yugoslavia. But other factors are also involved. Bette Denich has drawn attention to the importance of socio-economic organization for gender relations in the Yugoslav context: in her view, pastoral societies, specifically Serbia, Macedonia, Montenegro, and Kosovo, tend to be more patriarchal and more sexually stratified than agricultural communities, such as Slovenia and Croatia. Without exaggerating the relative advantage enjoyed by Slovenian and Croatian females, one may at least concede that the definite transition from traditional extended families to nuclear families in these parts has worked to the advantage of females (both adults and children). "In Montenegro"—by contrast—"daughters are not even reckoned by fathers enumerating their children."[3]

What accounts for this difference between pastoral and agricultural societies in Yugoslavia and elsewhere? Anthropologist Andrei Simic highlights the association of the institution of the extended famility with enhanced status for older women. He notes that as Serbian women age, they come to enjoy status, authority, and freedoms which would have been unthinkable for them at an earlier age. Related to this is a magnified status for mothers. Simic relates, for example, that adult Serbian males frequently consult their mothers before making important decisions, while ignoring their wives' views on the issues at hand.[4] In pastoralist Serbia, in fact, the mother exerts an authority over her children which the father cannot rival. The Serbs themselves say, Even God has a mother (*Majku i Bog ima*)—an aphorism which emphasizes the centrality of the mother. Ironically, however, the pivotal role of the mother in the family fuels patriarchy and machismo. In Serbia, for example, sentimental songs about mothers are highly popular with men—even moving them to tears—even though those same men repeatedly feel the need to "prove" their masculinity by engaging in rowdy, macho behavior in which the following elements typically figure:

open-handed hospitality and the seemingly heedless expenditure of money
. . . ; heavy drinking, usually in the company of a small group of male
friends but sometimes including prostitutes, bar girls, or female singers; the
destruction of property, most often glasses, tableware, and bottles, but
occasionally tables, chairs, and other barroom fixtures as well; trancelike
ecstatic behavior induced by a combination of alcohol and the performance
of erotic love songs; and not infrequently, brawling and more serious forms
of physical violence.[5]

As sociologist Nancy Chodorow has noted, women's role as the primary
socializers of men results in a pervasive "dread of women" among adult
males.[6] Margaret Mead claims that girls gain a sense of female identity
more easily than boys acquire their sense of male identity, because for
girls, the closeness with the mother facilitates the acquisition of the
relevant identity, while for boys, it obstructs such identification.[7] Femininity is assimilated through attachment to the mother, while masculinity is defined through separation. Harvard Professor Carol Gilligan
says that this dynamic leads to a situation in which ". . . males tend
to have difficulty with relationships, while females tend to have problems
with individuation."[8] Moreover, the combination of maternal authority
and lower female status makes female roles and behaviors deeply
threatening, even disturbing, to boys, who, unlike girls, feel the need
to "prove" their masculinity by making "correct" choices, as prescribed
by the hierarchy. One consequence of this—well known—is that females
in such societies tend to enjoy greater sex-role freedom than do males:
the "tom boy" is smilingly acknowledged, while the "pansy" is ridiculed.
It is easy to understand how societies in which the maternal role is
enhanced (as in Serbia and Montenegro), tend to be characterized by
greater fear of women, and hence a stronger assertion of the patriarchy
and a more powerful tendency toward male chauvinism. In this regard,
Serbia is a classic case. As Chodorow notes, "Like violent behavior,
male narcissism, pride, and phobia toward mature women—[all] indi-
cations of compulsive assertion of masculinity—seem to be prevalent
in societies in which boys spend their earlier years exclusively or
predominantly with women, and in which the degree of physical or
emotional distance between mother and father as compared with that
between mother and child" is great.[9]

Machismo, then, should be seen as a violent backlash against maternal
authority, inspired by fear of women, and seeking "revenge" in the
denigration and subordination of women. Machismo is a specifically
male complex, for which no female equivalent exists.

Among the pastoralists (Serbs, Montenegrins, Macedonians, Albanians), women were traditionally expected to walk several paces behind

their husbands and to carry whatever burdens there were. If the couple had a donkey, the man would ride on it, and the woman walked behind. Among Albanians, female subordination extended even to the suppression of women's names: specifically, after marriage, an Albanian woman would be known only by the possessive form of her husband's first name.[10]

Against this backdrop, it should come as no surprise that it is precisely in "macho" Serbia that patriarchal backlash has been strongest (among Yugoslav republics) in the late 1980s and early 1990s. The entire Milosevic phenomenon is, in fact, rooted in *fear*: fear of Albanians, Croats, and even, eventually, Slovenes; fear of new political movements; fear of randomness, freedom, chaos; and fear of women. The primordial linkage of these fears is the explanation as to why Slobodan Milosevic's support comes overwhelmingly from males—middle-aged peasant males being the core and largest part of his support—while his opposition draws women as well as men to its ranks and to its rallies.

Fear, of course, readily translates into hatred, prejudice, chauvinism, and violence—all hallmarks of Milosevic's rule and following. Since his advent on the scene in 1987, feminist activity in Belgrade has dried up, men have been told that they deserve preferential hiring in times of economic duress, and women have been advised to return to their "traditional duties"—kitchen, children, Church.

I have even heard the demented Otto Weininger's *Sex and Character* (originally published in Vienna in 1903) cited with favor in Serbia. Weininger, it was, who told the world,

> Women have no existence and no essence; they are not, they are nothing. Mankind occurs as male or female, as something or nothing. Woman has no share in ontological reality, no relation to the thing-in-itself, which, in the deepest interpretation, is the absolute, is God. Man, in his highest form, the genius, has such a relation . . . [But] woman has no relation to the idea, she neither affirms nor denies it; she is neither moral nor anti-moral; mathematically speaking she has no sign; she is purposeless, neither good nor bad, neither angel nor devil, never egotistical (and therefore has often been said to be altruistic); she is as non-moral as she is non-logical. But all existence is moral and logical existence. So woman has no existence.[11]

PROSTITUTION

If there is a direct line from maternal authority to male complex to machismo, it is worth adding that the ready availability of prostitutes

TABLE 6.1   Number of Prostitutes Arrested and Charged in Serbia-proper, 1968–1975

1968	300
1969	180
1970	154
1971	n/a
1972	102
1973	78
1974	n/a
1975	99

Source: Dragan Radulovic, *Prostitucija u Jugoslaviji* (Belgrade: Filip Visnjic, 1986), p. 41.

is a natural concomitant of macho culture. Belgrade, the capital of Serbia, is said to have had some 600 prostitutes even in 1901, when the total population of the city came to only 60,000; by 1928, Belgrade had some 80 brothels—all illegal.[12] Obviously a high percentage of young females was engaged in prostitution—itself a sure clue to the presence of macho culture in turn-of-the-century Belgrade. Nor were the communists able to eradicate prostitution, and there continued to be arrests of prostitutes over the years. Table 6.1 shows the number of prostitutes arrested and charged in Serbia, 1968–75.

Prostitution is, of course, found in many parts of Yugoslavia. In 1964, for example, there were 431 registered prostitutes in Belgrade, 360 in Ljubljana, 169 in Rijeka, and additional numbers in Zagreb, Split, Skopje, and elsewhere.[13] Yugoslav prostitutes are typically of rural origin. A 1985 study found that 70 per cent of prostitutes in Belgrade had been born outside the city, most often coming from poorer parts of Bosnia or southern Serbia.[14] Prostitutes may come from nationality groups which are in the minority locally: for example, in Skopje in 1974, 70.2 per cent of prostitutes were non-Macedonians—more than half of them Serbs.[15]

AGRICULTURIST SOCIETY:
SLOVENIA AND CROATIA

In discussing pastoralist society, I have focused largely on Serbia, chiefly because most of the available data pertains to Serbia, but also with the awareness that Serbs are by far the largest nationality group in Yugoslavia. Much of what was said about Serbian patriarchy would apply equally to the Montenegrins, the Macedonians, and the Kosovar Albanians.

By contrast, Slovenes and Croats (together with the diverse peoples of Vojvodina) are agriculturists. (The Slovenes and Croats are also

Catholics—another contrast with the largely Orthodox and Muslim affiliation of the pastoralists—and were ruled for centuries by the Habsburgs, while the pastoralists were ruled by the Ottomans.) Although the agriculturists are likewise organized on patrilineal and patricentric lines, they exclude "extreme forms of actual and ritual subordination of women to men."[16] Traditionally, wives in Slovenia and Croatia have participated in family decision-making, in marked contrast to the situation outlined for pastoralist Serbia. Again, unlike Serbia, where the male asserts supreme authority even in the kitchen, in Slovenia and Croatia, the female is clearly in charge of her own kitchen. Slovenia and Dalmatia (regions earlier attached to the Austrian half of the Austro-Hungarian empire) have long been characterized by a toleration of female engagement in premarital sexual relations and even, in Slovenian villages, of illegitimate births. The traditional pastoralist custom of automatic execution of a woman suspected of marital infidelity is unknown among the agriculturists. Nor is infidelity escalated into an affair of the entire extended family. As Denich notes, "[female] adultery diminishes the honor of the cuckolded husband, but not the collective status of an entire kin group."[17] Consistent with patriarchy, however, the betrayed wife in this rectangle does not suffer diminution of honor, because male unfaithfulness is either tolerated or even considered (by males) to be "manly."

In the agriculturist republics, larger proportions of public officials and of workers in the social sector are women, though, of course, here too, women's share in public and economic life is less than men's. In 1986, for example, women accounted for 51.6 per cent of the Croatian population, but only 42 per cent of the labor force in the socialized sector and 29.7 per cent of delegates to the Seventh Congress of the League of Communists of Croatia.[18] Figures (for 1984) on the proportion of women in the central committees of the party organizations of the respective federal units largely confirm the expected pattern: Slovenia, Croatia, and Vojvodina are among the four units with the highest representation of women at this level, while Serbia, Montenegro, and Kosovo are decisively lower. Interestingly enough, where CC presidencies are concerned, only in Croatia and Vojvodina did women account for more than 15 per cent of the local presidency (see Table 6.2).

THE BROADER PICTURE

According to the 1981 census—the most recent census for which complete data is available—there were, at the time, 11,340,933 women and 11,083,778 men living in Yugoslavia. The average age of Yugoslav females (in 1987) was 35.2, and of males, 32.8. Female life expectancy

TABLE 6.2   Women in Leadership Organs of the LCY (1984)

	Pct. of women in party membership	Pct. of women in central committee (CC)	Pct. of women in CC presidency
LCY	27.0	14.1	0.0
Bosnia	29.2	19.5	7.7
Montenegro	26.1	13.2	11.1
Croatia	27.5	21.6	15.4
Macedonia	23.0	21.9	13.3
Slovenia	32.1	20.5	7.7
Serbia	27.5	17.8	4.8
Kosovo	13.5	14.7	7.7
Vojvodina	31.6	23.5	15.4

Source: Jasna A. Petrovic, "Zene u SK danas," in Zena, vol. 44 no. 4, (1986), p. 7.

(as of 1987) was 68.6 years—several years longer than men's.[19] As of 1982, women constituted only 36 per cent of the Yugoslav labor force, but accounted for a strikingly high 45 per cent of the Slovenian labor force. At that time, following a pattern established a long time ago, women were concentrated in very specific (less prestigious) occupations: in health and social services, 75 per cent of the labor force was female; in hotels and tourism, 60 per cent. At the same time, 55 per cent of all persons registered as unemployed were female.[20] The latter figure was unchanged at the end of 1988.[21]

The education of women has long been a problem, as patriarchy has tried to enforce conditions in which women would accept household work as their "natural lot." An extreme reflection of this tendency is the fact that, at the end of World War Two, 93 per cent of all illiterates in Kosovo were women.[22] Even in 1981—across Yugoslavia as a whole— 15.0 per cent of women remained illiterate, as compared with only 6.7 per cent of men.[23] The education of women is marked by steady attrition, so that the proportion of females declines the higher up the educational scale one goes. Of pupils in elementary schools, thus, 48 per cent were females in 1982. But females constituted only 45 per cent of middle school students and 43 per cent of high school students.[24] The figures for universities and graduate schools were even smaller. In some communities, especially in Kosovo, there were continued difficulties even in the 1980s in assuring that village girls (in this case, Albanian village girls) attended primary school regularly.[25]

One consequence of the lower education of women is the disproportionate acquisition of skills necessary to obtain non-agricultural jobs. This translates into the steady, incremental femininization of the agricultural labor force in the post-war period.[26]

The lower valuation, lower education, and lower skills of women all contribute to their greater difficulty in making gains in the job sector. Indeed, Yugoslav sources repeatedly concede that even where women's skills are equal to or better than men's skills, men are frequently given preference in hiring. This results in a situation not unknown in the West: viz., when economic trends take a downturn, women are laid off first. This has occurred several times in Yugoslavia's post-war development. In the years 1949–51, for example, after several years of steady growth marked by the expanded hiring of women, the number of women employed in the social sector declined in absolute terms, dropping precipitously from 465,166 in 1949 to 375,166 by 1951.[27] Slow economic recovery after 1952 was associated with a revived expansion in the employment of women. By the early 1960s, the economy was becoming bottlenecked and stagnant. The economic reforms of 1963–65 assured temporary economic recovery, but at the expense of layoffs. As could have been predicted, women were the hardest hit by the rise in unemployment in the mid-1960s.[28] The cultural dimension of this was a resurgence of traditional values, which meant that economic liberalization was associated with a revival of cultural traditionalism.

The short-lived economic boom of the 1970s had ended by 1978, as high inflation, creeping unemployment, soaring foreign debts, and general economic inefficiency combined to drive the economy downwards. The result was a steady rise in the proportion of women unemployed, reaching 55 per cent throughout the 1980s. Alongside this was another problem: the systematic underpayment of the female labor force. In fact, Yugoslav women in the industrial sector earn about 80 per cent of what men earn.[29]

Turning now to the representation of women in positions of managerial responsibility, the figures are discouraging. Of the 445,539 delegates elected to serve on communal, political, and economic assemblies, only about a quarter (107,322) were women (as of 1986).[30] Of the 441,816 members of workers' councils that same year, about a third (142,375) were women.[31] Among presidents of workers' councils, only 6 per cent were women (in 1982).[32] Women occupied 8.4 per cent of leadership positions in middle schools and only 3.5 per cent of such positions in high schools, even though some 52.9 per cent of total faculty in these two branches were women. Women comprised 41.9 per cent of the employed sector in scientific institutes, but only 5.5 per cent of the managerial positions in these institutes were occupied by women.[33] As of 1987, only 28.8 per cent of the Yugoslav diplomatic service was female, and only two women had risen to the rank of ambassador.[34] The authorities themselves saw the problem, and from time to time, one could read public admissions that the representation of women in the political system was disproportionately low,[35] and so forth.

And yet, Yugoslav officials insisted that the "woman question," as they called it, was in some sense "solved." Thus Veljko Vlahovic already in 1961: "The basic problems of the legal and political position of women in our country have been solved."[36] With this self-congratulation as a basis, Yugoslavia's communists could proceed to declare themselves opposed to feminism, "because it is a movement which is always expressive of partial interests and demands, because it is in favor of dividing women from men in a formal-legal way, and because it devalues the class question."[37] Some observers went so far as to claim that Yugoslav society had already reached a "post-feminist" stage, on the argument that the right to obtain an abortion, improved access to professional careers, and other gains constituted a total solution of the problem of equality.[38] Would males show equal equanimity if only 6 per cent of the presidents of workers' councils were *men,* if males held only 14 per cent of the seats in the nation's top decision-making body, if only two Yugoslav ambassadors were males, and if male illiteracy were three times as high as female illiteracy?

YUGOSLAV WOMEN IN TROUBLED TIMES

As Yugoslavia faltered in the 1980s, politicians increasingly found themselves confronted with the trying issues of pressure for political freedom, economic instability, gender equality, ethnic toleration, environmentalism, etc. In Slovenia, whose relative prosperity reduced social pressure, communist politicians dealt with the issues on their own terms. Elsewhere, the situation was more complicated. In Serbia, Slobodan Milosevic owed his success to his ability to manipulate ethnic chauvinism and swept other issues to the side. Concomitantly, male chauvinism acquired new strength in Milosevic's Serbia. From time to time, women protested the shift from a policy of promoting gender equality to one of upholding so-called "traditional values."[39] But they have had increasing difficulty even being heard. The typical reply of the unconscious: "There are more important things to worry about right now than women's equality." Translated: "There are more important things to worry about now than human dignity."

In this context, lesbianism clearly figures—as it often does elsewhere as well—not merely as a matter of sexual preference but also as a political alternative. To be a lesbian is to opt out of patriarchal society, to refuse to play the game. In Ljubljana, a lesbian working group was organized in 1987—linked to the feminist organization, Lilith.[40]

Political organization is another alternative to which Yugoslav women have had recourse. This has taken two chief forms: feminist groups, and political parties. The former date from 1976, and exist essentially in three cities—Ljubljana, Zagreb, and Belgrade—although there is some interest in feminism in other cities as well. Yugoslavia's feminists tend to be professionals, intellectuals, middle class. They have concentrated on organizing open discussions of sensitive issues and on publishing articles and books advocating the feminist alternative.[41] It would be easy enough to dismiss Yugoslavia's feminists as ineffective and unsuccessful. Yet, as Barbara Jancar points out, they have succeeded in generating an "interest in feminist ideas [that] goes beyond a small collection of feminist intellectuals."[42]

Feminists also took advantage of the partial opening of the political system in 1990 to create their own political parties: a Croatian League of Women (founded in Zagreb in March 1990), a Democratic Movement of Women (founded in Kragujevac and registered in November 1990), and the Women's Party of Belgrade (also registered in November 1990).[43]

But ironically, just as economic crisis hit women hardest, so too the alternative responses to crisis—whether chauvinist authoritarianism (as in Serbia) or democratic pluralism (as in Croatia)—have also posed new threats to women's interests. In Serbia, women find their voices stilled and their organizations pushed into the corner,[44] while married couples without children have been threatened with a punitive tax. In Croatia, the Catholic Church has taken advantage of the new political situation to try to push women more firmly into their "traditional" role of housekeeper, targeting abortion as the arena for struggle. Belgrade feminist Sonja Licht commented in 1990, "Conservative attitudes toward women are resurfacing throughout Eastern Europe, usually with strong ties to nationalism. I often call the newly emerging democracies *male democracies.*"[45]

BEYOND MALE DEMOCRACY

Feminism in Yugoslavia, as elsewhere, faces a serious challenge: how to replace a system based on the subordination of women and the use of force to defend interests, with one based on genuine equality and consensus. Obviously, political struggle is one aspect of feminism. But the struggle cannot be won at that level. It can only be won at the cultural level, so that new ideas, new attitudes, new behaviors can percolate upwards, affecting politics in their wake. Collective action and organization are essential, as feminists realize, but they must ultimately transform not just laws and regulations, but the family, the community, and eventually, the nation. Such a change can only occur over generations, as each new generation assimilates new ideas. It is for this reason that Yugoslavia's feminists have concentrated much of their efforts on analyzing, critiquing, and revising school books, in order to present children with a new image of human society.

Feminism's focal task, thus, is *cultural*. But, to return to the themes developed at the outset, with distinct gender cultures for women and men, feminism is inevitably confronted with the dual task of changing the rather different cultures of the sexes. To do this, Yugoslav feminists have challenged the news organs to revamp their portrayals of women,[46] and have examined the language itself for semantically embedded prejudice.[47]

The Seventh Congress of the LCY (held in Ljubljana in April 1958) was seen at the time as a bold and radical departure, defining better than had been done previously, a genuine Yugoslav alternative. In addressing the question of the status of women, the Congress confronted the problem directly:

> The equality of the women in Yugoslavia is no longer a political problem or a problem of the legal status of the woman in society. It is now mainly a problem of economic backwardness, primitivism, religious conceptions and other conservative prejudices, [and] private property relations, all of which still affect family life. Backward housekeeping technique and the existing material problems of the family prevent the woman from full participation in the economic and social life of the country and cause a conflict between her role in society and her role in the house.[48]

PART THREE

◆

Religion

CHAPTER SEVEN

◆

The Catholic Church

IN AUGUST 1990, FRANJO TUDJMAN, the newly-elected noncommunist President of Croatia, gave a television interview, in which he addressed the subject of Catholicism. The Catholic Church, Tudjman argued, had been the only organized force which had provided consistent resistance to communist rule and which had nurtured Croatian national consciousness.[1] In communist times, the Catholic Church was kept on the defensive, subject to harassment and the target of endless small "stings" from Titoist officialdom. Now, in post-communist Slovenia and Croatia, the newly installed governments look on Catholic interests with favor, and the Catholic Church has revealed an ambition to return to conditions of the pre-communist era. This, in turn, prompted Zdenko Roter, a distinguished Slovenian sociologist of religion with demonstrated sympathies for the Catholic Church, to express concern that some Church leaders might try to turn the new post-communist political order into "a servant of the Catholic Church."[2]

THE SYMBOLOGY OF THE CHURCH IN YUGOSLAVIA

Relations between the Catholic Church in Yugoslavia and the communist regime were colored by three central symbols: Strossmayer, Stepinac, and the Vatican II Council. For the regime, Bishop Josip Juraj Strossmayer of Djakovo (1815–1905) represented the spirit of "Yugoslavism" (promoting the cultural and political unity of Serbs, Croats, Slovenes, and Macedonians) and of cooperation between Church and state, while Alojzije Cardinal Stepinac (1898–1960) symbolized exclusivist Croatian nationalism and the spirit of defiance. For the Church, on the other hand, Strossmayer is remembered also as an active missionary, as an ecclesiastical "liberal" who opposed introduction of the principle of papal infallibility, and as a champion of Slavic (vernacular) liturgy in

Catholic churches in Croatia; Stepinac is associated, in Church eyes, with heroic efforts to protect Serbs and Gypsies from slaughter by the *Ustasha* fascists during World War Two, with defiant outspoken criticism of both the *Ustasha* and the communists, and with unflinching loyalty to the Church. In certain ways, thus—for both regime and Church— twentieth century Stepinac symbolized the Church's traditional pastoral care for the nation, while nineteenth century Strossmayer symbolized adaptability, liberality, and hence modernity. It is worth noting, however, that through his progressive social programs and his use of Church funds for charitable programs, Stepinac may be said to have anticipated the "Church of the poor" of the Vatican II period.

The Vatican II Council (1962–1965) was a watershed for the Church, and, more particularly, the point at which modernizing currents within the Church received strong encouragement, in certain aspects, from the Holy See. The results were a new impetus to self-assertion in the Church, a new direction for the Church in its social presence, and a deepening of the division within the Church between traditionalists and modernizers. Interestingly enough, while the Belgrade regime expressed enthusiasm for the "modernizing" Strossmayer, it felt threatened, according to Zlatko Markus, by the reformist wing of the Church, which it viewed as "dangerously" active.[3] Far more to the liking of at least some elements in the regime, was the opinion once expressed by Archbishop Frane Franic of Split (retired in 1988), to the effect that the Church is called upon "to administer the sacraments and to conduct Church services, but political and social revolution should be left to others. That is not our calling."[4] The result is that theological conservatives in the Church (including the mixed conservative, Franic, and the generally conservative onetime Archbishop of Sarajevo, Smiljan Cekada) enjoyed better relations, than have some of their theologically more liberal colleagues, with those elements in the communist regime who sought to constrict Church activity.

In Yugoslavia, as elsewhere, the traditional/modern dichotomy manifests itself against the backdrop of another—partly reinforcing, partly crosscutting—dichotomy between hierarchy and lower clergy. In the early post-war years, tensions between hierarchy and lower clergy centered on the establishment of priests' associations—a move encouraged and supported by the regime. More recently, tensions developed between the episcopal conference and the Christianity Today Theological Society, over the latter's unilateral decision, in 1977, to reorganize itself as a self-managing enterprise and thereby obtain certain tax exemptions. The Society is responsible for running a formidable publishing house and for issuing the "AKSA" news bulletin.

THE DAWN OF COMMUNIST RULE

Although the communist regime would later try to portray the Catholic Church's role during World War Two monochromatically as the advocacy of Croatian independence and *Ustasha* rule, a rather substantial number of Catholic clergymen actually cooperated with or fought on the side of the Partisans, including Archbishop Kuzma Jedretic, Fr. Franjo Pos from Prezid, Franciscans Bosiljko Ljevar and Viktor Sakic, and the pastor of St. Mark's Church in Zagreb, Msgr. Svetozar Rittig, lauded by one Yugoslav author as "the most important figure in the people's liberation struggle, among Catholic priests."[5] Rittig, who joined the Partisans in 1943 and later became first president of the Croatian Commission for Religious Affairs, remaining active on the political scene until his death in July 1961, is said to have been devoted, in particular, to the ideas of Bishop Strossmayer. By contrast, according to Ciril Petesic, "only a part of the clergy, and a small part at that" actually endorsed the *Ustasha* program, mostly young priests, while most of the older clergy are said to have been pro-Yugoslav.[6]

From the beginning of Partisan warfare, the Partisans had need of priests to cater to the religious needs of their combatants, and this led to the establishment of a Religious Department of the AVNOJ[7] Executive Committee in December 1942. Behind Partisan lines, where religious schools were concerned, the Partisans were eager for religious instructors to teach about Cyril and Methodius (who created the Glagolitic alphabet), Sava Nemanjic (founder of the autocephalous Serbian Orthodox archdiocese), and Bishop Strossmayer.[8]

After the trying experiences under the Kingdom of Yugoslavia,[9] the Croatian Catholic hierarchy initially welcomed the establishment of a separate Croatian state.[10] Some clergy, such as Archbishop Ivan Saric of Sarajevo, remained sympathetic to the *Ustasha* until the very end. Other hierarchs were more critical, on the other hand. Bishop Alojzije Misic of Mostar, for instance, began condemning *Ustasha* oppression of Serbs as early as 1941.[11] Similarly, Zagreb Archbishop Stepinac repeatedly contacted Minister of the Interior Andrija Artukovic (e.g., in letters dated May 22, 1941 and May 30, 1941) to register his objection to the new legislation affecting Catholics of Jewish descent, declared membership in Catholic Action and the *Ustasha* movement to be incompatible (in December 1941), worked quietly to obtain the release of Orthodox believers from prison, and spoke out in his sermons against racism, genocide, and *Ustasha* policies (for example in his sermon of October 25, 1943).[12]

But if the local clergy were divided in their attitudes toward the *Ustasha,* and some frankly ambivalent about the Croatian state, the

Vatican had a clear line where *communism* was concerned. The difficulties experienced by the Church in the USSR provided a troubling precedent, and Pope Pius XII adopted a forcefully anti-communist stance. *Katolicki list* (April 24, 1937) had put it this way: "Communism is in its very essence evil. Therefore, the person who values Christian culture will not cooperate with [communists] in a single thing. If some are seduced into error and on their part help communism to grow stronger, they will be the first to be punished for that error . . . "[13] Thus, there was no basis, at that time, for a relationship of trust between the Vatican and the emerging communist parties in Eastern Europe.

Meanwhile, as the Partisans captured districts of Croatia, they massacred both civilians and priests, including more than two dozen unarmed Franciscans at the monastery of Siroki Brijeg.[14] The Independent State of Croatia collapsed in May 1945 and the communist party now set up its administration in the remaining parts of the country.

On June 2, 1945, communist party General Secretary Josip Broz Tito, Croatian President Vladimir Bakaric, and Msgr. Rittig held a meeting with Catholic bishops Franjo Salis-Seewis and Josip Lach. Tito's statement on that occasion has given rise to so much subsequent controversy that it is worth quoting at length. Replying to a statement presented by Bishop Salis, Tito said:

> As I have already explained to Msgr. Rittig, I would like to see a proposal worked out, as you see fit, as to how to solve the question of the Church in Croatia, the Catholic Church, because we shall be discussing the same thing also with the Orthodox Church. On my own part, I would say that our Church needs to be national [*nacionalna*], that it be more responsive to the [Croatian] nation. Perhaps that will seem a bit strange to you when I so strongly support nationality . . . I must say openly that I do not want to undertake the right to condemn Rome, your supreme Roman jurisdiction, and I will not. But I must say that I look at it critically, because [Church policy] has always been attuned more to Italy than to our people. I would like to see that the Catholic Church in Croatia now, when we have all the preconditions there, would have more independence. I would like that. That is the basic question. That is the question which we want to see resolved, and all other questions are secondary questions which will be easy to work out.[15]

Given the consistency with which communists in other East European countries were pressing Catholic hierarchs to break with the Vatican,[16] it seems reasonable to interpret this statement along the same lines (though Tito later denied that that was his intention). After all, the so-called Old Catholic Church in Croatia had already provided a precedent. Indeed, this Church, which had formed in reaction to the proclamation of the doctrine of papal infallibility in 1870, was even able to set up additional independent organizations after World War Two in Slovenia, Serbia, and Vojvodina.[17]

The following day, Tito and Bakaric received the papal delegate, Abbot Ramiro Marcone, together with his secretary, Don Giuseppe Masucci, who complained that the communist media were relentlessly attacking the clergy and the Vatican, even claiming that the Vatican had wanted a Nazi victory, and that the children were being taught in the schools that there is no God and trained to sing, "We will fight against God! There is no God!"[18]

On June 4, Tito and Bakaric received Stepinac and, on this occasion, Tito praised Pope Leo XIII for having backed Strossmayer in a dispute with the Court of Vienna about Russia and asked Stepinac to support Belgrade in its dispute with Italy in Istria. Stepinac, in turn, urged Tito to meet with representatives of the Croatian Peasant Party and even those of the *Ustasha* movement, and to try to heal the emotional wounds of war.[19] In spite of this meeting, the communist government continued to arrest Catholic priests and believers, including the bishops of Krizevci, Split, and Krk.

Archbishop Stepinac was receiving hundreds of appeals from Croats, asking him to intercede with the new authorities on behalf of imprisoned relatives. On June 28, 1945, he took up the matter with the President of the Croatian government and urged the authorities to drop the campaign against "collaborators" because, as Stepinac noted, it would be necessary then to imprison ordinary workers, peasants, and so forth. But part of the reason for the campaign was sheer opportunism on the part of particular individuals in the party, including their desire to seize the opportunity to settle old scores.[20] Stepinac also criticized the secret trials being conducted at the time, calling it inconsistent with the regime's claim to be a "people's" government.

Meanwhile, the regime decided to abolish all private high schools, following completion of the 1945–1946 school year, and moved to eliminate religious instruction from the curriculum of state elementary schools. In late summer 1945, the authorities began bulldozing the cemeteries in which combatants from other sides were buried, stirring protests from believers in the areas affected. Within a month of the war's end, the communist authorities also began forcible confiscations of Church property in Krizevci, Zagreb, Remete, and elsewhere, seized Caritas property and property of the Zagreb archbishopric, and outlined a more extensive program of agrarian land reform, which promised to produce further confiscations. When Stepinac complained about these developments in a letter to Tito, the latter replied by alluding to his interest in receiving a reply from the Catholic bishops with respect to "the possibility of coming to an agreement about certain matters between Church and state."[21]

In these circumstances, the first episcopal conference in Yugoslavia in six years was convened by Stepinac September 17–22, to discuss the new situation in which the Church found itself. Immediately upon convening, the episcopal conference sent a letter to Tito, asking for withdrawal of the law on agrarian reform, respect for Christian marriage, respect for continuation of religious instruction in elementary schools, and respect for Catholic cemeteries, and offering to consult with the state on a new law on agrarian reform. The following day, after further discussions, the conference sent a second letter to Tito, asking for the release from detention of Bishop Janko Simrak, freedom of the press, continuance of the private schools, and the return of confiscated property to the Church.[22] And at the close of the conference, the assembled bishops issued a joint pastoral letter, recounting the hardships suffered by the Church at the hands of the communists (243 priests and four nuns killed over four years, 169 priests still in prison, and 89 unaccounted for), and demanding complete freedom for Church activities, institutions and press. This pastoral letter was read in the churches, with copies sent to the Commissions for Religious Affairs in each of the federal units.[23]

The letter convinced the communist authorities that Archbishop Stepinac would be as much a thorn to them as he had been to *Ustasha* leader Ante Pavelic. They therefore reached a decision, shortly after the letter was issued, that a case would be prepared against him and that he would be put away in prison.[24]

THE TRIAL OF ARCHBISHOP STEPINAC

The authorities continued to try to persuade Archbishop Stepinac to break relations with Rome; instead, Stepinac denounced the proposal in yet another pastoral letter.[25] The authorities then tried to persuade the Vatican to remove Stepinac from his seat in Zagreb; the Vatican refused.[26] The archbishop was therefore arrested on September 18, and put on trial together with 15 other persons who were being tried on criminal charges connected with the excesses of the NDH. On September 30, the charges against Stepinac were read in court. Specifically, he was accused of collaborating with the *Ustasha* in the calculated hope of enriching the Church and the upper clergy, of allowing the *Krizari* (Crusaders) and Catholic Action to work for fascism, of using traditional religious celebrations as political manifestations in support of the *Ustasha*, of encouraging the coercive conversion of Orthodox Serbs to Catholicism, of serving as a rallying point for enemies of the communist state after the war, and of concealing *Ustasha* archives and materials of the Croatian Foreign Ministry, under an agreement concluded with Ante Pavelic.[27]

The *official* (edited) record of the trial shows Stepinac refusing to cooperate with his interrogators:

> *Presiding judge: Nedjelja* no 15 of April 27, 1941 carries a report with the following content: "Archbishop Dr. Alojzije Stepinac, as representative of the Catholic Church and Croatian metropolitan, visited General Slavko Kvaternik as deputy of the Poglavnik in the homeland and conducted a lengthy conversation with him. In that way, as Radio Zagreb reports, the most cordial relations were established between the Catholic Church and the Independent State of Croatia."
> Why did you consider it necessary, only two days after the establishment of the Independent State of Croatia and the occupation of our country by the enemy, to hurry to visit the *Ustasha* commander, Slavko Kvaternik?
> *The accused*: I have nothing to say.
> *Presiding judge*: Did you visit Pavelic on April 16, 1941, four days after the occupation of our country but two days before the capitulation of the Yugoslav army, which was at war with the enemy?
> *The accused*: I decline to answer . . . .
> *Presiding judge*: . . . Did you, immediately in the first days of the occupation, i.e., in mid-April or early May, take part in a meeting to which you invited *Ustasha* emigrants, returnees?
> *The accused*: I have nothing to say. If necessary, the defense lawyers appointed for me can answer that.[28]

The prosecution made use of a string of citations from Catholic and *Ustasha* press to try to incriminate the archbishop. But most of the Catholic periodicals cited by the prosecution in substantiation of its charges were published in dioceses lying outside Stepinac's jurisdiction: in particular, the Franciscan publication *Andjeo cuvar,* the Jesuit publication *Glasnik Srca Isusova,* the Sarajevo weekly *Katolicki tjednik,* and the Sarajevo publication *Glasnik sv. Antuna.*[29] The prosecution claimed that Stepinac and other clergy had received decorations from the Croatian government in gratitude for their political support and produced pictures showing the archbishop together with *Ustasha* ministers on official occasions and at official receptions.[30]

Chief prosecutor Jakov Blazevic dwelled at length on the Church's cooperation with the *Ustasha* in carrying out forced conversions of Orthodox believers. The archbishop defended himself by insisting that the Church had exerted no pressure on the Orthodox and could not be held responsible for coercion applied by others, and by pointing out that a large number of Catholics had converted to Orthodoxy, under pressure, during the period of the Yugoslav kingdom.[31] Against the archbishop's denials, Blazevic insisted that between 1943 and 1944, Archbishop Stepinac became involved in vaguely defined "conspiratorial work" with Pavelic and Croatian Peasant Party leader Vlatko Macek, and—in a bizarre turn—"charged" the archbishop with having sent Christmas wishes to Croatian prison laborers in Germany.[32]

L'Osservatore Romano, the Vatican newspaper, scoffed at the charges and held that the real reason for the trial was the pastoral letter of September 22, 1945.[33] By continually returning to the subject of this letter, the authorities seemed to confirm this interpretation:

> *Presiding judge*: In the pastoral letter of last year, of 1945, one finds, among other things, the claim that the Franciscans at Siroki Brijeg were well-known anti-fascists. Here is a photograph, taken at Siroki Brijeg, showing *Ustasha* colonel Jure Francetic with Fr. Bonaventura Jelacic, an "'anti-fascist' from Siroki Brijeg." Also in the photograph are [other] Franciscans of Siroki Brijeg together with *Ustasha* and Italian officers. Is this the famous anti-fascist stance of the Franciscans from Siroki Brijeg?
>
> *The accused*: I have nothing to say.
>
> *Presiding judge*: You could correct your declaration in the pastoral letter— were they not, maybe, fascists?
>
> *The accused*: I think that we have nothing to correct.[34]

Blazevic later returned to this subject in order to assail the idea of freedom of the press:

> *J. Blazevic*: . . . . Defendant Stepinac, in connection with the facts which have been revealed and established in this trial, I ask you please, for what purpose did you convene the episcopal conference in September 1945 and for what purpose did you write the pastoral letter?
>
> *The accused*: I have nothing to say.
>
> *J. Blazevic*: I will cite some passages from the pastoral letter to you and then I will ask you some questions about it. Speaking of the persecutions of priests etc . . . , you say this: "And when we explain all this to you dearest believers, we do not do so in the hope of provoking a battle with the state authorities. We neither desire such battles nor do we seek them." Defendant, you say that you have always sought peace and stable political life and you say, "That peace is so necessary to everyone today, but we are deeply convinced that that peace can only be founded on the pacification of relations between Church and state." What do you say to that, defendant Stepinac?
>
> *The accused*: I have nothing to say.
>
> *J. Blazevic*: You have nothing to say, because you are ashamed. In the

pastoral letter, in order to realize the principles that you stress, you seek complete freedom for the Catholic press. Is that freedom for the press we have been reading? . . .

The accused: I have nothing to say.

J. Blazevic: You have nothing to say. In the pastoral letter you write, "Only under those conditions can circumstances be put in order in our state and can lasting internal peace be achieved." So, you demand freedom for your press, that is, the Catholic press which you commanded and which you converted completely into an instrument of fascism. That press could only return if fascism would return, if the *Ustasha* were to return . . . It's clear that you seek to introduce fascism in our country anew, that you seek [foreign] intervention in the country . . .[35]

The court rejected most of the witnesses proposed by the defense; on the other hand, most of the 58 witnesses summoned by the prosecution to testify against Stepinac were not from his archdiocese. The trial ended on October 11, when the court found all but three of the defendants guilty,[36] and sentenced Archbishop Stepinac to 16 years at hard labor, followed by five years' deprivation of civil and political rights. *L'Osservatore Romano* condemned the proceedings as a complete sham, whose outcome had been determined in advance and whose script had been drafted to serve political ends, and challenged the authenticity of some of the documents produced by the prosecution.[37]

Some time after the trial, Milovan Djilas—then still a prominent member of the political establishment—admitted in private conversation that the real problem with Stepinac was not his politics vis-a-vis the *Ustasha,* but his politics vis-a-vis the communists themselves, and in particular his fidelity to Rome. "If he had only proclaimed [the creation of] a Croatian Church, separate from Rome," said Djilas, "we would have raised him to the clouds!"[38] More recently—in February 1985—Blazevic himself admitted this in an interview with the Croatian youth weekly, *Polet.* Admitting that Tito had wanted Stepinac to cut the Croatian Church's ties with Rome, Blazevic commented, "That trial of Stepinac was forced on us. If Stepinac had only been more flexible, there would have been no need of a trial."[39]

THE PRIESTS' ASSOCIATIONS

Since it had proved impossible to coopt the Church hierarchy, the authorities quickly pursued an alternative policy of trying to sow divisions and discord within the Church, and to win over *portions* of the clergy into a cooperative relationship. One token of this was the regime's response to the pastoral letter of September 22, 1945. *Borba,* for example, reported that many Catholic priests in Bosnia-Herzegovina refused to read the letter in their churches,[40] while other papers carried a story claiming that Archbishop Nikola Dobrecic of Bar had criticized those bishops who had signed the pastoral letter.[41]

A more tangible symptom of this strategy was the promotion of priests' associations which would lie outside the authority of the bishops. However, after the controversial trial and imprisonment of Archbishop Stepinac, the clergy, especially in Croatia, were ill disposed to cooperate with the regime. All the same, the first Catholic priests' association was created in Istria in 1948, under the presidency of Dr. Bozo Milanovic, and most Istrian priests joined. That same year, an attempt was made to set up an association in Slovenia. The first attempt failed, however, and the matter had to be taken up again the following year. These first two associations were more or less spontaneous on the part of the priests, though actively encouraged by the government.

A third priests' association was set up in January 1950 in Bosnia-Herzegovina. The government set up health insurance for members and pressured priests to join, for example by making permission to give religious instruction contingent on membership (a policy adopted in 1952 but eventually abandoned). By the end of 1952, nearly all the priests in Istria were association members, along with 80 per cent of priests in Bosnia-Herzegovina and 60 per cent of priests in Slovenia.[42]

The bishops were opposed to these associations and, in a statement dated April 26, 1950, declared them "inexpedient." Two and a half years later, after consulting the Vatican, the bishops issued a decision forbidding the clergy altogether to join the associations. This move provoked a crisis in Church-state relations when the Yugoslav government sent a note of protest to the Holy See on November 1, 1952. The Holy See replied on December 15, detailing the troubles being experienced by the Church, but this note was returned unopened. On December 17, the Yugoslav government terminated diplomatic relations with the Vatican.[43]

By the end of 1953, three more priests' associations for Catholic clergy were created—in Croatia, Serbia, and Montenegro. The associations thus paralleled the federal structure of the political system, with one association per republic. These associations served as conduits for state subsidies—which were welcome given the destruction caused by the war. The Bosnian Franciscan Province, for example, began receiving state subsidies through this source in 1952, and in the period 1952–1964, received a total of 63 million old dinars in subsidies (estimated as equivalent to 315,000 West German marks).[44] Nor were the Franciscans the only ones to receive state aid: other institutions of the Catholic Church also received aid, such as the Theological Faculty in Ljubljana (which received several state subventions), the diocese of Djakovo (where Strossmayer once presided, which received a subsidy to restore the cathedral), and the diocese of Senj (which received a state subsidy to restore the episcopal palace).

In addition to health insurance, subsidies, and better relations with the bureaucracy, the priests' associations also enjoyed preferential treatment where publications were concerned. Thus, "Dobri pastir," the Bosnian association, was able to publish a religious periodical and a calendar beginning in 1950, i.e., even at a time when almost all of the rest of the Church press was suppressed.[45]

The priests' associations are integrated into the structure of the Socialist Alliance of Working People of Yugoslavia (SAWPY) and are officially viewed as a means for clergymen to protect and realize their "professional interests." Despite claims by various observers[46] that the associations have benefitted the Church, the hierarchy has remained deeply suspicious. In 1970, for example, Archbishop Frane Franic of Split wrote that the Franciscans, insofar as they constitute three quarters of Dobri pastir's membership, were "true collaborators with the people's authorities."[47] A meeting of representatives of clergymen's associations in 1978 showed that the antagonism felt by the hierarchy toward the associations was working against the latter. Vinko Weber, Secretary of the Society of Catholic Priests of Croatia, told that meeting that his once vibrant organization was "now in its last gasp," that it had not been allowed to distribute its publications on Church premises, and that it had subsequently even lost its printing facilities. Weber continued,

Unfortunately, the days of "non licet non exedi" are still with us. This ban has remained in force right up to the present day. And let me tell you why this is so! Our society has its own statutes, and these statutes include the famous article 3, which, inter alia, states that members of the Society of Catholic Priests shall promote the brotherhood and unity of our peoples, defend the achievements of the national liberation struggle, promote ecumenism, and so on. And this is the crux of the matter, that is, they cannot forgive us for incorporating this article into our statutes, and this is why they keep trying to foil us in everything we do. Things have finally reached the point where even certain Catholic societies in other republics are starting to refuse to have anything to do with us, thinking that we are some kind of black sheep, and this is only because they have been misinformed. But the upshot of all this is that nowadays our society is barely managing to keep itself together.[48]

Similarly, the Association of Catholic Priests of Montenegro, which attracted more than 20 of the 30 Catholic priests serving in that republic in 1954, could count only six members as of 1978—and all of them retired priests. Thus, far from being able to serve as an effective mediary between Church and state, the priests' associations turned out to be at the most a useful mechanism for health insurance and other material benefits, or, on the other hand, irrelevant vestiges of a failed strategy. In Slovenia, by contrast, the Catholic priests' association has always been weak and marginal, and figures today chiefly as the publication outlet for a quarterly newsletter and for a series of religious books for children.

PHASES IN CHURCH-STATE RELATIONS

The years 1945–1953 were the most difficult period for the Church. The Catholic press shriveled, and where there had been about a hundred periodical publications prior to the war, the Church could count only three publications now: *Blagovest* (in Belgrade and Skopje), *Dobri pastir* in Bosnia, and *Oznanilo* in Slovenia, which appeared as a two-page (front and back) bulletin from 1945 to 1946, and as a four-page bulletin, 1946–1952. (As of 1987, by contrast, the Catholic Church was publishing 134 periodicals in Croatia alone.[49]) Catholic hospitals, orphanages, and homes for the aged were seized and closed, and Catholic secondary schools were nationalized. Seminaries were likewise confiscated, for example, in Zagreb, Split, Travnik, Sent Vid, Ljubljana, Maribor, and Sinj.[50] Some 600 Slovenian priests were imprisoned. The faculties of theology of the Universities of Ljubljana and Zagreb were separated from the universities by governmental decree in 1952.

The passage of a special Law on the Legal Status of Religious Communities (April 27, 1953) stirred hope for change, insofar as it guaranteed freedom of conscience and religious belief. Perhaps as important was Tito's call, in a speech at Ruma that same year, for a "halt to physical assaults on the clergy"[51]—partly in concession to Western public opinion, now that Tito's Yugoslavia had broken with the Soviet bloc. The years 1953–1964 saw some reduction in the pressures against believers, though as Paul Mojzes notes, "excesses—such as torture, imprisonment on false charges, and even murder by the secret police—were still practised from time to time, more in some parts of the country than in others."[52] Both Church and state were clearly groping toward a *modus vivendi* during this period. And hence, when Yugoslavia's bishops submitted a memorandum in September 1960, detailing their complaints and demands (including the unhindered prerogative to build and repair churches), they also included a calculated invitation to dialogue, noting that "the Constitution guarantees freedom of faith and conscience to all citizens, while the Law on the Legal Status of Religious Communities [gives form to] and defines this constitutional provision more closely. These legal provisions contain the nucleus of all that is necessary for relations between the Church and the State to develop in line with the principle of a free Church in a free State."[53]

By early 1964, there were unmistakable signs of a new atmosphere in Church-state relations, by 1965 Belgrade and the Holy See were engaged in negotiations, and on June 25, 1966, Belgrade and the Vatican signed a Protocol and exchanged governmental representatives. In the Protocol, Belgrade guaranteed the Roman Catholic Church "free conduct of religious affairs and rites," confirmed the Vatican's authority over Catholic clergy in Yugoslavia in religious matters, and guaranteed the bishops the right to maintain contact with the Vatican. On the other side, the Vatican undertook that priests in the country would respect Yugoslavia's laws and that the clergy "cannot misuse their religious and Church functions for aims which would have a political character."[54]

The hierarchy in Yugoslavia welcomed the Protocol. Archbishop Franic saw in it the promise of "a new era for our Church,"[55] while Franjo Cardinal Seper, then Archbishop of Zagreb, commented in 1967, "The Catholic community cannot escape being engaged. But that presumes a greater amount of freedom. We hope that that freedom will steadily increase for the Catholic Church as well as for other social communities . . . In the Belgrade Protocol, the Catholic Church accepted the existing legislation of Yugoslavia as a starting point. That at least presumes the possibility of legislative development in religious questions, so that [religious policy] would not lag behind the development of reality and become an anachronism."[56] Four years later, Yugoslavia reestablished full diplomatic relations with the Vatican, and in March 1971 Tito paid an official visit to the Vatican.

The general liberalization in Yugoslavia in the late 1960s permitted the launching of a series of Church periodicals, including the fortnightly newspaper (now weekly), *Glas koncila,* which has become an important organ for Church opinion. The Church also began to revive its social programs for youth, not only in Croatia and Slovenia, but also in Bosnia, where the authorities showed especial misgivings at the Church's new self-confidence.[57] Catholic clergy in Rijeka, Split, Zadar, and Zagreb responded enthusiastically to the Croatian liberal-nationalist groundswell of 1967–1971, and in Bosnia-Herzegovina, Franciscan priests gathered data on the number of Croats occupying administrative posts in that republic.[58]

It was this renewed self-assertion of the Church, combined with the purge of the liberal faction in the party, 1971–1973, rather than the Protocol and exchange of emissaries, which colored Church-state relations at the outset of their fourth post-war phase, 1970–1989. On the Church's part, the tenth anniversary (in 1970) of the death of Cardinal

Stepinac was commemorated as demands emerged for his canonization.[59] For the regime, however, the rehabilitation of Stepinac seemed fraught with danger, since his trial had converted him into something of a Croatian mythological hero. Accordingly, Croatian sociologist Srdjan Vrcan warned a seminar at Krapinske Toplice, in January 1973, that "viewpoints, completely political and totally nonreligious in spirit, have again been revived as the widest ideological base, viz., viewpoints that the Croats and Serbs are two completely separate worlds between which no kind of stable and positive form of unity can be established."[60] Stepinac became the focal point for the self-defense of the Croatian Catholic Church (as witnessed in Franjo Cardinal Kuharic's annual sermons in defense of Stepinac), and the foundation of the attempted self-legitimation of the regime.

In the period 1970-89, there were at least six issue areas which complicated the Church-state relationship.

First, the Church never reconciled itself to the inclusion of courses in atheism and Marxism in the school curricula and repeatedly asked for equal time or, alternatively, the removal of these courses from the schools. The point of view of the League of Communists of Yugoslavia (LCY) was summarized by *Nedjeljna Dalmacija* in 1972 when it wrote: "The LC cannot accept the concept of an ideologically neutral school nor a school pluralism based on the individual right of each parent, because the educational system is the social obligation and affair of a social institution."[61]

The Church, however, complained that it was dissatisfied "with the method [of teaching], with the content, with the textbooks, with the sundry provocations through which believing children . . . are indoctrinated and atheized."[62] And in late 1987, the Episcopal Conference of Yugoslavia issued a statement calling on the government to respect the right of parents to obtain a religious education for their children.[63]

In autumn 1987, the Episcopal Office set up a theological institute in Mostar, Herzegovina, in cooperation with the Franciscan Province in Mostar. The institute planned to offer a three-year theological program to lay persons, and quickly registered 45 students for the 1987–88 academic year. Despite the fact that there were precedents for such an institute (in Zagreb, Split, Ljubljana, and Maribor), republic authorities closed it down already in November 1987. The Yugoslav news agency TANJUG explained that the establishment of the institute was "directly opposed to the law on the legal position of religious communities in the Socialist Republic of Bosnia-Herzegovina which, in article 20, states emphatically that religious communities can form religious schools only for the training of religious officials. Scientific and educational treatment of believers outside the church itself is, therefore, not in conformity with the law."[64] The Catholic paper, *Glas koncila,* issued a strong protest of this action.[65]

Second, the Church from time to time questioned the legitimacy of excluding believers from the ranks of the LCY. In 1971, for instance, the Slovenian Catholic weekly, *Druzina,* published an article urging that the opportunities provided by SAWPY to Christians were inadequate and that their exclusion from the party was a token of political inequality.[66] Again, in 1987, Cardinal Kuharic raised this issue in an interview with the Catholic journal, *Veritas,* adding that believers were excluded from high posts in various sectors of public life.[67] The party repeatedly repudiated this interpretation, however, and even urged party members to eschew marriage with believers and to stay away from Church ceremonies.[68] On the other hand, a 1988 article about religious life in Serbia found that only a third of party members in Serbia called themselves atheists, with most giving a positive description of religion.[69]

Third, the Church repeatedly challenged the regime over human rights—whether civil, national, or even the human rights of believers qua believers. In a public statement, Kuharic used his 1987 Easter sermon to plead on behalf of 26-year old Croatian dissident Dobroslav Paraga. Paraga had been charged with "slandering the state" after he gave an interview to the Slovenian youth magazine, *Mladina,* in which he discussed the treatment he had received during a three-year prison sentence for anti-state activity.[70] The defenselessness of believers in the face of slander by the secular press also preoccupied the Church, which deplored the lack of objectivity and fairness in the mass media, and the inability of those calumniated to reply in the same media.[71] *Glas koncila* figured as probably the Church's single most important vehicle for self-defense against insinuations and distortions in the communist press.

Fourth, the Church continued to complain that believers were, in other ways, treated as second-class citizens by the communists, who, the Church claimed, treated religious belief as an *alienable* right. In particular, the Church complained of the fact that military personnel were not allowed to attend Church services in uniform or to receive Church newspapers or religious books in the barracks. The Church also long sought to obtain access to incarcerated believers, regardless of the issue for which they are in prison.[72] The Church also expressed concern about continued discrimination against believers in hiring practices in the public sector: this issue was raised by the Split archdiocesan journal, *Crkva u svijetu,* in late 1987 and by a special commission of the Provincial Episcopal Conference of Slovenia in 1988.[73]

Fifth, some elements in the communist political establishment periodically tried to foster and aggravate internal divisions within the

Church. For a while, the Christianity Today Publishing House seemed to some to be the ideal beneficiary of official favor in its "liberal defiance" of the hierarchs. Earlier, *Glas koncila* expressed concern that *Nedjeljna Dalmacija* was seeking to drive a wedge between the Archbishop of Zagreb and the Archbishop of Split and to set them at odds, manipulating the latter's statements to suggest opposition to or divergence from the policy of the Zagreb archbishopric.[74] This strategy was epitomized by the rival formula that recurrently praised the "vast majority" of the clergy, while condemning the "political extremism" of a "reactionary minority."

And sixth, the legislation governing religious practice was itself an important bone of contention between Church and state, both in the preparatory stage and in discussions about the execution of policy. With the passage of the 1974 Constitution, the Religious Law of 1953 was suspended and the republics were entrusted with the task of passing their own legislation in this domain. The new religious laws took effect in Slovenia on May 26, 1976 and in Bosnia-Herzegovina on January 4, 1977. After a vocal debate, Croatia was the last of the eight federal units to pass a new law, which took effect on April 17, 1978. Among the issues in contention were the ban on Church sponsorship of recreational activities, the absence of legal sanction for Church access to radio and television, and an article requiring the consent of the minor before parents could enroll her or him in religious instruction. *Glas koncila* objected, "Many citizens who are believers quite properly observe that neither they nor their minor children are asked for consent to be introduced in the course of their schooling to Marxism in its emphatically atheistic form."[75] The authorities compromised on the last point mentioned and the final version of the Croatian law required the child's consent from age 14 on, rather than from age 7, as specified in the draft.

INTERNAL DIVISIONS

In an earlier study, I described the presence of three opinion groupings within the communist establishment where religious questions were concerned, viz., orthodox Marxists (who had no interest in genuine dialogue with the Churches and believed that they should disappear under communism), passive contract Marxists (who were willing to adopt a passive attitude toward religion provided that the Churches adopted a passive posture toward society and politics), and liberals (who were interested in dialogue and believed the Churches could make a positive contribution to society).[76] These divisions inevitably had consequences for Church-state relations.

In this section, I propose to focus on three sources of internal discord within the Catholic Church in Yugoslavia: the heterogeneity of responses to the Vatican II Council, the controversy surrounding Christianity Today, and the rivalry in Herzegovina between the secular bishop and the Franciscan Order.

Some 25 of Yugoslavia's 29 Catholic bishops (at the time) participated in the Second Vatican Council. Four Yugoslav bishops also participated in the work of the commissions, viz., Archbishop Franjo Seper of Zagreb and Archbishop Frane Franic of Split in the Theological Commission, Archbishop Gabrijel Bukatko of Belgrade in the Commission for Eastern Churches, and Bishop Alfred Pichler of Banja Luka in the Liturgical Commission.

Two things quickly became clear: first, that the more general division between theological traditionalists and theological progressives was replicated within the ranks of Yugoslavia's bishops; and second, that certain bishops espoused a mix of "traditional" and "progressive" views. On the whole, Seper figured as a "progressive," Archbishop Smiljan Cekada of Sarajevo as a "traditionalist," and Franic as a mixture. In fact, Franic himself conceded that while he took a "traditional" stance on some issues, on others he was innovative and prepared to try new approaches.[77]

Seper and Franic favored introduction of the vernacular for Holy Mass, for example, with Franic favoring use of the vernacular for all Church rituals; Cekada preferred to retain Latin as the universal language of liturgy. Again Seper and Franic both supported ecumenism and efforts to patch up old conflicts with particular Churches. But when a specific application of the ecumenical spirit came up—namely, a proposal to build a cathedral in Skopje for joint use by Catholics and Orthodox—Cekada resisted, calling this "an infantile and romantic ecumenism." Seper and Franic split on the proposed introduction of married deacons, on the other hand, with Seper favoring it but Franic and 15 other Yugoslav bishops opposed; Franic argued that people had more respect for a celibate minister than for one who married. Franic also found himself among the traditionalists in defending the notion of the personal primacy of the pope, and proposed that the vow of poverty, hitherto taken only by orders, also be extended to secular clergy. Much of the discussion during the Council centered on proposals to expand the role of the laity in the Church generally and in the liturgy in particular. Predictably, Cekada spoke out against laicization.[78]

The Second Vatican Council ended in a compromise between the traditionalist and progressive wings, but not without strengthening the latter current and reinforcing the self-awareness of the former tendency.

The result was a reinforcement, within Yugoslavia, of a polarization of opinion among clergy that goes back well over a hundred years.[79]

In some ways, the Theological Society Christianity Today is a product of the Vatican II Council.[80] Founded in 1968 as a research and publishing center, Christianity Today soon became a haven for theologically progressive clergymen. In May 1977, the society reorganized itself as a self-managing association in order to free itself from the rather overwhelming tax burden to which it had been liable previously. Several of the bishops condemned this move, arguing that it had not been cleared by an episcopal authority and that it opened the prospect for the society to come under communist party supervision and thus figure as a "Trojan horse."[81] Archbishop Franic became one of the most vocal critics of Christianity Today, banned priests in his archdiocese from having any contacts with the association, and told *Glas koncila,* in an interview in 1981,

> Some of our theologians tell us that the Church has in its history adapted to all social systems, and that it can and must adapt today, say, to self-managing socialism . . . It is also said that this is in fact the doctrine of the Second Vatican Council.
>
> I hold that this is an altogether mistaken interpretation of the council and of Church history. The Church has, to be sure, adapted to all social systems, for example, even to slave-owning society and feudal society, and today to capitalist and socialist society . . . . However, the Church did not introduce into its structures either the slave-owning system or the feudal system or the capitalist system. So, accordingly, it cannot introduce the system of self-managing socialism into its structures either. In this sense, neither the Church nor its theology nor its pastoral work can be based on the principles of self-managing socialism, nor can they enter into self-managing socialism as a part or branch, since this socialism of ours, although it is a more humanist form of Marxism and of the dictatorship of the proletariat, is still essentially aimed at creating a new civilization which is supposed to be atheist.[82]

Priests in Croatia and Bosnia-Herzegovina have been divided over this decision by Christianity Today, with the Jesuits tending to be among the most critical. Moreover, with the issuance of the encyclical "Quidam Episcopi" on March 8, 1982, directed against the Czechoslovak priests' association, Pacem in Terris, the Episcopal Conference wielded yet another weapon in its battle with the progressive theologians of Christianity Today.[83] The danger, as the bishops saw it, was that the publishing house would carry out its tasks "outside Church structures," and foster clerical independence of episcopal authority.[84] The danger, as the

Christianity Today theologians saw it, was that a traditionalist view of episcopal authority would result in the strangulation of a perfectly pragmatic adjustment to fiscal realities. And thus the controversy surrounding Christianity Today was simultaneously a controversy between traditionalist and theologically progressive points of view, a controversy between hierarchy and theologians, and a controversy about possible channels of regime penetration of Church institutions.

The third and final focus of internal Church discord to be treated here is the long-standing rivalry between the diocesan clergy in Bosnia-Herzegovina (most particularly the Bishop of Mostar) and the Franciscan Order. The Franciscans are (with 1094 members in 1978) the largest order in Yugoslavia, far ahead of the next largest order—the Salesians (103 members in 1978).[85]

A delicate balance prevailed in Franciscan-diocesan relations. Hence, in the period 1945–1978, of the 17 new parishes established within Bosnia-Herzegovina, eight were entrusted to the Franciscans, seven to the diocesan clergy, and two were split between them.[86] Beginning in the mid-1960s, there were repeated clashes between pro-Franciscan parishioners and diocesan clergy over efforts to place Franciscan parishes in the hands of diocesan clergy, or to redraw parish boundaries.[87]

Starting in 1976, the present Bishop of Mostar, Pavao Zanic, pressed hard to roll back Franciscan jurisdiction. In early 1981, two young Franciscans—Ivica Vego and Ivan Prusina—refused to relinquish their posts in Mostar and became the center of considerable strife and controversy. Bishop Zanic declared them "suspended" and initiated action to obtain their expulsion from the order. Shortly thereafter, six youngsters whom these two Franciscans had been counseling began to report apparitions of the Madonna, who, they said, was endorsing the Franciscans and blaming the Bishop of Mostar for his "severity."[88] The apparitions continued on a daily basis, with Franciscans taking the lead in ministering to the thousands upon thousands of pilgrims who have been flocking to the site of the apparitions in the Herzegovinan village of Medjugorje. In these circumstances, it became inopportune for the bishop to take any further steps against the Franciscans. Zanic, thus frustrated by the Franciscans, referred to the apparition as the "Franciscan miracle" and was said to have stacked the initial investigative commission with skeptics, in order to defuse the miracle as fast as possible.

Even this brief elaboration of three important sources of internal discord should make it clear that the Catholic Church in Yugoslavia cannot be considered a monolith, and that Church-state relations must accordingly be diffracted by this political complexity.

TABLE 7.1 Proportions of Believers and Nonbelievers in Yugoslavia, 1953–1984 (percentage)

	1953	1964	1969[a]	1984[a]	1984[b]
Believers	87	70.3	53.1	45	51.9
Indifferent or undecided		0.5	32.1	37	27.4
Atheists	13	29.2	14.2	18	18.6
No answer			0.6		2.1

[a]Zagreb region.
[b]Secondary school children in Split.

Sources: Zlatko Frid, Religija u samoupravnom socijalizmu (Zagreb: Centar za drustvene djelatnosti omladine RK SOH, 1971), p. 33; Branko Bosnjak and Stefica Bahtijarevic, Socijalsticko drustvo, crkva i religija (Zagreb: Institut za drustvena istrazivanja Sveucilista u Zagrebu, 1969), p. 29; Nedeljni vjesnik (April 1, 1984); and Slobodna Dalmacija (Split, March 2, 1987).

BELIEF AND UNBELIEF

In the years since the communist takeover of Yugoslavia, religiosity has declined overall. This decline has been sharpest among the traditionally Orthodox[89] and least noticeable among the Muslims, while the smaller neo-Protestant sects such as Seventh Day Adventists and Jehovah's Witnesses have probably grown in membership, if anything. In varying degrees, as the figures in Table 7.1 make clear, the trend has been unmistakably toward the secularization of society, especially of the urban areas.

A 1960 survey, conducted among youth, found that Croats recorded the greatest proportion of believers, followed by Slovenes and Muslims (both 10 percentage points behind the Croats), Macedonians, Serbs, and Montenegrins.[90] A 1985/86 survey among more than 6,500 Yugoslav young people found similar results. Of those from Catholic families, 62.3 per cent said they were religious, as compared with 43.8 per cent of those from Muslim families and only 26.2 per cent of those from Orthodox families.[91] Among the traditionally Catholic republics of Croatia and Slovenia, moreover, while the 1970s and 1980s have seen a continued decline in religiosity in Slovenia, the same period (1968–1985) recorded an increase in religious observance in Dalmatia: where 32 per cent of Dalmatian youth declared themselves religious in 1968, 52 per cent did so in 1985.[92] A 1985 survey of obituary notices in the press confirmed these results, showing 46 per cent religiosity and 54 per cent indifference or atheism.[93]

Following a pattern typical of transitional societies, urban residents and young people are less likely to be religious. The difference between

TABLE 7.2 Responses to the Question, "Do You Accept Marxism?" (1969, percentage)

	Yes	No	Partly	Not acquainted
Believers	18.5	2.3	10.7	66.0
Undecided	32.8	0.0	23.8	41.9
Nonbelievers	61.1	0.0	15.0	23.9
Atheists	82.7	0.0	4.7	12.6

Source: Bosnjak and Bahtijarevic, *Socialisticko drustvo, crkva i religija* (Zagreb: Institut za drustvena intrazivanja Sveucilista u Zagrebu, 1969) p. 122.

city and village, when it comes to religiosity, is reflected, for example, in the recent report that while 95 per cent of young Catholics in Yugoslav villages obtain religious instruction, only 10 per cent of those in cities do so, averaging 60 per cent for the country as a whole.[94] And for reasons unclear, a 1986 survey in Belgrade showed that the proportions of *both* atheists and believers were shrinking, with an increasing number of people reporting themselves "agnostics."[95] Already in 1975, a group of Zagreb sociologists found that 40 per cent of respondents had no definite or clear worldview.[96] The persistence and even increase of agnosticism was probably related to the more general failures of Yugoslav ideology and socialization.

For all that, party members have tended, at least until recently, to see religion as an unwelcome social phenomenon. Branko Bosnjak and Stefica Bahtijarevic conducted an extremely comprehensive survey of attitudes toward religion among residents of Zagreb and its immediate vicinity in 1969. Their results showed that 28.7 per cent of LCY members viewed religion as actually "damaging," as compared with 18.7 per cent of government functionaries, 15.8 per cent of World War Two veterans, 10.3 per cent of members of administrative organs, and 8.5 per cent of SAWPY members.[97]

Other results showed a clear relationship between atheization and socialization to accept Marxism and to respond positively to the communist system, thus confirming LCY suspicions of religion, though perhaps only with circular logic. In Table 7.2, for example, three times as many nonbelievers as believers accepted Marxism, while believers were the most likely to report nonacquaintance with the Marxist creed. Table 7.3 shows a clear inverse correlation between religious belief and participation in public meetings. And asked if Church teachings influenced their participation in public life, 33.2 per cent answered in the affirmative.[98]

Other questions touched on the practice of religion in Yugoslavia. Of the sample polled, 46.8 per cent said they felt that they could practise their faith freely in Yugoslavia, versus 6 per cent who felt they

TABLE 7.3 Responses to the Question, "How Often Do You Participate in Public Meetings?" (1969, percentage)

	Regularly, or very often	Sometimes	Never
Believers	17.5	40.0	40.9
Undecided	30.6	48.6	19.5
Nonbelievers	39.5	47.2	13.3
Atheists	51.7	37.4	10.9

Sources: Bosnjak and Bahtijarevic, *Socijalisticko drustvo, crkva i religija* (Zagreb: Institut za drustvena istrazivanja Sveucilizta u Zagrebu, 1969) p. 101.

TABLE 7.4 Proportion of Population Reporting Religious Belief (November 1985), by Federal Unit

Federal unit	Percent
Kosovo	44
Croatia	33
Slovenia	26
Macedonia	19
Bosnia-Herzegovina	17
Serbia	11
Vojvodina	10
Montenegro	10

Source: Intervju (March 28, 1986), as reported in AKSA (April 4, 1986), in *AKSA Bulletin* (August 5, 1986), p. 8.

could not. (7.8 per cent answered with a qualified "yes," adding that they avoided conversations about religion, while 37.8 per cent were not believers, and 1.6 per cent declined to answer.)[99] Asked if they considered it easy to safeguard their faith in an atheist environment, 25.1 per cent of the sample replied in the negative, with an additional 16.4 per cent replying merely that they did not reveal their religious belief to others: this makes for a composite negative reply of 41.5 per cent.[100]

And finally, when asked if believers are more moral than nonbelievers, 1.6 per cent of party members answered in the affirmative—indicating that not all LCY members were convinced "atheists."[101] A more recent poll, conducted anonymously in 1987, found that 7.7 per cent of communist party members surveyed (in the Zagreb region) were believers, and that 12.5 per cent admitted that they were sending their children to religious instruction.[102] Table 7.4 shows the proportion of Yugoslavs reporting religious beliefs in 1985.

Yugoslav society is a partly secularized and partly secularizing society—and not merely because of LCY rule. In this context, the

Catholic Church has had to adapt to changed circumstances and to discover new strategies for maintaining and propagating the faith. Many clergymen have called for coexistence, such as Croatian theologian Tomislav Sagi-Bunic who, in his *Ali drugog puta nema* (1969), wrote: "The political community and the Church are independent and autonomous of each other, each in its own sphere. Both stand in service, although for different reasons, at the personal and social summons of the very same people. Thus, . . . appropriate cooperation between them is necessary, so that they can better carry out their service toward people."[103]

THE STRUGGLE FOR A NEW YUGOSLAVIA

As Serb-Croat polemics heated up in the course of 1989–90, the Catholic Church was ineluctably drawn into the fire. Serbian politicians revived the old communist canard that the Catholic Church had been pro-*Ustasha* in the war, and stirred up fears of partition, by talking of the supposedly Orthodox origins of Dalmatia.[104] The Church rebuffed these attacks, and replied with a sharp article that suggested that Serbian revanchists may still nurture dreams of including as much as 70 per cent of the territory of Yugoslavia within the borders of an enlarged Serbia.[105]

Not surprisingly, it was Slovenia—where both Strossmayer and Stepinac are largely irrelevant—that Church-state relations first acquired a somewhat friendlier tone. This was signalled in December 1986 when Ljubljana's Archbishop Sustar became the first Yugoslav hierarch in the post-war period to be allowed to wish his flock a Merry Christmas over public radio.[106] The decision sparked a lively national debate, but privately Slovenian clergy expressed confidence that Christmas would soon be declared a public holiday, if not in 1987, then by 1988—at least in the Republic of Slovenia.[107] Sustar's Christmas greetings were once again broadcast in December 1987, but only amid massive controversy and discussion in the press. Meanwhile, Mitja Ribicic, a prominent Slovenian politician, suggested that rather than engaging in endless debate about the rectitude of broadcasting the prelate's Christmas greetings, it would be better to discuss how to improve the access of believers to jobs in both local and federal governmental agencies.[108] This was followed by the announcement in 1988 that the Catholic Faculty of Theology in Ljubljana, which was forced to separate from the university shortly after the war, would shortly be reincorporated into the University of Ljubljana.[109]

Slovenes started to talk openly of the liquidation of priests by Tito in early post-war Slovenia.[110] Slovenian society was opening up. In

February 1989, it was announced that Catholic journalists would be allowed to join the Society of Journalists of Slovenia.[111] Four months later, a Society of Catholic Journalists in Yugoslavia was established in Zagreb.[112]

As the communist monopoly broke down, Catholic prelates joined in the general debate about the country's future. In November 1989, for example, the Iustitia et Pax Commission of the Episcopal Conference of Yugoslavia published a statement urging progress in repluralization, stressing, in particular, the central importance of the establishment of an independent judiciary.[113]

When the first free elections were conducted in Slovenia and Croatia, the Catholic bishops of Ljubljana and Zagreb issued a statement supportive of democracy, but declining to endorse any particular party. On the contrary, Church elders warned clergy not to become involved in partisan politics.[114] But in other ways, the Catholic Church has taken advantage of the new liberalism to stretch its wings. In July 1990, already, Franciscans in Herzegovina asked for a lifting of the ban on associations based on religious and ethnic affiliation. In Croatia and Slovenia, Catholic authorities have talked about restoring religious instruction as a regular school subject and have, as elsewhere, targeted abortion. Nor has the Church held aloof from the most burning questions of the day. Kuharic, in particular, took up the subject of confederalization, in an article for *Vjesnik,* and argued that "the question of confederation does not pass by the religious communities."[115]

Ever more secure, the Catholic Church has recently also revived its efforts to obtain a judicial review of the Stepinac trial, a review which prelates feel confident would be sure to lead to a full rehabilitation of the hapless cleric.[116]

CHAPTER EIGHT

———————◆———————

The Serbian Orthodox Church

BETWEEN 1984 AND 1987, there was a dramatic transformation of the status of the Serbian Orthodox Church. Long treated as a despised pariah, whose gospel was the dispensation of depraved reactionaries, the Serbian Orthodox Church regained some of its earlier stature and prestige, and has, more recently, been treated—as in the interwar kingdom—as the most constant defender of the Serbian people and their culture.

THE SOUL OF THE CHURCH

Prior to 1984, however, the Serbian Orthodox Church became accustomed to vilification. Over time, this affected the psychological state of Orthodox clergy, who came to see themselves as embattled warriors for their Christ, profoundly threatened by a dangerous world. For much of the postwar period, it was more or less routine for the communist press in Yugoslavia periodically to assail the Serbian Orthodox Church for chauvinism, Greater Serbian nationalism, and reactionary attitudes. The sensitivity with which that Church often reacted to such attacks betrayed a psychological vulnerability fostered by the vicissitudes in the Church's fortunes during the twentieth century and by the erosion of its power on several fronts, and expressed in the hierarchy's self-image as a *suffering* Church, even of a Church marked out for *especial* suffering. Having lost a fourth of its clergy and many of its churches during World War Two, the Serbian Church had to endure the postwar harassment of its priests and the continued obstruction of church construction. Having lived to see the extinction of the artificially created Croatian Orthodox Church, the Belgrade patriarchate had to deal with two further schisms, resulting in the loss of effective jurisdiction over part of the American and Australian congregations as well as the Macedonian dioceses. And while most of the Serbian clergy resisted the Nazis and their allies tenaciously, they found themselves strangely isolated, derided, chastened—until quite recently. The Serbian Church remained defiant, but there was a sense of pessimism or perhaps of impotence to that defiance. Accordingly, in the new arcadia of Church-state rapprochement created by Slobodan Milosevic, the Serbian priests behave as if they are unsure whether these "freedoms" are here to stay, and privately express concern that everything could be rescinded and retracted overnight. The Church, thus, retains a sense of insecurity and has not forgotten that, in the greater scheme, it remains impotent.

It was not always this way. In the early part of the century, the Serbian Church took its numerous privileges for granted and identified the purposes of the Serbian kingdom so totally with its own purposes as to be incapable of comprehending differences of interest, except as misinterpretations of their common interest. Yet it should be stressed that the comparatively weak position of the Serbian Church since the war is not the result merely of the decimation of World War Two, let alone of communist rule, but has its roots deep in the past.

The second suppression of the Serbian patriarchate of Pec in 1766 no doubt undermined the institutional power of the Church. Thus, at the opening of the twentieth century, the Serbian Orthodox Church was organized differently in the different political systems in which it had dioceses and lacked a centralized authoritative head. In the Kingdom of Serbia, for instance, the leading Church figure was the metropolitan of Belgrade, assisted by a synod, and the clergy received state salaries. In Montenegro, the Montenegrin government set up a synod, in 1903, as the highest Church authority in that principality, including in its membership all Montenegrin bishops, two archimandrites, three protopriests, and a secretary. In Hungary, Orthodox Church affairs were regulated autonomously by a national Church council over which the Metropolitan of Karlovci presided. And in Bosnia-Herzegovina, the Orthodox clergy again regulated the internal life of the Church independently, although the Austrian emperor appointed its bishops.[1]

More significant for the vitiation which began in the late nineteenth century were the ideas of materialism, positivism, and progressive secularism, which infected even some of the clergy (e.g., Jovan Jovanovic, rector of the Orthodox Theological Seminary in Belgrade), and the persistent encroachments by the state on ecclesiastical turf. Repeated intellectual attacks on the Serbian Church, combined with the increasingly poorer training given to Serbian clergy, eventually resulted in a sapping of religiosity among the Serbs. Meantime, infused with notions of social activism, many of the clergy became involved in Serbian political parties, which encouraged the state to interfere ever more and more in ecclesiastical affairs. By 1881, with the dismissal of Belgrade

Metropolitan Mihailo and the passage of a new law, whereby the government was able to pack the Church synod with its own lay delegates, the state had effectively taken over the Church, reducing it to something akin to a state agency; even the reinstatement of Mihailo in 1889 did not reinvigorate the Church's power.[2] The very organization of the Serbian Orthodox Church was eventually regulated by a law on Church districts passed by the state with the consent of the Church.

Yet there were benefits for the Church in the old Kingdom of Serbia too. For one thing, under the Serbian constitution of 1903, Orthodoxy was recognized as the official state religion and all state and national holidays were celebrated with Church ritual. Orthodox religious instruction was mandatory throughout Serbia. And all bishops, Serbian Church officials, religious instructors, and army chaplains received state salaries. Moreover, after the establishment of a unified Yugoslavia at the end of 1918, and the revival of the patriarchate, the Serbian patriarch would sit on the Royal Council, while several Orthodox clergymen had seats in the National Assembly as deputies of various political parties.

Given the disunity in Church organizations that existed in the first two decades of this century, it was inevitable that the Serbian Church viewed the unification of the South Slavs as *also* a unification of the Serbian Orthodox Church, and thus perhaps even as a great turning point. Within six months of the establishment of the interwar Kingdom of Serbs, Croats, and Slovenes (as Yugoslavia was initially called), the Serbian bishops convened in Belgrade and proclaimed the unification of all the Serbian Orthodox provincial churches into a single unified ecclesiastical structure. The following year, on 12 September 1920, the bishops completed the process by solemnly proclaiming the reestablishment of the Serbian patriarchate, in the presence of the highest dignitaries of both Church and state. These moves were fully canonical, undertaken with the concurrence and blessing of the Ecumenical Patriarchate.

The state's interest in this was clear from the outset. Even before the unification conference, a governmental delegate, Dr. Vojislav Janic— later to become the Minister of Faiths—revealed that it was "the wish of the government that the reestablishment of the patriarchate be accomplished as soon as the Church is unified."[3] Furthermore, once the patriarch had been elected, the government lost little time in drafting a law that would have imposed greater legislative and judicial unity on the Church and thus made it simpler to regulate and control. Because this draft bill provoked immediate protests from all sides, but especially in the metropolitanate of Karlovac and in Bosnia-Herzegovina, where the local clergy dreaded the diminution of their autonomy, it was withdrawn and a different bill was submitted to the assembly at the end of 1923. This draft also failed to be passed, and two further drafts were likewise defeated before the government finally succeeded, in 1929, in passing a law drafted by the Minister of Justice, Milan Srskic. The prolonged controversy over this law revealed the existence of considerable differences of opinion between Church and state regarding state jurisdiction over the Church, and also considerable division within the Serbian Church itself.

In the meantime, the Serbian Church and the government signed an agreement in 1926 (between the Episcopal Synod and the Ministry of Faiths) which was the equivalent of a concordat, arranging many questions pertaining to their mutual relations. The state now discovered that instead of simplifying its control over the Church, the reestablishment of the patriarchate gave the Church new resources; and in the course of the 1920s, as a result both of the passage of a new Church constitution (in 1924) and of the fluidity produced by the drawn-out controversy over the Church law—as well as the financial strength derived in part from state subventions to the Church—the Serbian Orthodox Church improved its position vis-à-vis the state and showed itself willing to confront the state over matters of importance. The Church became, at the same time, a unified structure, as differences between provincial Churches disappeared.

Under Yugoslavia's King Alexander (1921–34), "not only was the dynasty Serbian, but all the important ministries were monopolized by Serbs, the bureaucracy was predominantly Serbian, the police were controlled by Serbs, [and] the high ranks of the military were occupied by Serbs."[4] The monarchy gave the Serbian Orthodox Church generous subsidies. As a result of these, the Serbian Church was able to establish a metropolitanate in Zagreb and to contruct three churches in Catholic Slovenia.[5] There was even talk, in the early 1920s, that the Serbian Orthodox Church might open a theological faculty in Zagreb.[6] During the 1920s, non-Orthodox believers repeatedly complained that the Serbian Church was manipulating the state to serve its own confessional objectives, and reports that the Royal Dictatorship (established in 1929) was persecuting Catholic schools only deepened the alienation of the Catholic sector of the population.[7]

Although it enjoyed, thus, in some ways, a privileged position in the interwar kingdom, or perhaps precisely *because* it did, the Serbian Church was deeply troubled by the Roman Catholic Church's quest for a concordat, which, it feared, would greatly strengthen the position of the Catholic Church throughout Yugoslavia. Catholic Archbishops Bauer and Stepinac were very much in favor of the concordat, and Vlatko Macek, chair of the Croatian Peasant Party, lent his endorsement to the Holy See's efforts to secure it. The concordat was finally signed on

25 July 1935, shortly after Milan Stojadinovic became prime minister, though its contents were not published by the state. The Serbian Orthodox Church, however, published what purported to be a complete draft of the concordat, together with a point-by-point critique.[8]

The Serbian patriarchate claimed that the concordat was designed to give the Catholic Church exclusive privileges in Yugoslavia. These privileges were said to include: the guarantee that Catholic bishops, clergy, and believers would enjoy complete freedom of direct contact with the Vatican, whereas in the case of the Serbian Church, only the patriarch was guaranteed such access to fellow Orthodox clergy abroad; an extension to Catholic clergy of the same state protection enjoyed by state employees and the protection of the privacy of the confessional; the right to retain buildings and property even in hypothetical cases in which the local congregation should convert en masse to another faith; privileged exemption from the payment of telegraph tax; the assurance that Catholic bishops would enjoy unlimited rights to inspect religious instruction, whereas the Serbian Church could conduct such inspections only once a year, and the Islamic community only twice a year; the guarantee that Catholic schoolchildren not be obliged or even invited to attend religious instruction of any non-Catholic denomination, and that the school program be arranged so as not to obstruct Catholic students from carrying out their religious obligations; and the exemption of Catholic priests and monks, but not Orthodox clergy, from military conscription, except in case of general mobilization.[9] The Serbian Church also objected to Article 8 of the proposed concordat, because it would have banned *all* clergymen in *all* Churches from participation in political parties, even though the Serbian Orthodox Church had not been consulted in this regard.[10] Finally, the patriarchate claimed that in the broad sense, the guarantee in Article 1, that the Catholic Church might carry out its "mission," could embrace a right of proselytization "which is contrary to Article 16 of the state constitution and which can disturb the interconfessional balance."[11]

The Serbian Orthodox Church created a huge uproar over the bill. The Serbian Church even allied itself with opposition Serbian parties in efforts to bring down the pro-concordat administration. The government offered to guarantee the Serbian Church the same privileges, but the uproar did not die down. On 23 July 1937, despite violent confrontations between Orthodox believers and police, Stojadinovic pushed the bill through the Assembly (the lower house in the bicameral legislature), by a vote of 166 to 128. The same night, the patriarch died, and rumors spread that the government had had him poisoned. The Orthodox Synod refused the state funeral that would have been customary for a deceased patriarch, and punished the Orthodox parliamentary deputies who had supported the concordat by suspending their rights in the Church.[12] These additional pressures broke the government's will to continue, and Stojadinovic decided not to present the document to the senate for approval. On 27 October 1937, Stojadinovic informed the Catholic episcopate that the concordat was decidedly dead. The concordat was formally withdrawn on 1 February 1938. This constituted a major victory for the Serbian Orthodox Church, which had been fighting the concordat for more than twelve years.[13] Thus, on the eve of World War Two, the Serbian Church could congratulate itself on two major victories—in the controversy over the Church law and in the struggle over the concordat.

THE GREAT CATASTROPHE

The systematic destruction of hundreds of monasteries and church buildings, the liquidation of hundreds of Serbian Orthodox clergy, and the wartime deaths of at least six of the Church's top hierarchs[14] (three murdered by the *Ustasha*) had a traumatic effect on the Serbian clergy, and even today they live with a complex of bitterness rooted in the wartime debilitation. The Serbian Church had shared in the Serbian nationalist enthusiasm to see Croatia as a zone for Serbian political, economic, cultural, and confessional expansion, and viewed Catholicism as a degenerate form of the true faith; this orientation made it all the more painful for the Serbian Church to bear the fruit of wartime Croatia's program of eliminating all traces of Serbdom and Orthodoxy from Croatia. The fact that the program of forced exile and liquidation was supplemented by the coercive conversion to Catholicism of part of the Orthodox population in the fascist Independent State of Croatia (*Nezavisna Drzava Hrvatska*, or NDH), in order to "Croatize" them, deepened both the identification of Serbdom and Orthodoxy in the consciousness of the Serbian Church, and the sense of threat from the *Ustasha* party of the NDH. Moreover, the Catholic Church by and large seemed to welcome the conversions, even if it sometimes distanced itself from the coercion employed. Mile Budak, NDH *Doglavnik* (second-in-command to Ante Pavelic) told an assemblage of representatives of the Catholic Action organization on 8 June 1941: "The Orthodox came to these districts as guests. And they should now leave these parts once and for all. Of course, many will not be able to leave, but in that case they will want to convert to our faith."[15]

In April 1941, there had been 577 Serbian Orthodox clergymen in the territory of the NDH. By the end of 1941, all of them had been removed from the scene: three were in prison, five had died of natural causes, 217 had been killed by the *Ustasha*, 334 had been deported to Serbia, and 18 had fled to Serbia earlier.[16] Serbian clergy were treated in a similar fashion in parts occupied by other powers. In Vojvodina, there was pressure on Orthodox believers. In Bulgarian-occupied Macedonia, the Bulgarian Orthodox Church asserted its jurisdiction (in the conviction that Macedonians are Bulgarians rather than Serbs, as the Serbian Church has always insisted), expelled or arrested those clergy who considered themselves Serbs, and sent in about 280 of its own clergy to administer the faith in Macedonia.[17] In the Italian-occupied littoral, Orthodox clergy were imprisoned and executed, and numerous church edifices were destroyed.[18]

The losses suffered by the Serbian Church during the war were colossal both in real terms and in psychological terms. Of the more than 4,200 churches and chapels and 200 monasteries owned by the Serbian Church in Europe prior to the war,[19] almost 25 per cent had been completely destroyed and 50 per cent of those in Yugoslavia were seriously damaged. As much as a fifth of the clergy in Yugoslavia as a whole had been killed (perhaps as many as seven hundred), and another three hundred had died of natural causes during the war. Of a total of 8.5 million believers before the war, Slijepcevic claims that 1.2 million had lost their lives.[20] The communist government later claimed that 1.7 million Yugoslavs had lost their lives in the war. At war's end, without any assured income and with an estimated wartime damage of 2.4 billion dinars, the Serbian Church still had 2,100 parish priests, 537 lay employees, and about 1,000 retired priests (on pension).[21] Under these circumstances, the Serbian Church was faced with a difficult challenge. The Church wanted to rebuild its world as it had been before, but the preconditions for that world no longer existed.

THE COMMUNIST ASSAULT
AND THE EFFORT TO REBUILD

Understandably, the Serbian clergy had taken an active part in the resistance against the occupation, and some of its clergy, including Patriarch Gavrilo and Bishop Nikolaj Velimirovic, had been incarcerated in German concentration camps. But the Serbian Church had naturally viewed the resistance in quite different terms from the Communist Party. For the Church, the resistance was a nationalist cause of the Serbian people against traitorous Croats and imperialist Nazis. For the communists, on the other hand, the war—which Yugoslav communists henceforth referred to as the national liberation struggle (*narodnooslobodilacka borba*)—was at the same time a social revolution whereby the different peoples of Yugoslavia would subordinate their divisive ethnic interests to joint class interests and through which exploitative "vestiges of the past," such as the Serbian Orthodox Church, would be pushed into an inferior position, in which they could subsequently be snuffed out. Serbian nationalism, which has always been close to the heart of the Serbian Church, was seen by the communists not merely as an archenemy of the new Yugoslavia but even as an enemy of the Serbian people itself.

The aims of the Communist Party of Yugoslavia (CPY) diverged from those of the patriarchate in a number of ways. The CPY wanted, first of all, to legitimize its federation and most especially its reconquest of Macedonia in every possible way. Hence, if there were Orthodox clergy in Macedonia eager to set up an autonomous or autocephalous Church, so much the better, as this would reinforce the image of a distinctive Macedonian ethnicity. The patriarchate, which was an expression of union achieved only with some difficulty in 1920, was hostile to any assault on its unity.

Second, the CPY wanted a tame and cooperative Church which would eschew anything smacking of opposition but be available to support CPY policies when such support was desired. To this end, the government revived the priests' associations (which actually traced a tradition back to 1889), hoping, with some cause, to use these associations to control the Church. The patriarchate was prepared to cooperate with the new regime but not to be its tame and obedient tool. Thus, while there were those on each side who desired to reach an accommodation, there was much less agreement as to the form that that accommodation should take.

Third, the CPY, then still in its Stalinist phase, wanted to uproot religion and to resocialize the population according to the precepts of atheistic dialectical materialism. That is, it was willing to tolerate Churches as institutions, but not as teachers and leaders of the people. The regime therefore initiated a policy of obstructing religious education, confiscating Church buildings, and fining the clergy on various pretexts. Orthodox clergy were, in the early postwar years, harassed, beaten up, and imprisoned on trumped-up charges. And, in the hope of compromising the prestige of the Church elders, the regime began a practice—which continued until Slobodan Milosevic seized the reins of power in Serbia in late 1987—of accusing various Serbian hierarchs of wartime collaboration with the Nazis, such as Bishops Irinej Djordjevic and Nikolaj Velimirovic, though in fact, both of these bishops had been interned by the Axis and were as antifascist as they were anticommunist.[22] But therein lay another problem, for the communist regime was strongly opposed to an anticommunist clergy. Velimirovic was, moreover, an outspoken Serbian nationalist.

There were, at the same time, two respects in which the Serbian Church could be useful to the communist regime. First, insofar as the patriarch of the Serbs would be seen to be on decent terms with the regime, this would tend to give the lie to accusations that the regime was anti-Serb; this was especially important in the early period, when the regime was preparing to put Chetnik leader Draza Mihailovic on trial. Second, the Serbian Church could be useful as a vehicle for maintaining contacts with other communist countries in which there were prominent Orthodox Churches, i.e., the Soviet Union, Romania, and Bulgaria.

There was thus an ambivalence in the communist attitude toward the Serbian Church—an ambivalence not shared by the patriarchate, though it must be emphasized that many lower clergy felt disposed to strive for accommodation with the regime and at least a part of the membership of the priests' associations seems to have felt this way. Reformist lower clergy met as early as November 1942, to revive the Orthodox priests' association, and at war's end, priests' associations were set up, with government backing, along federated lines, corresponding to the federal units erected by the regime. According to Stella Alexander, these Orthodox priests' associations were, in the beginning, "completely under government control."[23] By mid-1952, *Borba* would claim that some 80 per cent of the remaining active clergy (approximately 1,700) were members of priests' associations.[24] It was these associations which were now authorized to publish the newspaper *Vesnik,* which began publication on 1 March 1949. *Vesnik,* supposedly a Church paper, immediately published attacks on the Serbian Church synod and on Bishops Irinej of Dalmatia and Nikolaj of Zica (both in emigration) and, in other ways, showed itself to be a pliable tool for the regime. Understandably, the synod repeatedly turned down the association's application for official recognition and the patriarchate remained formally opposed to the associations, though this opposition was, over time, tempered by some forms of accommodation. Indeed, a number of bishops have been elected from the ranks of the association.[25]

In May 1953, the communist regime passed a new Law on Religious Communities. Prior to issuing this bill, communist authorities consulted with Orthodox and Muslim clergy, though not with either Catholics or Protestants.[26] Despite this limited consultation, the bill represented communist interests, not Church interests. Among the more controversial stipulations in the law was one guaranteeing that no child could be forced by her or his parents to attend religious instruction. The years 1945 to 1955 were the most difficult of the entire postwar period for the Serbian Church. During these years, Belgrade gave a strict interpretation to clauses of laws curtailing the activity of Churches, imposing heavy penalties on clergymen for any infractions but light punishment, at the most, on those infringing on the rights of religious believers.[27] In a striking illustration of the mood of this period, Bishop Nektarije of Tuzla was roughed up by a mob after he pointed out that the Law on the Legal Status of Religious Communities (1953) expressly permitted the holding of religious services.[28] Under the Law on Agrarian Reform and Colonization (27 May 1945), the state seized 173,367 hectares of land belonging to the religious organizations (85 per cent of their total); 70,000 hectares of what was seized had belonged to the Serbian Orthodox Church. The Serbian Church had had considerable investments in apartments, affording it a tangible rental income, but by 1958, the regime completed the nationalization of apartments, depriving the Serbian Church of 1,180 buildings, worth 8 billion dinars.[29] The Church's two printing presses were also expropriated after the war, without compensation,[30] and various difficulties were encountered in the re-opening of religious seminaries and in their maintenance, due to bureaucratic pressure.

Yet despite all this, the Serbian Church was able to rebuild. Between 1945 and 1970, the Church built 181 churches and restored 841, built 115 chapels and restored 126, and built eight monasteries and restored 48. Even in the Zagreb Eparchy, 20 churches were restored and two new chapels built.[31] By 1949, a makeshift seminary was operating in the Rakovica monastery near Belgrade, and shortly thereafter, the Church was able to reopen its seminary in Prizren. Subsequently, in 1964, Orthodox seminaries were also opened in Sremski Karlovci and at Krka, in the Dalmatian hinterland. Meantime, the Theological Faculty in Belgrade had, by 1966, developed a permanent staff of eight professors and lecturers and had about 120 students.[32] As of 1982, there were about 100 to 110 students in each of the Church's four seminaries, which was close to the capacity of 120, and there were about 70 students studying at the Theological Faculty in Belgrade. While the number of male clergy has held almost steady at about 2,000 for the past two and a half decades, the number of Orthodox nuns inched upward from 468 in 1965 to 519 in 1966 to about 700 in 1980.[33]

Although the Serbian Church had had a lively and plentiful press in the interwar period, with numerous Church magazines, newspapers, and journals, established in the 1920s and 1930s,[34] its publishing activity had to be rebuilt essentially from scratch after World War Two. Initially this activity was limited to a single official organ. *Glasnik,* the Serbian Church's oldest journal, was being published in 2,100 copies in 1955 and, beginning in 1965, in 3,000 copies. The Church established the quarterly educational magazine *Pravoslavni misionar* in 1958, and by 1968, it was being printed in 50,000 copies. The patriarchate brought out its first popular newspaper, *Pravoslavlje,* on 15 April 1967 which, as of summer 1987, was being printed in 23,000 copies (of which 1,500 went to foreign subscribers). A monthly children's magazine, *Svetosavsko zvonce,* was added in 1968 and had a circulation of 15,000 in 1982. The wartime deaths of a number of leading theologians complicated the task of the resumption of theological publication, and *Bogoslovlje,* the scholarly journal of the Theological Faculty, which had ceased publication during the war, did not resume until 1957, although three special collections of articles (*Zbornik radova*) were issued in 1950, 1953, and 1954. A decade later, the archbishopric of Belgrade-Karlovac created its own theological journal, *Teoloski pogledi.* In addition to these theological periodicals, there is also *Pravoslavna misao,* a magazine for Church questions, which, in 1970, had a circulation of 2,000.[35] Book publication resumed slowly, after hesitation, in 1951, but by 1982, the patriarchate was literally boasting of its fine editions, scholarly tomes, ample publications, and so forth.

WHITTLING THE CHURCH DOWN

To understand the Serbian Orthodox Church is to comprehend it as an institution that has repeatedly been whittled down—sometimes unsuccessfully, sometimes successfully. The first twentieth-century challenge to the Serbian patriarchate in this sense was the establishment of the Croatian Orthodox Church in April 1942. Although no Serbian hierarch would accept office in this artificial Church (so that two Russian emigre clergymen had to be contracted to head the dioceses of Zagreb and Sarajevo), a number of Serbian Orthodox clergy did in fact join and cooperate with that structure, in the vain hope of saving themselves and their parishioners. The attempt of the Bulgarian Orthodox Church to "annex" the faithful in Macedonia, like the shortlived Croatian Orthodox Church, likewise met ultimate defeat.

On the other hand, the Serbian patriarchate lost its jurisdiction over its Czechoslovak dioceses between 1945 and 1948, and in 1951, these became the Czechoslovak Orthodox Church. Some Serbian parishes lying within Romania's borders were similarly transferred to the Romanian Orthodox Church in 1969, though the Diocese of Timisoara is still administered by the Serbian Church. The Serbian Church suffered a formal schism in 1963, when Bishop Dionisije Milivojevic of the American-Canadian diocese summoned an assembly to declare that diocese an autonomous Church. Only much later, in 1989, would there be a rapprochement between the Serbian patriarchate and the American diocese.[36] And finally, on 17 July 1967, the Macedonian clergy, in open defiance of the Serbian patriarchate to which it had taken oaths of

loyalty, unilaterally declared itself an autocephalous Macedonian Orthodox Church, electing a Smederevo native, Dositej, as Archbishop of
Ohrid. It is natural, then, that the Serbian patriarchate was anxious
whenever the communist regime gave encouragement to ecclesiastical
separatism in Montenegro, as it did in the early postwar years,[37] and
in this context, Patriarch German's comment, in 1970, that Montenegrins
are simply Serbs by another name, becomes readily intelligible.[38]

Although the Serbian Church remained apprehensive of a regime-
backed Montenegrin schism at least into the early 1970s, it is the
Macedonian schism which has caused the Church the most grief. And
despite its inability to do anything to change the situation, the Serbian
Orthodox Church has refused to recognize the schismatic Macedonian
Church.

The collaboration of the Macedonian clergy with the communists
stretches back to the war. At the end of 1943, the Partisan high command
appointed a Macedonian, Rev. Veljo Mancevski, to take charge of religious
affairs in liberated areas. Shortly after the occupation forces were driven
out of Belgrade, three Macedonian clergy (Metodije Gogov, Nikola
Apostolov, and Kiril Stojanov) presented themselves to the Serbian
synod as representatives of the Orthodox Church in Macedonia and
members of the Organizing Committee for the Founding of an Independent Church in Macedonia. A premature declaration of autocephaly
at this point in time was stymied, but relations between the Serbian
patriarchate and the CPY remained tense as long as the patriarchate
refused to compromise. The Orthodox priests' association, often inclined
to take a stance at odds with the patriarch, supported Macedonian
autocephaly all along, despite the misgivings among some Serbian
members. Finally, in 1958, after the Macedonian clergy declared themselves an "autonomous" Church on their own initiative, the new Serbian
patriarch accepted the fait accompli, though he underlined that it should
go no further than autonomy. Directly as a result of the patriarch's
acceptance of Macedonian ecclesiastical autonomy, the Serbian Church's
relations with the government improved markedly, and by 1961, the
regime's encouragement of intraecclesiastical divisions generally seemed
to have died down.[39] The interest of the government in the Macedonian
Church was shown in its hints of a subvention of 60 million dinars
to the Serbian Church if it came to terms with the Macedonian clergy.[40]

The Communist Party was, at this time, seriously divided between
advocates of "organic Yugoslavism," led by Slovenian party ideologue
Edvard Kardelj, who wanted to knit the country together by making
generous allowances to the cultural and national distinctiveness of its
component peoples, and advocates of "integral Yugoslavism," led by
Vice President Aleksandar Rankovic, who wanted to encourage the

development of a Yugoslav consciousness in the ethnic sense and who tended to view non-Serbs as "less reliable" than Serbs. The former group thus favored decentralization to the federal units, while the latter favored political and administrative centralism. Rankovic, whose Serbian nationalism was never much below the surface, was known for having promoted discriminatory practices against non-Serbs in Croatia, Bosnia, Vojvodina, and Kosovo.[41] The fall of Rankovic in July 1966 proved instrumental in fostering a change of regime policy vis-a-vis the Serbian Church, as Rankovic had wanted to prevent the erosion of the Serbian position in any sphere, including the ecclesiastical. He dealt with the Church roughly, and used threats to obtain ecclesiastical compliance.[42] But as long as he was in office, the Macedonians were unable to obtain full autocephaly.

Rankovic was removed from office on 1 July 1966. The Macedonian clergy immediately began preparations for declaring complete autocephaly, and were ready in a matter of four months. On 18 November 1966, at a joint meeting of the Serbian and Macedonian synods, the Macedonian clergy demanded full autocephaly. When the Serbian synod demurred, the demand was renewed on 3 December, with the attendant threat of unilateral action if the Belgrade patriarchate did not concur. Since the patriarchate refused to accept this, the Macedonians declared autocephaly on their own authority at an ecclesiastical assembly in Ohrid in summer 1967. Although the communist government repeatedly encouraged the two Churches, throughout the late 1960s, 1970s and much of the 1980s, to resolve their differences, and advised the Serbian patriarchate that its failure to recognize this latest fait accompli had a negative impact on the political climate, more particularly on Serb-Macedonian relations, as well as in the party's dispute with communist Bulgaria over the ethnicity of Macedonians, the patriarchate unbudgingly insisted (and insists today) that Macedonians are Serbs and that the Macedonian Orthodox Church has no canonical raison d'être, basing the latter position on the fact that the Macedonian Church was not established on the basis of pan-Orthodox agreement, as prescribed by ecclesiastical tradition.[43]

CHURCH-STATE RELATIONS, 1970–1986

It is a remarkable fact that communist regimes, which always talked about wanting the complete separation of Church and state, were consistently the most eager to assert state control or influence over Church policies and appointments. In Yugoslavia, the communists hoped that their backing of the priests' associations would lead not merely to the cooptation of those associations, but to the cooptation of the

Churches themselves, i.e., to the revival of the situation in old Serbia, when the Serbian Orthodox Church functioned in effect as a bureaucratic department of the state.

Instead, however, the Serbian patriarchate's relations with the associations have remained complex, and the continued activity of the latter provided yet another element of internal opposition within the Serbian Church. The communist regime repeatedly praised the cooperation it received from the Orthodox association,[44] and occasionally presented awards to its members,[45] but the patriarchate itself remained cool and distrustful toward the priests' association.[46] Indeed, this distrust occasionally provoked outbursts of frustration from convinced members of the association. In 1978, for example, Archpriest Ratko Jelic, a representative of the Croatian wing of the Orthodox Association, told members of a committee of the Socialist Alliance of Working People of Yugoslavia, which was concerned with religious matters, that the patriarchate (presumably through its organ, *Pravoslavlje*) was presenting a distorted picture of the work of the association, and proposed to increase the circulation of the association's organ, *Vesnik,* as a foil to *Pravoslavlje.* He continued:

> We have been publishing our *Vesnik* for the past 30 years. True, the number of copies printed per issue is small, a mere 3,000 copies, but I believe that there is no more positive periodical among all of those published by the Church press in this country, especially among those put out by the Serbian Orthodox Church. But this periodical is, unfortunately, not accessible to the public at large. For this reason, I believe that the situation would be entirely different if we were able to inform the members of our faith as to the true nature of our association. As things now stand, it is directly and falsely suggested to them that we are some kind of communist association which wants to destroy the Church and so on and so forth. Thus, people know nothing at all about the work that is being done by our association.[47]

On the same occasion, Archpriest Milutin Petrovic, president of the Central Union of Orthodox Priests of Yugoslavia, complained that some clergy had declined to join the association because they feared reprisals from the hierarchy (although 83 per cent of all Orthodox priests in Yugoslavia were, in 1978, members of the association), while Veselin Cukvas, president of the Montenegrin wing of the Orthodox association, accused the hierarchy of frustrating and ignoring the work of the associations.[48]

But even in 1889, the priests' association was conceived in the spirit of opposition to the hierarchy; over the years, the association has felt free to arrive at conclusions that have diverged from the policies of the patriarchate. Hence, it should come as no surprise that the patriarchate has viewed the Orthodox Association as an internal opposition, even as a Trojan horse.

Another species of internal opposition was highlighted by *Vesnik* in 1971. *Vesnik* charged that there was no practical ecclesiastical unity in policy matters and painted the patriarchate as a kind of bodyless head, "presiding" over a collection of eparchies that operate according to the discretion and wishes of local archpriests. According to *Vesnik,* the episcopal council was failing to reconcile these divergent views and functioned as no more than a sounding board for adamantly held positions.[49]

With only half the clergy it had before the war and a tangibly diminished income, the Serbian Church has been conscious of its weakness. Despite this, it never allowed itself to be coopted by the communist regime—at least not until 1987—and has assumed an oppositional posture from time to time. In this respect, one could speak of two realms: the assertion of Church interests and the demand for policy change, even if Church interests appear to be in opposition to the regime's; and actual opposition by the Church in matters pertaining to the Serbian nation and its culture. That is to say, the Serbian Church was an opposition force insofar as it was (and is) a nationalist institution.

Although the Catholic Church and the Islamic community experienced little difficulty in the early 1980s obtaining official approval for the construction of places of worship, and although the Macedonian Orthodox Church too did well during this time period in the area of church construction, the Serbian Orthodox Church complained of difficulties in obtaining building permits, especially in the cities.[50] Styling itself as a "patient" Church, it nonetheless spoke out in May 1977 in a petition addressed by the Holy Synod to the presidency of the Republic of Serbia and signed by Patriarch German and two other bishops. The letter asked, inter alia, for (1) routinization of permission to build new churches; (2) extension of the state social insurance to the teaching staff and students at theological faculties and seminaries; (3) an end to discrimination against children enrolled in Orthodox religious education; (4) an end to state interference in Church matters; (5) an end to the practice of libeling and slandering clergymen, both living and deceased, in the media; (6) unhindered celebration of funeral rites according to the wishes of the bereaved; and (7) the return of confiscated Church property.[51]

Since then, the Church has chalked up some gains. In 1984, Serbian authorities granted permission for the Church to resume construction of the monumental Church of St. Sava (started 1935–41, but subsequently left unfinished).[52] The following year, the Republic of Croatia returned various icons, books, manuscripts, and sacred objects from the thirteenth to the nineteenth centuries to the Church; they had been confiscated at the end of World War Two and kept in state museums for four decades.[53] And in 1986, permission was granted for reconstruction of the historic monastery of Gradac in central Serbia.[54] In an even more striking move, the ideological commission of the Serbian Socialist Youth Federation declared subsequently that young believers could enjoy full equality in the youth organization, even serving in leadership positions, and proposed to support an initiative to create a postgraduate program in religious studies at the University of Belgrade.[55]

Patriarch German had a reputation, both at home and abroad, for being cautious and circumspect in his dealings with the government. That this reputation was both deserved and open to diverse interpretation was suggested by the sending of an impassioned letter to the patriarch, on 26 February 1982, on the part of Orthodox priests from the Raska-Prizren diocese in Kosovo. Their letter touched on matters concerning Kosovo in particular, such as the harassment of Orthodox clergy and believers by local Albanians, and issues affecting the Church's life in other parts, such as their allegation that officials in the Sabac-Valjevo diocese were interrogating and harassing families that attempted to send their children to Orthodox catechism classes. They pointed out that the Roman Catholic Church was faring tangibly better in this regard, and expressed their dismay that *Pravoslavlje* had ignored these problems and had limited itself to bland announcements that Church representatives and state authorities were conferring about matters of "mutual interest." Their letter was not published in the Orthodox religious press, but appeared in print abroad.[56] Perhaps partly in response to this critical latter, the patriarchate's news organ, *Pravoslavlje,* published a long critique of the regime's policy in Kosovo in its 15 May edition, appealing for the protection of the Serbian population and Orthodox shrines in Kosovo.[57]

The Serbian Church's clashes with the communist regime over the Macedonian Orthodox Church and over regime policy in Kosovo both stemmed from the Church's self-appointed guardianship over the Serbian people—a guardianship which the communist regime wanted to deny but which both the Church and the state label as "nationalist." The Serbian nationalism of the Serbian Church, expressed in numerous ways over the decades, confronted the communist regime as a challenge both to its nationality policy and to its claim to be the *exclusive* representative of the political interests of the population. As a nationalist institution, thus, the Serbian Church was, de facto, in opposition, even if in *loyal* opposition.[58]

REHABILITATION

The seizure of power, in Serbia, by Slobodan Milosevic in mid-December 1987 had a direct impact on the fortunes of the Orthodox Church. True, Milosevic's predecessor, Ivan Stambolic, was responsible for setting in motion what was, in his day, a limited rapprochement with the Serbian Church. But Milosevic extended and deepened this rapprochement. A very explicit token of this rapprochement was Milosevic's meeting with a high-ranking Serbian Orthodox delegation in July 1990.[59] Where the pre-Milosevic Serbian press had excoriated the Serbian Church for meddling in nationalism, under Milosevic, *Politika* praised the Serbian Orthodox Church for its service to the Serbian people, and even declared that Orthodoxy was "the spiritual basis for and the most essential component of the national identity [of Serbs]."[60]

The Orthodox Church has benefitted from Milosevic's rule in concrete ways. First of all, it has been allowed to undertake a vigorous church construction program, to include the construction of churches in areas from which it had long been barred (e.g., Novi Beograd). Again, in December 1989, permission was granted for *Pravoslavlje* to be sold at public newsstands. Third, in January 1990, Orthodox Christmas was publicly celebrated in downtown Belgrade for the first time in four decades. And again, in June 1990, the Serbian government removed Marxism classes from school curricula and replaced them with religious instruction.[61] In token of the new atmosphere, the Serbian Orthodox Church cooperated with the Milosevic government in marking the 600th anniversary of the battle of Kosovo, on 28 June 1989. In Orthodox services connected with the commemoration, pictures of Milosevic could be seen among religious icons.

Not everyone was happy with this state of affairs, and some Serbian nonbelievers quietly registered concerns that the authorities were becoming too friendly with the hierarchy. Charges of collaboration between Serbian Orthodox Church hierarchy and the Milosevic government were more volubly registered by Croatian Catholics, and in November 1990, the Serbian Orthodox Church news organ, *Pravoslavlje,* replied to these accusations by asserting that the Church's contacts with the government's Commission for Relations with Religious Communities were entirely correct and should not be interpreted as active "cooperation," let alone partnership.[62]

As noted in the preceding chapter, the disintegration of Serb-Croat relations affected the religious realm as well. Where Orthodoxy is concerned, one may note that the Serbian Church repeatedly polemicized with the Catholic Church after 1989, and only, finally, in May 1991, did the new Orthodox patriarch, Pavle, respond positively to overtures from Catholic Cardinal Kuharic and agree to a meeting.[63]

As in the case of the Catholic Church in Croatia, the Orthodox Church has played a visible role in the debate about both the federal constitution (still under discussion in spring 1990) and the proposed draft for a new constitution for Serbia. The Church has not been entirely satisfied with either draft document. In the case of the federal draft, the Church indicated that it wanted a constitutional provision to guarantee property and to provide for the return of property confiscated after World War Two.[64] In the case of the Serbian draft, *Pravoslavlje* published a tough criticism by Fr. Dragan Terzic in its August 1990 issue, expressing concern above all about the proposed retention of a clause barring the "misuse of religious beliefs for political purposes."[65]

CONCLUSION

What I have tried to produce here was not an exhaustive history of the Serbian Orthodox Church in recent times, but rather an interpretation of the meaning of that history. To understand the Serbian Orthodox Church today is to understand its mind set, its set of working assumptions about the world, that are the product of the problems, privileges, conflicts, advantages, and setbacks experienced by the Church over the years.

The central experience of this century that colors the entire outlook of the Serbian Orthodox Church even today is the savage assault suffered in World War Two. This assault, which was experienced as trauma, has both stiffened the resolve and defiance of the Church and, reinforced by the communist takeover, deepened its pessimism. The Serbian Church views itself as identical with the Serbian nation since it considers that religion is the foundation of nationality. The hierarchs of the Serbian Church deny that Macedonians are anything but "south Serbs." For the Serbian patriarchate, then, the Macedonian Orthodox Church is, in essence, a reincarnation of the spirit of the Croatian Orthodox Church since, in the view of the patriarchate, the one, like the other, represents an endeavor to reduce the Serbian nation by transforming the religious affiliation of a part of its number. The Serbian Church might well repeat the words of the poet Tanasije Mladenovic, who, in a controversial poem, asked,

Serbia, poor and wretched . . .
will you be able,
as in time past,

to renew your strength with a sudden crack?
Or will you,
discouraged and feeble,
disappear among the mountains and nations . . .
torn to pieces by apocalyptic forces?[66]

CHAPTER NINE

◆

Islam

IN SEPTEMBER 1989 I VISITED Yugoslavia for the sixth time. As always, there was electricity in the air, and as always, the national question, as Yugoslavs fondly call it, had a great deal to do with that electricity. Serbs fear everyone (so it seems these days), everyone fears Serbs, Macedonians and Montenegrins fear Albanians, and Montenegrins fear each other. Typical of this atmosphere was a conversation in which I found myself, at a Belgrade cafe, as two local journalists drew and redrew maps of the Balkans, showing a menacingly large arrow projecting northward from Istanbul through Serbia, while they told me of their fears of a Muslim threat to European civilization. "Albanian Muslims and Bosnian Muslims are in this together," they told me, deadly earnest. "They have big families in order to swamp Serbia and Yugoslavia with Muslims, and turn Yugoslavia into a Muslim republic. They want to see a Khomeini in charge here. But Belgrade is not their final goal. They will continue to advance until they have taken Vienna, Berlin, Paris, London—all the great cities of Europe. Unless they are stopped."

Psychiatrist Jovan Raskovic told *Intervju* magazine in September 1989 that Muslims are fixated in the anal phase of their psycho-social development and are therefore characterized by general aggressiveness and an obsession with precision and cleanliness. (Croats, by contrast, suffer from a castration complex, according to Raskovic.)[1]

Non-Muslims in Yugoslavia recall Libyan dictator Qaddafi's generosity in providing for the Yugoslav Islamic community's mosque-building program, note Bosnia's long-term interest in building economic and cultural contact with Syria, Iraq, and other Arab states, point to the Muslims' efforts to align Yugoslavia with the Arabs during the October 1973 war in the Middle East, and underline the on-going contacts between Islamic clerics and believers in Bosnia and their co-religionists in the Middle East, as, for example, in the case of young Yugoslav Muslims who go to the Middle East for Islamic theological training.

TABLE 9.1 Proportion of Ethnic Muslims, Serbs, Croats, "Yugoslavs," and Other Nationalities in Bosnia-Herzegovina, 1948–1981 (percentage)

	1948	1953	1961	1971	1981	1991
Muslims	30.7	31.3	25.7	39.6	39.5	43.8
Serbs	44.3	44.4	42.9	37.2	32.0	31.5
Croats	23.9	23.0	21.7	20.6	18.4	17.3
"Yugoslavs"	n/a	n/a	8.4	1.2	7.9	7.0
Others	1.1	1.3	1.3	1.4	2.2	1.4

Sources: Ante Markotic, "Demografski aspekt promjena un nacionalnoj strukturi stanovnistva Bosne i Hercegovine," in *Sveske,* nos. 16–17 (1986), p. 292; and Tanjug (30 April 1991), translated in Foreign Broadcast Information Service, *Daily Report* (Eastern Europe), May 1, 1991, p. 53.

For some non-Muslims, these are all signs that the Muslim community is in some sense a foreign implant, that Muslims are not fully integrated into Yugoslav society, that they should be feared.

Hence, when, after repeated delays, permission was finally granted to Muslims, in 1981, to construct a new mosque in Zagreb, to replace the one closed down after the war, controversy was inevitable. Like the Serbs, Croats expressed concern that their republic would be Islamicized. Three years later—in June 1984—when much of the construction on the mosque had been all but completed, a fire set by arsonists destroyed much of what had been built up to then. Finally, in September 1987, the mosque was opened, with considerable fanfare.[2]

Needless to say, this fear of the Muslims has aggravated inter-communal relations within Bosnia, and sharpened the recent debate about Bosnia's place in the federation. Bosnian Muslims have repeatedly talked of wanting Bosnia declared a "Muslim republic," while Serbs and Croats have from time to time hinted that Bosnia might best be divided between Serbia and Croatia. Within Sarajevo, one hears people declare for a united Yugoslavia, on the argument that for inhabitants of Bosnia, there is no other realistic option: any attempt at dividing it up—so they argue—would stir up inter-communal violence in this divided republic.

BASIC FACTS AND RESOURCES

Some 44 percent of Bosnia's population registered as "ethnic Muslims" in the 1991 census, as against 31 percent Serbs, 17 per cent Croats, and 6 per cent ethnic "Yugoslavs" (the latter usually the product of mixed marriages).[3] That makes Bosnia the only federal unit in Yugoslavia in which no single nationality group constitutes a local majority (see Table 9.1). More broadly, however, ethnic Muslims remain a relatively small minority in this country—tallying about 9 per cent of the total population in 1981.[4] In religious terms, one may speak nominally of about 3.8 million confessional Muslims in Yugoslavia, accounting for about 16 per cent of the total population of the country. Religious Muslims include not only the greater portion of ethnic Muslims, but also varying numbers of Albanians, Turks, and Macedonians, as well as some Gypsies, Montenegrins, Croats, Serbs, and even small groups of Pomaks in the region surrounding Pijanac.[5]

The Islamic community in Yugoslavia is organized into four administrative regions: *Sarajevo Region* (Bosnia-Herzegovina, Croatia, and Slovenia, with its Supreme Headoffice in Sarajevo); *Pristina Region* (Serbia, Kosovo, and Vojvodina, with its Supreme Headoffice in Pristina); *Skopje Region* (Macedonia, with its Headoffice in Skopje); and *Titograd Region* (Montenegro, with its Headoffice in Titograd). The Reis-ul-ulema, the head of the entire Yugoslav Islamic community, has his office in Sarajevo.

At the dawn of the post-Tito era, the Islamic community disposed of the following institutional resources and facilities:[6]

Sarajevo Region:
- 1,092 mosques
- 569 mesdzids (smaller places of worship)
- 394 places for religious instruction
- 2 medresas (religious schools)
- 5 tekijas according to usage (cemeteries)

Pristina Region:
- 445 mosques
- 125 mesdzids
- 35 places for religious instruction
- ? tekijas
- 1 medresa

Skopje Region:
- 372 mosques
- 19 mesdzids
- 10 places for religious instruction
- ? tekijas
- 1 medresa

Titograd Region:
- 76 mosques
- 2 mesdzids
- 36 other buildings

- 4 turbe (mausoleums)
- ? tekijas

In addition, every Muslim town or village has a separate graveyard for Muslims. The figures for mosques would be much higher today, having passed the 3,000 mark in 1986 and given the energetic building program which the Yugoslav Islamic community has been able to maintain.

As of 1980, some 120,000 children were receiving Islamic religious instruction at the primary school level. This instruction is provided free of charge to believers. Secondary religious instruction is available at two medresas: Gazi Husrefbey's medresa in Sarajevo, and Alaudin medresa in Pristina. The former is more than 450 years old. In addition, an Islamic Theological Faculty opened in Sarajevo in 1977, and a women's department was created the following year.

The Gazi Husrefbey Library in Sarajevo is an important repository for Islamic materials, and contains several thousand original manuscripts in Arabic, Turkish, and Persian. Courses in Arabic are offered in Sarajevo, Pristina, and Belgrade.

Each of the four regions also has a clerical association, known as an Ilmija. These associations were integrated into the work of the Socialist Alliance of Working People of Yugoslavia, and in this way acquired a legitimate role in the public arena.

The Islamic community naturally maintains a number of periodical publications. The chief ones are: *Preporod,* a fortnightly newspaper published in Serbo-Croatian, in Sarajevo; *Islamska misao,* a monthly journal devoted to theological reflections and news of the community, likewise published in Sarajevo; *El-Hilal,* a Skopje journal, published in Macedonian, Turkish, and Albanian; the bimonthly journal *Glasnik,* the official bulletin of the Supreme Headoffice of the Yugoslav Islamic Community, published in 15,000 copies; *Takvim,* an annual publication; *El-Islam,* which concentrates on religious information; *Edukataiislam,* an Albanian-language publication of the Pristina office; and *Zemzem,* a newspaper published by the Gazi Husrefbey medresa and which is said to have won credibility among young people. All four regional headoffices also have extensive book-publishing programs for religious literature.[7]

Many Bosnian Muslims emigrated abroad, some of them prior to World War One. Today there are Muslims who trace their origins to the lands of present-day Yugoslavia, living in the US, Canada, Australia, Turkey, and in smaller numbers, in several West European countries, including Austria and Germany. In 1977, Yugoslav Muslims in Canada sent a request to the Islamic Community of Yugoslavia to send a delegate to help organize their religious life. A similar request was subsequently submitted also by the Yugoslav Muslim community in Australia.

Yugoslav Muslims have also taken employment, at certain times, in Libya, Iraq, and Kuwait. This experience must be presumed to have strengthened the affinity of at least some Yugoslav Muslims for the Middle East.

THE SOCIAL PRESENCE
OF ISLAM

Despite this formidable institutional base, the Islamic leadership has adopted a much lower profile than either the Roman Catholic Church or the Serbian Orthodox Church. While the two Christian Churches have been able to celebrate Christmas quite openly for several years, with Christmas Day finally declared a state holiday in Slovenia as of 1989,[8] one cannot imagine the Islamic community obtaining the same access to the media, let alone seeing its festivals declared state holidays in multi-confessional Bosnia.

A comparison of the leading Muslim newspaper, *Preporod,* with its Croatian Catholic and Serbian Orthodox counterparts—*Glas koncila* and *Pravoslavlje,* respectively—is telling. Whereas *Glas koncila* has for years struck a defiant posture, openly polemicizing with the communist press on a regular basis and publishing highly informative interviews, as well as articles about state atheism, Christian-Marxist dialogue, proposals to change the laws governing religious life in Yugoslavia, and other social issues, with *Pravoslavlje,* for its part, becoming ever more strident (since 1981) in its defense of Serbian interests in Kosovo and its advocacy of Serbian nationalism in general,[9] *Preporod* has rarely if ever entered into the social arena, restricting itself by and large to reports on the construction of mosques and the observance of religious holidays, along with information about Islamic teachings.

This same pattern carries over into the behavior of religious leaders. Catholic prelates (such as Zagreb's archbishop Franjo Cardinal Kuharic) have delivered sermons defending human rights activists (e.g., Dobroslav Paraga) or demanding an official exoneration of the late Alojzije Cardinal Stepinac, archbishop of Zagreb 1937–60 (tried and convicted in 1946, on charges of collaboration with the *Ustasha* fascists). Serbian Orthodox prelates have been somewhat less bold, but have been found celebrating Serbian heroes such as Tsar Lazar,[10] Tsar Dusan, and Vuk Karadzic, and taking part in commemorations of Serbian national holidays—most pointedly, the 600th anniversary (in 1989) of the famous Battle of Kosovo polje. One cannot imagine Islamic leaders being allowed to celebrate the anniversary of the Ottoman conquest of Bosnia (or considering such a celebration wise, for that matter), or feeling sufficiently confident to undertake to speak out on human rights issues— at least not in the years prior to 1990.

On the contrary, the Islamic community has often found itself on the defense. For example, in November 1987, the Republican Conference of the Socialist Alliance of Working People of Serbia discussed the activities of the Islamic community and concluded that Islamic fundamentalism "had reached Yugoslavia and . . . threatened to spread all over Europe."[11] There have also been rumors and charges from time to time, whether in Bosnia, or Macedonia, or Serbia, that Islamic religious education is inspired by nationalist and separatist orientations. (This will be taken up below.)

In fact, the Islamic community adopted a more quiescent and defensive posture—by comparison with the Catholic and Orthodox Churches— from the very beginning, and from an early time, was able to boast smooth relationos with the authorities. In the initial years—roughly 1945 to 1966 —religious policy was basically worked out in Belgrade, which meant that religious policy throughout the country was guided, within some limits, by a single vision. The decentralization of the political and administrative system which began in the late 1960s and which was designed to satisfy irresistible pressures on the ethnic level, inevitably had consequences for the religious communities. Hereafter, the Catholic Church, with most of its believers living in Slovenia and Croatia, had to worry principally about the orientation of secular authorities in Ljubljana and Zagreb, authorities who, at least in Slovenia, generally showed themselves to be more liberal than their counterparts elsewhere in the country. The Orthodox, living predominantly in Serbia, Macedonia, and Montenegro, had an entirely different set of authorities to deal with. At times, a kind of alliance between Church and party developed at the republic level—as, for example, has occurred in Serbia under Slobodan Milosevic. And for the Muslims, with their largest concentrations inhabiting Bosnia and the autonomous province of Kosovo—the authorities in Sarajevo and Pristina have been their principal reference points for coexistence. This has made for a more complex situation for Muslims for two reasons. First, the authorities in Bosnia tended toward the dogmatic side through much of the 1970s and 1980s. (This is not the case in post-communist Bosnia, obviously.) This meant that Bosnian Muslims were more likely to be attacked in the press than were, for example, Slovenian Catholics or Macedonia's Orthodox, and more likely to find their newsorgan subjected to pressure. Second, Bosnia and Kosovo are the two regions in Yugoslavia with the most delicate inter-communal relations. And while these relations are usually defined in terms of ethnic groups, there are also religious dimensions—as was patently clear in 1981 and 1982, for example, after Albanian Muslims desecrated the Orthodox shrines of Kosovar Serbs, setting fire to the monastery at Pec. An "alliance" between the Muslim community and secular authorities in either Sarajevo or Pristina—on the model of Milosevic's "alliance" with the Serbian patriarchate or even on the model of the friendly relationship which emerged between the Catholic Church and the communist authorities in Ljubljana—is obviously ruled out, as Bosnia has followed the lead of Slovenia and Croatia and adopted a multi-party system. The result has been liberalization and the spirit of compromise and negotiation.

Yet despite the tradition of dogmatic rule in Bosnia and despite the complexities arising from the republic's ethnic fragmentation, Muslims were able to maintain a vigorous mosque construction program throughout the postwar period. In Bosnia-Herzegovina alone, some 400 new mosques were built between 1945 and 1985, and some 380 mosques were renovated. By 1986, there were some 3,000 mosques in Yugoslavia as a whole.[12]

From time to time, the communist press would attack the Muslim community for allegedly misusing religious training. For example, in 1973, officials of Tetovo *opstina* in Macedonia estimated that some 20 per cent of students were receiving religious instruction after regular school hours. The officials claimed, however, that religious instruction was not being used strictly to instruct children in matters of faith and worship. On the contrary, *Nova Makedonija* charged that "in some places, religious education is even used to orient the children in a direction entirely different from our social system, in broadening national intolerance, and in promoting other anti-socialist manifestations." But efforts to reach some understanding with local clergy proved unavailing, according to the Macedonian newspaper. "The measures that we have implemented in this respect have not brought any particular results. We have had discussions on this subject with the Islamic religious community which has claimed the opposite."[13]

Aside from questions of the authorities, it is clear that in a multi-confessional society (e.g., Bosnia), individual religions may have to be more circumspect than would be the case in a religiously homogeneous society (such as Slovenia).

For that matter, the Islamic community in Yugoslavia is itself internally divided, insofar as the leaders of the Yugoslav Islamic Community have given the cold shoulder to the dervishes (or, as they are more formally known, the Community of the Islamic Alia Dervish Monastic Order). The dervish order was introduced in Yugoslavia in 1974, and by 1986, numbered 50,000 followers, organized in 70 monasteries across southern

Yugoslavia (53 in Kosovo, 10 in Macedonia, and seven in Bosnia).[14] At one point, the Islamic Community ordered Sheikh Jemaly Haxhi-Shehu, senior leader of the dervishes, to disband the order. Shehu replied by registering his order as a "self-managing" organization, thus giving himself legal protection—a move paralleled in Croatia, if for different motivations, by the Catholic "Christianity Today" Publishing House.

WOMEN AND ISLAM

In the course of the 1980s, Muslim women began taking a more independent role in public life. The fact that a large group of Albanian Muslim women organized a large protest, independently, in late 1989 (to protest deteriorating conditions in Kosovo) is a sign of increased self-awareness and self-confidence. Another sign of change came earlier, in 1981, with the graduation of the first woman (Nermina Jasarevic) from the Islamic Theological Faculty in Sarajevo.[15]

By 1986, the first female imams had been educated in Skopje, and were delivering sermons (the first being in the Kumanovo mosque). In the course of 1986, Albanian men in Kumanovo went to the authorities to protest the appearance of women at the mosque, since, according to Islamic teaching, women and men should not mix at the mosque. It turned out that the sudden appearance of the women was the result of direct pressure from the Islamic Central Board in Skopje, whose elders were intent on upholding the equality of women and who pointed to the tradition that every mosque has a special, separate room for the women. Why had the women not come earlier? Isa Ismaili, leader of the Islamic community in Kumanovo, blamed space problems:

> For two reasons: first, until now we did not have female imams; now we have them and they are capable of delivering their sermons. Secondly, we in Kumanovo have only a single mosque, which is too small to hold even all the males; this is why we did not insist that the women come. . . . Long ago we asked the authorities for permission to build a new mosque, but we unfortunately never got an answer. . . . If our women are forbidden to go to the mosque, we will ask the men not to go either. Why should the men [be allowed to] pray and not the women? This is an attack on equality.[16]

RECENT DEVELOPMENTS

In 1989, a small publishing house in Zagreb brought out a *Bibliography of Croatian Writers of Bosnia-Herzegovina between the Two Wars*. The publication at once stirred controversy, because of its inclusion of a number of Muslim literary figures in the ranks of "Croatian writers." The Islamic Community was outraged, and its organ, *Preporod,* published a lengthy commentary, in which it excoriated the bibliography for the "Croatization" of some 38 Muslim writers. Among this number were such Islamic-sounding names as Salih-beg Bakamovic, Enver Colakovic, Abdulatif Dizdarevic, Husein Dubravic Djogo, Mustafa H. Grabcanovic, Kasim Gujic, Osman Nuri Hadzic, Muhamed Hadzijahic, Mehmed Handzic, Ahmed Muradbegovic, and others. *Preporod* called this a "negation of the cultural independence of a national tradition."[17]

This controversy was symptomatic of a deeper problem which has serious implications for the Islamic community—viz., the tendency of the Croatian and Serbian nations to want to claim the land on which the Muslims live, for their own nations, and to absorb or suppress Islamic culture. Both Croats and Serbs have claimed large parts of Bosnia in the past, and Serbs have viewed Kosovo as their ancestral heartland, depicting the Albanian Muslims as intruders. Hence, while Serbs sometimes betray a desire to suppress or eject Islamic culture from Kosovo, where Bosnia is concerned, Serbs and Croats have long registered rival claims to "annex" the Muslim community, claiming alternatively that Muslims are "really" Serbs, or Croats.[18]

It is against this background that periodic Muslim pressures to declare Bosnia a "Muslim republic" must be seen. Such a move would provide a small legal reassurance to the Muslims. It also reflects the fact that, as of October 1991, Bosnia's Muslims have good reason to be apprehensive at the prospect of seeing Serbia and Croatia fight over the partition of Bosnia. It is impossible to speculate as to what the long-term effects of the civil war will be for the country's Muslims. Be that as it may, it is quite clear, all the same, that there have been some sharp differences in the past, in the orientation of Bosnia's Muslims, versus Kosovo's Muslims,[19] toward the question of the preservation of a Yugoslav federation/confederation. Bosnia's Muslims, at any rate, long resisted the idea that there was any reasonable alternative.

The repluralization of Yugoslavia has affected the Islamic Community just as it has affected all other areas of public life. From 1946 to 1990, the Reis-ul-ulema (chair of the Islamic Council) was always a political appointee, beholden to the communist regime. But in March 1991, Jakub Selimoski, a Macedonian Muslim, was elected to that post by a special 96-member electoral body, established by the Islamic community itself.[20] The Islamic community simultaneously adopted a new constitution, and elected new presiding officers to head its Supreme Assembly.[21] In January 1991, in token of its new independence and new-found courage, the Islamic Supreme Assembly issued a resolution denouncing the Serbian government's policies in Kosovo and demanding the restoration of the natural rights of Kosovo's inhabitants, including a cessation of political interference in the work of the institutions of the Islamic community in Kosovo.[22]

Epilogue

YUGOSLAVIA HAS ALWAYS BEEN a Tower of Babel, with its builders not only speaking different languages but talking past each other. In many ways, the diverse peoples of Yugoslavia have failed to comprehend each other's cultures. Disintegration seemed to be sewn into the very fabric of state.

Part of the excitement that Yugoslav politics has long generated in the West was, I think, attributable to the awareness, even if only at an unconscious level, that here were people struggling to find a way to make something work which seemed incapable of working.

There were, of course, signs of trouble from the very beginning. When Serbian armies entered Dubrovnik at the end of World War One, for example, they hoisted Cyrillic banners to celebrate the event—even though Croatian locals could not read Cyrillic and viewed that alphabet as completely foreign. The Belgrade government followed this up by making Cyrillic mandatory throughout the land. This was a sign of things to come.

In the post-war period, the real troubles began around 1980, when the economy started to fall apart. Coincidentally, 1980 was also the year in which Tito died.

By the early 1980s, the gathering economic, ethnic, political, and moral crisis was already pushing the country toward disintegration. Croatian historian Dusan Biber told a group of historians in Zagreb, in October 1983, that if the trends then prevailing should continue, "we will turn into a second Lebanon."[1] I echoed this warning a month later, writing that, as a result of the mishandling of liberal currents in 1971 and the ensuing political line, "it is probably only a matter of time before another bloodbath occurs between Serbs and Croats."[2]

It would be a tricky business, and, in part, no doubt, artificial, to try to pinpoint any single event as a turning point in the disintegration of Yugoslavia. Certainly, the rise of Slobodan Milosevic provided a strong push toward civil war. But he did not create the hatreds in Yugoslavia. He catered to them, manipulated them, and amplified them.

1989 and 1990 were years of clear disintegration, and by early 1991, it was clear that the country was seriously threatened by civil war. As I wrote at the time, "As of late February, 1991, it appears likely that within a matter of weeks, Yugoslavia could be in the grip of a full-scale civil war centered in Croatia, Bosnia, southern Serbia (specifically, Sandzak of Novi Pazar), and Kosovo. The most dangerous of these flashpoints has been Croatia . . . "[3]

Again, events have proven me right.

Yet, until the explosion came, on 26 June, the sheer complexity of the situation, with diverse political groupings within each republic and province, factions within each grouping, and sometimes factions within factions, left part of the picture in the shadows and left open the possibility of a sudden change of the scenario. For example, when the Serbian opposition took to the streets of Belgrade in March 1991 to protest the drift toward war and economic catastrophe, the possibility that Milosevic might be forced to retire and that the political deck in Serbia might be reshuffled seemed to have been opened. And coloring *everything,* as ever in Yugoslavia, was the national question, that prickly and seemingly insoluble dilemma. As late as May 1991, veteran Yugoslav observer Dennison Rusinow portrayed the situation as "a perilous and accelerating hesitation waltz: two steps forward (to strident notes from competing nationalist horn sections) and then one step back (somber strings and woodwinds foreshadowing or confirming violence)."[4]

The Yugoslav National Army (JNA) had been playing a coy game for a few years, at first repeating over and over that it was not going to interfere in the natural political processes, then warning that it would not tolerate political chaos or inter-ethnic violence, and ultimately deciding to play a dramatic role in the effort to counter Croatia's declaration of independence, thus risking political chaos and, perhaps ironically, both intensifying and prolonging inter-ethnic violence. Earlier, in 1988, the JNA underwent restructuring, and merged the Ljubljana Military District with the Zagreb Military District—a move that appeared to reflect the military's growing disgruntlement with Slovenian political trends at that time. That reorganization notwithstanding, many Western observers were skeptical about the JNA's capacity to move against wayward republics. As late as March 1991, British expert James Gow wrote,

. . . the composition of the army does not favor use of the army to impose rule throughout Yugoslavia . . . The only viable use of military force to control the internal situation would be inside Serbia. . . . [All in all,] the military is unlikely to intervene [elsewhere] because of its physical difficulties in doing so, because of its political reluctance to do so, and because of the political realities which determine that reluctance: to intervene would be to destroy the fragile chances of keeping Yugoslavia together—which objective remains the first priority of the military leadership.[5]

When the army first began military operations in Croatia in late June, some observers discounted the possibility that the violence could continue for more than a month or two. Either Croatia would succumb, or the JNA would reconsider its policy, or, having shown they meant business, Croatia's Serbs would find the Croatian leaders ready to sit down and talk about the surrender of territory, or, in the most optimistic scenario, the European Community would impose effective diplomatic, psychological and economic sanctions, and prevent the Yugoslavs from doing any serious harm to each other. None of these scenarios ultimately had much to do with reality. By the end of October, Vukovar, once a bustling Danubian town with a population of about 50,000, had been reduced to rubble, and many other Croatian cities, including Dubrovnik, Zagreb, and Osijek, as well as various smaller towns and villages, had been damaged, some of them seriously. In late October, aircraft of the JNA even bombed a village in Hungary by mistake. But the war continued.

For Bosnia and Macedonia, the crisis had a particular edge. Serbia and Montenegro had sought to tighten up the federation. Slovenia and Croatia had sought, first, to transform the federation (quasi-confederation, in some ways) into a full-fledged confederation, and, when that proved impossible, to secede. Bosnia and Macedonia, by contrast, did not have any particular agenda other than live and let live. They were on the whole satisfied with the Yugoslav federation as it was set up, believing that structural reforms and policy adjustments were the most promising paths to bring the country out of its economic and political doldrums. They felt that they needed Yugoslavia as a guarantee of their internal stability. The Macedonians were, as I discovered when I visited Skopje in September 1989, Yugoslavia's last "Titoists," still trying to defend a system that everyone else had abandoned and preaching dialogue and reason at a time when other republics were becoming impatient. Bosnia, for its part, has always been so complex a mix of peoples and religions that stability has seemed a fragile and delicate commodity; the other side of the coin is that the risk of civil war has always been, at least potentially, the most frightening to Bosnians, with their complex intermixture of Muslims, Serbs, and Croats.

THE ARMY TAKES ACTION

On 27 May, Yugoslav President Stipe Mesic delivered a confident speech in Krasic, at a ceremony to mark Croatian statehood. Mesic reviewed the failed efforts to topple the Markovic government,[6] and said that any recourse to the army had "no chance." He concluded that it was "quite unlikely" that the army would take any steps to block the secession of Slovenia and Croatia.[7] Two days later, the Serbian parliament refused to take up Croatian Serbs' appeal for annexation to Serbia—thus giving some encouragement to Croatia.[8]

However, scarcely a month later, the army moved, first against Slovenia, turning later against Croatia. By the beginning of July, mediation by the European Community had obtained JNA agreement to pull its troops out of Slovenia,[9] though the process was only completed in October.

But no sooner did things calm down in Slovenia than tensions flared in Croatia, where the local secessionist Serbian council was said to enjoy the confidence and support of all Serbs living in the "Krajina."[10]

From July to October, Serbian militias in Croatia seized large chunks of Croatian territory, destroying villages and towns, and setting the local population to flight. By the end of October, Serbian insurgents controlled more than a third of Croatia and continued to press forward. About that time, a Serbian spokesperson from Croatia declared, "The Serbs in Croatia [less than 12 per cent of the republic's population] are not a minority and the [European Conference] on Yugoslavia has understood that."[11]

Aside from Vukovar, which by October had been completely destroyed by the fighting, Serbian militias, backed by the JNA, also laid siege to Osijek (population 200,000, of which 30,000 Serbs),[12] Dubrovnik (population 60,000, of which fewer than 6,000 Serbs), Petrinja (which fell to Serbs after a struggle), Glina (which *Danas* reporter Jasmina Kuzmanovic dubbed the "Croatian Alamo,"[13] Okucani (14 km. from the Bosnian border), Vinkovci (a city near Vukovar in eastern Slavonia), and other Croatian towns and villages. Zagreb, Karlovac, Osijek, Vukovar, Borovo, and others were subjected to aerial bombardment,[14] and in early October, air strikes were carried out against the presidential palace in Zagreb, nearly killing Croatian President Tudjman. In the midst of the fighting, Serbian President Milosevic accused Croatia of trying to pursue a "policy of genocide."[15]

By mid-November, at least 3,000 persons had been killed in the war, and thousands more wounded. As of late September, more than 230,000 persons had been driven from their homes, about a quarter of them fleeing abroad (chiefly to Germany and Hungary).[16] Not all the refugees were Croats; thousands of Serbs abandoned their frontline villages to take refuge in Vojvodina or Serbia proper.

Between July and mid-November, some twelve ceasefires collapsed. Peace plans by the European Community proved unacceptable to Serbia and peace plans proposed by Serbia proved unacceptable to other republics.[17]

In early August, Milosevic called for a meeting of the representatives of the three republics which, as of then, had not seceded from Yugoslavia, i.e., Serbia, Montenegro, and Bosnia. The purpose of the meeting was to discuss the restructuring of the Yugoslav state.[18] The meeting took place on 12 August and was attended by: Milosevic, president of Serbia; Aleksandar Bakocevic, president of the National Assembly of Serbia; Momir Bulatovic, president of Montenegro; Risto Bukcevic, president of the Assembly of Montenegro; and Momcilo Krajisnik, president of the Assembly of Bosnia. Alija Izetbegov, president of Bosnia, had of course been invited to attend, but he had refused; Krajisnik's participation, thus, reflected intra-elite division at the highest level in Bosnia.[19] The meeting issued a call for a new constitution, enumerating a number of bland principles.[20] Krajisnik, hailed in Belgrade, faced severe criticism back in Bosnia for having attended the Belgrade meeting at all.[21]

Macedonia and Bosnia at first held back from issuing any declarations, but under the pressure of events, first Macedonia, then Bosnia, declared their intention to secede. And in October, the Albanian opposition conducted a referendum among Kosovo's Albanian population: an overwhelming majority of those taking part voted for secession and annexation to Albania. For them, the Yugoslav option was likewise dead.

At the same time, demands were heard in Serbia that historic Dubrovnik be taken away from Croatia. The Belgrade magazine *Intervju* published an interview with academician Miroslav Pantic, demanding that the Dubrovnik area be set up as an "independent" republic, separate from Croatia. Pantic blamed Austria and the Catholic Church for Croatizing Dubrovnik, and claimed that a group of Dubrovnik citizens— how many he did not say—had framed a demand in 1945 that the city be set up as an autonomous province, if not as a republic.[22] Despite international protests, the Serbian-dominated army kept a stranglehold on historic Dubrovnik, reinforcing its siege force in late October. The army informed the city's defenders that "only surrender can save Dubrovnik."[23]

In July 1991, the federal government issued a statement that it was slashing the military budget from $34 billion to just $15 billion.[24] This decision was quickly countermanded and Belgrade began printing money, without backing, to pay the army.[25] As a result, instead of shrinking, the military budget increased, as a proportion of the total federal budget, from 40 per cent to 65 per cent by October.[26] A Western diplomat assigned to Belgrade commented, "Only 25 per cent of the budget is covered [by reserves]. They are printing the rest."[27] At the same time, Serbia was losing hard currency income on sales of electric power to Italy and Austria, because the grid that ran through Croatia was closed down by the war. Croatia also shut down the oil pipeline to Serbia.[28] Industrial production slumped everywhere, as a result of the war, including in Serbia, and Western credits dried up.[29]

By late September, there were confirmed reports that the JNA was experiencing growing problems recruiting soldiers.[30] But on 7 November, the Serbian government took the first step toward establishing a specifically Serbian army.[31] Moreover, in Serbia itself, critical voices could not be silenced.[32] Some members of the opposition also expressed the conviction that Milosevic would ultimately fail. "Milosevic is not a man of vision," said Milos Vasic, editor of the privately owned Belgrade magazine *Vreme* and one of Milosevic's more deadly critics. "The Greater Serbia that he is trying to create will be undefendable and unsustainable."[33] Dragan Veselinov, head of the opposition Serbian Peasant Party, linked Milosevic's fortunes to the war: "The moment Milosevic stops his territorial campaign, he will face social unrest in Serbia."[34] And Zoran Djingic, leader of the opposition Democratic Party in Serbia, seconding this point of view, told an American correspondent, "It's impossible to defeat Milosevic in Serbia. All our internal problems have been dissolved in the war. Milosevic, like Napoleon, will be defeated on the battlefield. The army in Croatia will come back to Serbia and they will overthrow Milosevic . . . The only question is how long it will take to defeat him."[35]

REFLECTIONS

This book has argued that political dynamics are reflected in, and even adumbrated by, changes in the cultural sphere, and that the religious sphere underpins and legitimizes actions and decisions taken in the political sphere. The political, cultural, and religious spheres do not exist apart from each other; they are, rather, organic parts of a religio-politico-cultural system, in which activity in one part has intentions, reflections, and consequences in other parts. Hence, the Serbian Orthodox Church's endorsement of the Serbian military campaign in 1991[36] heightened the political profile of that Church, deepened and cemented its growing alliance with the Serbian government of Slobodan Milosevic, and distorted the Church's Gospel itself. Yet so involved did the Serbian Church become in the Serbian nationalist revival and in support for the military campaign, that the Vatican, which was overtly sympathetic to the Croatian aspirations for independence,[37] sent its Secretary for Foreign Relations, Jean-Louis Toran, to Belgrade on 7 August, to confer with Patriarch Pavle about the crisis.[38]

More broadly, the disintegration of the political fabric in Yugoslavia was presaged by a deterioration of inter-ethnic relations in various spheres, including in ecumenical contacts, in the media, and even, as outlined earlier in this book, in rock music. Later, the rise of nationalist movements in Serbia, Croatia, and Slovenia was reflected in sundry spheres, including in rock music, where the strident tones of Laibach served as a warning, with Bora Djordjevic as the self-appointed rock bard of Serbian nationalism, and in the sphere of gender relations, where the new chauvinists expressed disdain for feminists and impatience with demands that women be treated with dignity.

Some cultural figures sought to assail the very cultural underpinnings of each other's nation. For example, *Politika* reported disapprovingly about claims made by certain Serbian figures at Croats' expense. Milan Paroski, a deputy in the Serbian parliament, told that body that "Croats did not have any literature except for Serbian literature," while Serbian writer Antonije Isakovic declared, "Seeing that they could not constitute a nation on the cakavian and kajkavian dialects (spoken in Croatia), Croats got the idea to take our language (Serbian)."[39] The denigration of the culture of the "enemy" nation may even extend to disparagement of specific songs. For example, the Serbian daily *Politika* claimed, in August, that Croats were singing patriotic songs honoring wartime fascist leader Ante Pavelic.[40] The denigration of the other's culture is, thus, one side of the politico-cultural coin.

The other side of the coin is that political atavism invariably entails cultural atavism. And hence, recent calls, in Serbia, for a restoration of the alleged glory of the interwar Kingdom of Serbs, Croats, and Slovenes, including the restoration of its laws, have been accompanied not merely by renewed interest in the Karadjordjevic dynasty, and especially Crown Prince Alexander, but also by calls for the restoration of the old Serbian coat of arms and anthem.[41]

In fact, inter-communal political conflict necessarily has a cultural dimension. And victory or defeat in the political sphere may entail as well corresponding victory or defeat in the cultural and religious spheres.

The Titoists had some sense of this, and this is why they argued, back and forth, in the 1950s and early 1960s, as to whether they should aspire to create a new culture, a Yugoslav culture, which would melt down and assimilate the "partial" cultures of the component peoples of this country, or whether they should rather extend toleration to all component cultures, while promoting a thin overlay of "Yugoslav culture," based ultimately on Partisan mythology from World War Two and notions of self-management. In 1964, at its Eighth Party Congress, the League of Communists opted for the second strategy: toleration while promoting a thin overlay of "Yugoslavism." The internal contradiction here, not noticed at the time, was that in tying this Yugoslavism to the Partisan mythology, this strategy entailed constant reminders of the inter-communal internecine strife of that war. Hence, even while trying to build a concept of "Yugoslavism," Yugoslavia's communists constantly stirred up the old fires of inter-group hatred. Viewed in this way, civil war is the logical outcome of this strategy.

Could the alternative approach—energetic homogenization—have worked? Successful instances of this approach in Europe tend to involve cases where unification and adoption of this policy occurred much earlier (e.g., England, France, Spain). Twentieth-century European attempts to pursue such a policy (the USSR, interwar Czechoslovakia, interwar and early post-war Yugoslavia, and Romanian Transylvania) have all run up against serious difficulties.

A recent article by Andrei Simic sheds additional light on the dynamics of these processes. Describing the concept of a "moral field" (defined as "an interactional sphere where those engaged typically behave towards each other with reference to ethically-perceived imperatives, that is, rules that are accepted as being 'good,' 'God-given,' 'natural,' 'proper,' and so forth),"[42] Simic argues that the membership of a moral field depends on criteria of recruitment that generally are functions of kinship, tribe, or nation. "Within a moral field," Simic points out, "members are expected to act towards each other with reference to a common set of shared ideas by which behavior is structured and evaluated. In contrast, behavior outside the moral field can be said to be *amoral* in that it is primarily idiosyncratic, and as such may be purely instrumental or exploitative without being subject to sanctions. Thus, for the individual, those belonging to other moral fields can be said to form part of his or her *amoral* sphere."[43] And hence, actions which might be deemed morally reprehensible when committed against a fellow member of the moral field (such as murder, torture, rape, confiscation of goods) may be seen as morally commendable when committed against persons not included in the group's moral field.

Viewing the issue in this way, it is apparent that the Titoists failed to create a common moral field in which all Yugoslavs would be included. Instead, moral fields remained coincident with ethnic communities, heightening the risks and dangers of political disintegration. Morality, molded and manipulated by politics, culture, and religion alike, ultimately has lain at the heart of the breakdown of the Yugoslav system and the breakup of Yugoslavia itself.

Notes

CHAPTER ONE

This chapter is a revised version of an earlier article, "The Limits to Political Change in a Communist Country: The Yugoslav Debate, 1980–1986," originally published in *Crossroads,* No. 23 (1987). The author wishes to thank the editors of *Crossroads* for granting permission to reproduce the article here.

1. Pedro Ramet, "Apocalypse Culture and Social Change in Yugoslavia," in Pedro Ramet (ed.), *Yugoslavia in the 1980s* (Boulder, Colo.: Westview Press, 1985).

2. The *Sporazum* established an autonomous "banovina" of Croatia, comprising roughly 30 per cent of the territory and population of Yugoslavia, and enjoying budgetary and administrative independence, and independent authority in most spheres of domestic policy. The monarchy was in fact the sole remaining constitutional link between Croatia and the rest of Yugoslavia.

3. *Start* (26 March 1983), trans. in Joint Publications Research Service (JPRS), *East Europe Report,* no. 83734 (22 June 1983), p. 54; and *Vjesnik* (Zagreb), 6 April 1985.

4. Miroslav Stojanovic, "Opstepartijska debata o ulozi Saveza komunista," in *Socijalizam,* Vol. 27, Nos. 7–8 (July–August 1984), p. 996.

5. *Borba* (Belgrade), 20 November 1984.

6. Milan Dimitrijevic, "Samoupravne interesne zajednice," in *Opstina,* Vol. 29 (1976), Nos. 5–6, pp. 116–118.

7. For particulars, see Pedro Ramet, "Yugoslavia and the Threat of Internal and External Discontents," in *Orbis,* Vol. 28, No. 1 (Spring 1984), pp. 104–105.

8. Evidence for these characterizations will be provided in the text.

9. Interview, Belgrade, July 1982.

10. For details, see Pedro Ramet, "The Yugoslav Press in Flux," in Ramet (ed.), *Yugoslavia in the 1980s.*

11. *NIN,* no. 1601 (15 November 1981), p. 9.

12. *Ibid.,* no. 1645 (11 July 1982), p. 10.

13. M. Caldarevic, *Komunisti i samoupravljanje* (Zagreb: FPN, 1967), p. 486, as cited in Simo S. Nenezic, "Divergentne koncepcije u SKJ o demokratskom centralizmu," in *Socijalizam,* Vol. 18, No. 1 (January 1975), p. 53.

14. See, for instance, "Jugoslawischer Theoretiker für Zweiparteiensystem," in *Osteuropäische Rundschau,* Vol. 13, No. 12 (December 1967), pp. 19–21.

15. Rade Koncar, a Serb, was at the time chair of the Novi Beograd (city) party organization and a member of the party committee of the city of Belgrade. He was forced to resign these posts soon after the Congress.

16. CK SKJ Predsednistvo, *Ostvarivanje vodece uloge SKJ u drustvu i jacanje njegovog idejnog i akcionog jedinstva* (Belgrade: Komunist, 1984), pp. v–vii, as quoted in Wolfgang Höpken, "Party Monopoly and Political Change: The League of Communists since Tito's Death," in Ramet (ed.), *Yugoslavia in the 1980s,* p. 37.

17. See Vjekoslav Koprivnjak, "Protiv tendencije federalizacije Saveza komunista," in *Socijalizam,* Vol. 28, No. 1 (January 1985).

18. See, for instance, *Politika* (Belgrade), 17 January 1985.

19. For details, see Pedro Ramet, "Self-management, Titoism, and the Apotheosis of Praxis," in Wayne S. Vucinich (ed.), *At the Brink of War and Peace: the Tito-Stalin Split in a Historic Perspective* (New York: Brooklyn College Press, 1982), pp. 169–170, 1745–177, 192–193.

20. Svetozar Stojanovic, "Marks i ideologizacija marksizma—kritika jedne predrasudne moci" [based on a talk given in Novi Sad in December 1983], in *Gledista,* Vol. 25, Nos. 1–2 (January–February 1984), pp. 28–33.

21. *Radio Free Europe Research* (24 July 1985), pp. 19–22.

22. Edvard Kardelj, *Democracy and Socialism,* trans. by Margot and Bosko Milosavljevic (London: Summerfield Press, 1978), p. 69.

23. Stipe Suvar, "Sloboda misli—da, ideoloski i politicki pluralizam—ne," in *Socijalizam,* Vol. 27, Nos. 7–8 (July–August 1984), p. 1129.

24. Miladin Korac, "Branko Horvat: 'Politicka ekonomija socijalizma'—kriticka analiza treceg dela knjige," in *Socijalizam,* Vol. 27, No. 10 (October 1984), pp. 1518–1519, 1526–1530.

25. Vojislav Kostunica and Kosta Cavoski, *Stranacki pluralizam ili monizam* (Belgrade: Institut za drustvene nauke, 1983).

26. Radoslav Ratkovic, "Interes nije bazicna kategorija," in *Socijalizam,* Vol. 27, Nos. 7–8 (July–August 1984), p. 1057.

27. *Vecernje novosti* (Belgrade), 16 April 1985.

28. On the last of these points, see *Vjesnik* (19 March 1985).

29. See, for instance, *Politika* (8 January 1985).

30. *Borba* (7–8 April 1984); and *Duga* (Belgrade), 10 March 1984.

31. *Danas* (9 April 1984), trans. in JPRS, *East Europe Report,* Nos. EPS-84-076 (18 June 1984), p. 91.

32. *Borba* (7–8 April 1984).

33. For more details on these two proposals, see Ramet, "Apocalypse Culture and Social Change," in Ramet (ed.), *Yugoslavia in the 1980s,* pp. 19–20.

34. Quoted in Höpken, "Party Monopoly," p. 41.

35. *Politika* (24 November 1984).

36. *Dnevnik* (Novi Sad), 21 April 1985, p. 3, trans. in FBIS, *Daily Report* (Eastern Europe), 2 May 1985, p. 17.

37. *Politika* (20 December 1984), p. 5, trans. in JPRS, *East Europe Report,* No. EPS-85-012 (23 January 1985), p. 29.

38. *Borba* 12–15 October 1984). See the Editorial Report in JPRS, *East Europe Report,* No. EPS-84-135 (1 November 1984), p. 120.

39. Tanjug (14 November 1985), trans. in FBIS, *Daily Report* (Eastern Europe), 15 November 1985, p. 13.

40. Tanjug (18 November 1985), trans. in FBIS, *Daily Report* (Eastern Europe), 20 November 1985, p. 16.

41. *Ibid.,* p. 17; and Tanjug (18 November 1985), trans. in FBIS, *Daily Report* (Eastern Europe), 26 November 1985, pp. 16–18.

42. Tanjug (24 October 1985), trans. in FBIS, *Daily Report* (Eastern Europe), 1 November 1985, p. 19.

43. *Politika* (20 April 1986).

44. *Ibid.* (24 April 1986).

45. *Vjesnik* (30 June 1986); also Tanjug (16 February 1986), trans. in FBIS, *Daily Report* (Eastern Europe), 20 February 1986, p. 13; and *Vjesnik* (29 June 1986).

46. *Vjesnik* (30 June 1986).

47. *Ibid.* (27 June 1986).

48. *Ibid.* (24 August 1985).

49. For details and discussion, see Pedro Ramet, "Yugoslavia 1987: Stirrings from Below," in *South Slav Journal,* Vol. 10, No. 3 (Autumn 1987).

CHAPTER TWO

This chapter is a revised and expanded version of an earlier article, "Yugoslavia's Troubled Times," originally published in *Global Affairs,* vol. 5, no. 1 (Winter 1990). The author wishes to thank the editor of *Global Affairs,* for granting permission to reproduce the article here.

1. For details of Milosevic's biography and career, see Sabrina P. Ramet, "Serbia's Slobodan Milosevic: A Profile," in *Orbis,* Vol. 35, No. 1 (Winter 1991).

2. *Vecernji list* (Zagreb, 15 September 1989), p. 2; and *Politika* (Belgrade, 8 September 1989), p. 9. Latest census figures, as reported in Tanjug (30 April 1991) trans. in FBIS, *Daily Report* (Eastern Europe), 1 May 1991, p. 53.

3. *Vecernji list* (6 September 1989), p. 5, and (11 September 1989), p. 2; *Nedjeljna Dalmacija* (Split, 19 September 1989), p. 6; and *Vecernji list* (19 September 1989), p. 6.

4. On the last point, see *Vecernji list* (21 September 1989), p. 10.

5. *Vecernji list* (11 September 1989), p. 2, (15 September 1989), p. 5, and (24 September 1989), p. 4.

6. *Danas,* no. 394 (5 September 1989), p. 11.

7. *Vjesnik* (Zagreb, 28 August 1989), p. 5.

8. *Intervju* (Belgrade), no. 215 (1 September 1989), p. 19.

9. Ciril Ribicic and Zdravko Tomac, *Federalizam po mjeri buducnosti* (Zagreb: Globus, 1989), p. 183.

10. *Mladina* (Ljubljana, 1 September 1989), p. 4.

11. *Intervju,* no. 215 (1 September 1989), p. 32.

12. See *Politika ekspres* (Belgrade, 24 September 1989), p. 2.

13. Summarized in *Svet* (Belgrade, September 1989), pp. 50–51.

14. Gregor Tomc, "The Active Society," in *Independent Voices from Slovenia, Yugoslavia,* Vol. 4, No. 3 (July 1988), p. 6.

15. Interview, Ljubljana, 4 September 1989.

16. Interview, Ljubljana, 1 September 1989.

17. Interview, Ljubljana, 5 September 1989.

18. Interview, Ljubljana, 5 September 1989.

19. *Vecernje novosti* (Belgrade, 27 September 1989), p. 4.

20. *Vecernji list* (12 September 1989), p. 6.

21. *Vecernje novosti* (27 September 1989), p. 2.

22. Ivan Stambolic, *Rasprave o SR Srbiji, 1979–1987.* (Zagreb: Globus, 1988), p. 49.

23. *Ibid.,* p. 62.

24. Quoted in Wolfgang Höpken, "Party Monopoly and Political Change: the League of Communists since Tito's Death," in Pedro Ramet (ed.), *Yugoslavia in the 1980s* (Boulder, Colo.: Westview Press, 1985), p. 41.

25. *Intervju,* no. 213 (4 August 1989), pp. 23–25.

26. *Duga,* no. 406 (16 September 1989), pp. 82–83; and interview, Belgrade, 23 September 1989.

27. Radoslav Stojanovic, *Jugoslavija, nacije i politika* (Belgrade: Nova knjiga, 1988), p. 213.

28. In interview with the author, Zagreb, 8 September 1989.

29. See Pedro Ramet, "Yugoslavia 1987: Stirrings from Below," in *South Slav Journal,* Vol. 10, No. 3 (Autumn 1987).

30. Bora Djordjevic, *Necu, necu, necu, necu* (Belgrade: Knjizevna zadruga, 1989), pp. 11, 18–19.

31. E.g. Vanja Brkic's album, *Kosovo je moja domovina* [Kosovo is my homeland], released by ZKP RTV, Ljubljana.

32. *Glas crkve* (Sabac), quoted in *Borba* (Belgrade, 25 July 1989), p. 3, trans. in Foreign Broadcast Information Service, *Daily Report* (Eastern Europe), 4 August 1989, p. 43, my emphasis.

33. Yugoslav Situation Report, *Radio Free Europe Research* (26 May 1989), pp. 33–34.

34. Interview, Belgrade, 21 September 1989; and interview, Ljubljana, 4 September 1989.

35. Interview with Matija Beckovic, Belgrade, 21 September 1989.

36. Interview with Goran Bregovic, leader of *Bijelo dugme,* Sarajevo, 14 September 1989.

37. Interview, Ljubljana, 1 September 1989.

38. *NIN,* no. 2020 (17 September 1989), pp. 42–43.

39. *Slobodna Dalmacija* (Split, 22 September 1989), p. 16.

40. *Vecernje novosti* (18 September 1989), p. 3; *Vecernji list* (23 September 1989), p. 12; and *Frankfurter Allgemeine* (2 October 1989), p. 1.

41. *Vjesnik* (10 September 1989), p. 5; *Slobodna Dalmacija* (22 September 1989), p. 16; and *Politika* (25 October 1989), p. 7.

42. *Slobodna Dalmacija* (10 September 1989), p. 13.

43. Interview, Zagreb, 8 September 1989.

44. *Slobodna Dalmacija* (10 September 1989), p. 10.

45. *Politika* (20 October 1989), p. 7.

46. *Danas,* no. 401 (24 October 1989), p. 15.

47. See Sabrina P. Ramet, *Nationalism and Federalism in Yugoslavia, 1962–1991,* 2nd ed. (Bloomington, Ind.: Indiana University Press, 1992) and Sabrina P. Ramet, *Social Currents in Eastern Europe: The Sources and Meaning of the Great Transformation* (Durham, N.C., Duke University Press, 1991), chapter 7.

CHAPTER THREE

1. *Financial Times* (London), 26 June 1991, p. 1. See also editorial, p. 16.

2. For further discussion of Milosevic's role, see Sabrina P. Ramet, "Serbia's Slobodan Milosevic: A Profile," in *Orbis,* Vol. 35, No. 1 (Winter 1991).

3. For details, see Ivo Banac, *The National Question in Yugoslavia* (Ithaca, N.Y.: Cornell University Press, 1984).

4. *Ibid.,* pp. 298–299.

5. *Borba* (Belgrade), 6 March 1991, p. 3.

6. Franjo Tudjman, *Bespuca povijesne zbiljnosti: Rasprava o povijesti i filozofiji zlosilja* (Zagreb: Nakladni zavod Matice Hrvatske, 1989).

7. Interview with the author, Zagreb, 8 September 1989. The full text of the interview is published in *South Slav Journal,* Vol. 12, No. 3–4 (Autumn-Winter 1989), pp. 87–93.

8. Tanjug (1 October 1990), trans. in Foreign Broadcast Information Service (FBIS), *Daily Report* (Eastern Europe), 1 October 1990.

9. For details, see Sabrina P. Ramet, "The Breakup of Yugoslavia," in *Global Affairs,* Vol. 6, No. 2 (Spring 1991).

10. See, for instance, *Oslobodjenje* (Sarajevo), 25 February 1991, p. 3, trans. in FBIS, Daily Report (Eastern Europe), 1 March 1991, p. 38.

11. *Daily Telegraph* (London), 18 March 1991, p. 1.

12. *Danas,* no. 459 (4 December 1990), pp. 10–12.

13. *Daily Telegraph* (20 March 1991), p. 15.

14. *Frankfurter Allgemeine* (2 February 1991), p. 2. See also *Croatian Democracy Project,* news release, 7 February 1991.

15. *Danas,* no. 459 (4 December 1990), p. 18.

16. *Wall Street Journal* (18 March 1991).

17. *Neue Zürcher Zeitung* (Zürich), 29/30 March 1991, p. 18.

18. Tanjug (28 February 1991), in FBIS, *Daily Report* (Eastern Europe), 1 March 1991, p. 39.

19. See *Neue Zürcher Zeitung* (8 February 1991), p. 16, and (29/30 March 1991), p. 18.

20. *Oslobodjenje* (12 November 1990), p. 1, trans. in FBIS, *Daily Report* (Eastern Europe), 29 November 1991, p. 74.

21. Re. the 15 per cent shortfall, see *Borba* (26 December 1990), p. 3. Re. the layoff of 2,700 employees, see Tanjug (3 March 1991), trans. in FBIS, *Daily Report* (Eastern Europe), 4 March 1991, p. 41.

22. Tanjug (4 March 1991), trans. in FBIS, *Daily Report* (Eastern Europe), 5 March 1991, p. 56.

23. Tanjug (5 February 1991), in FBIS, *Daily Report* (Eastern Europe), 6 February 1991, p. 57. Also: *Borba* (7 September 1990), p. 3.

24. Tanjug (11 January 1991), trans. in FBIS, *Daily Report* (Eastern Europe), 15 January 1991, p. 57; and Tanjug (15 March 1991), in FBIS, *Daily Report* (Eastern Europe), 18 March 1991, p. 56.

25. Tanjug (21 February 1991), trans. in FBIS, *Daily Report* (Eastern Europe), 25 February 1991, p. 52.

26. Re. the Slovenes, see *Frankfurter Allgemeine* (27 December 1990), p. 2. Re. the Croats, see *Neue Zürcher Zeitung* (22 May 1991), p. 1. Re. the Albanians, see Belgrade Domestic Service (10 February 1991), trans. in FBIS, *Daily Report* (Eastern Europe), 12 February 1991, p. 59. Re. the Macedonians, see *Vjesnik* (Zagreb), 13 September 1990, p. 3; and Tanjug (23 February 1991), in FBIS, *Daily Report* (Eastern Europe), 25 February 1991, p. 55.

27. Re. Serbs in Bosnia, see Radovan Karadzic's interview in *Borba* (12 November 1990), p. 4.

28. For a full account of these riots and an analysis of the ethnic problems in Kosovo, see Sabrina P. Ramet, *Social Currents in Eastern Europe: The Sources and Meaning of the Great Transformation* (Durham, N.C.: Duke University Press, 1991), chapter 7.

29. *Borba* (17 August 1990)p. 3.

30. Re. the Serbs, see Tanjug (10 August 1990), trans. in FBIS, *Daily Report* (Eastern Europe), 13 August 1990, p. 56.

31. *Flaka e Vellazerimit* (Skopje), 27 January 1991, p. 4, trans. in FBIS, *Daily Report* (Eastern Europe), 31 January 1991, p. 57.

32. Tanjug (8 January 1991), in FBIS, *Daily Report* (Eastern Europe), 9 January 1991, p. 43.

33. *Zeri i Rinise,* as summarized in Belgrade Domestic Service (10 February 1991), trans. in FBIS, *Daily Report* (Eastern Europe), 12 February 1991, p. 59.

34. Tanjug (30 October 1990), in FBIS, *Daily Report* (Eastern Europe), 31 October 1990, p. 73.

35. *Borba* (12 November 1990), p. 4.

36. *Ibid.* (3 August 1990), p. 3; and Tanjug (23 February 1991), in FBIS, *Daily Report* (Eastern Europe), 25 February 1991, p. 55. See also *Vjesnik* (13 September 1990), p. 3.

37. *Borba* (6 March 1991), p. 3, trans. in FBIS, *Daily Report* (Eastern Europe), 8 March 1991, p. 56.

38. *Borba* (1 March 1991), p. 9.

39. In a poll conducted by *Mladina* among 265 people in summer 1990, 5.3 per cent favored an independent Istrian state, 22.2 per cent wanted to join Italy, 38.6 per cent preferred to be transferred to Slovenia, and 18.4 per cent preferred to remain in Croatia, but on the condition that the region be granted local autonomy. This poll is reported in Milan Andrejevich, "Relations between Croatia and Slovenia," in RFE/RL Research Institute, *Report on Eastern Europe,* Vol. 2, No. 12 (22 March 1991), p. 35.

40. Tanjug (11 March 1991), trans. in FBIS, *Daily Report* (Eastern Europe), 13 March 1991, p. 71.

41. *Nepszava* (Budapest), 26 February 1991, pp. 1, 2, trans. in FBIS, *Daily Report* (Eastern Europe), 1 March 1991, p. 39.

42. Full text in *Vjesnik* (12 October 1990), p. 5.

43. The republics' stands on these and other issues are compactly summarized in *Vjesnik* (2 February 1991), p. 4, trans. in FBIS, *Daily Report* (Eastern Europe), 12 February 1991, p. 47.

44. "Yugoslavia: The March 1991 Demonstrations in Belgrade," *Helsinki Watch: A Committee of Human Rights Watch* (1 May 1991), pp. 1–2.

45. *Globe and Mail* (Toronto), 11 April 1991, p. A7; and *Neue Zürcher Zeitung* (12 April 1991), p. 4.

46. *Delo* (Ljubljana), 21 February 1991, p. 3, trans. in FBIS, *Daily Report* (Eastern Europe), 7 March 1991, p. 33.

47. *Neue Zürcher Zeitung* (7/8 April 1991), p. 6.

48. Tanjug (7 April 1991), trans. in FBIS, *Daily Report* (Eastern Europe), 8 April 1991, p. 56.

49. *The Times* (London), 4 May 1991, p. 10.

50. Belgrade Domestic Service (31 March 1991), trans. in FBIS, *Daily Report* (Eastern Europe), 1 April 1991, pp. 49–50; and *Politika* (19 March 1991), p. 9.

51. Tanjug (3 April 1991), in FBIS, *Daily Report* (Eastern Europe), 4 April 1991, p. 25.

52. *Neue Zürcher Zeitung* (3 April 1991), p. 3.

53. *Croatian Democracy Project* news release, 13 May 1991.

54. Quoted in *Ibid.*

55. *The Independent* (London), 8 May 1991, p. 1.

56. *Croatian Democracy Project* news release, 13 May 1991.

57. *Neue Zürcher Zeitung* (4 May 1991), p. 2, and (5/6 May 1991), p. 1; *The Times* (4 May 1991), p. 6.; and *The Independent* (8 May 1991), p. 1.

58. Quoted in *New York Times* (19 May 1991), p. 8.

59. *Vjesnik* (17 April 1991), p. 4.

60. *Süddeutsche Zeitung* (Munich), 25/26 May 1991, p. 5.

61. Reported in *Neue Zürcher Zeitung* (29 May 1991), p. 5.

62. *Ibid.* (15 June 1991), p. 2.

63. *Daily Telegraph* (8 May 1991), p. 8.

64. *Neue Zürcher Zeitung* (4 June 1991), p. 2.

65. *Daily Telegraph* (8 April 1991), p. 11.

CHAPTER FOUR

This is an updated and revised version of a paper originally published in John B. Allcock, John J. Horton, and Marko Milivojevic, *Yugoslavia in Transition: Choices and Constraints—Essays in Honour of Fred Singleton* (Oxford and Hamburg: Berg Publishers; New York: St. Martin's Press, 1991). Reproduced

1. Interview with magazine editor, Belgrade, July 1982; and interview with newspaper editor, Ljubljana, July 1982.

2. See Pedro Ramet, "The Yugoslav Press in Flux," in Pedro Ramet (ed.), *Yugoslavia in the 1980s* (Boulder, Colo.: Westview Press, 1985).

3. Report by Vitomir Sudarski, in *Dvanaesti kongres Saveza komunista Jugoslavije, Beograd, 26–29 juni 1982,* Magnetofonske bileske (Belgrade: Izdavacki Centar Komunist, 1983), Vol. 3, p. 226; and *Handbook on Yugoslavia* (Belgrade: Exportpress, 1987), p. 214.

4. Report by Ivan Hocevar, in *6. Sednica CKSKJ. Sto godina od smrti Karla Marksa. Obrazlozenje uz Predlog poslovnika o organizaciji i nacinu rada CKSKJ. Idejna kretanja, problemi i pojave u oblasti informisanja i propaganda i zadaci SKJ* (Belgrade: Izdavacki Centar Komunist, 1983), p. 58.

5. Tanjug (30 March 1984), trans. in FBIS, *Daily Report* (Eastern Europe), 3 April 1984, p. I13.

6. *Handbook,* p. 219.

7. Marko Lolic, "Savez komunista i savremena uloga javnih glasila," in *Socijalizam,* Vol. 30, Nos. 10–11 (October-November 1988), p. 95.

8. Interview with former editor of a religious periodical, Belgrade, July 1987; confirmed in interview with former editor of a youth periodical, Ljubljana, July 1987.

9. One exception concerns the front-page of an issue of the Croatian weekly, *Hrvatski tjednik,* in late 1971, which its editors defiantly published with a blank page and a brief notice that the material intended for that page had been administratively suppressed.

10. Interview, Belgrade, July 1987.

11. Interview with staff members of *Vjesnik,* Zagreb, July 1982.

12. See *Oslobodjenje* (Sarajevo), 21 January 1982, p. 6; *Politika* (Belgrade), 16 January 1985, p. 6, and 25 December 1985, p. 6; *Komunist* (Belgrade edition), 20 December 1985), p. 17; *Borba* (Zagreb edition), 22–23 February 1986, p. 8, and 11 September 1987, p. 3; and *Vjesnik* (Zagreb), 9 July 1987, p. 3.

13. See, for example, *Politika* (19 December 1985), p. 6.

14. *NIN* (Belgrade), no. 1836 (9 March 1986), p. 9.

15. *Vecernje novosti* (Belgrade), 14 March 1986.

16. Discussed in Stevan Niksic, *Oslobodjenje stampe* (Belgrade: Mladost, 1982).

17. Tanjug's director, Mihajlo Saranovic, later complained about this in a speech reported in *Vjesnik* (14 March 1986).

18. *Komunist* (26 June 1987), p. 12.

19. Detailed in Ramet, "The Yugoslav Press in Flux", pp. 104–106.

20. *Politika* (30 March 1985), p. 6.

21. Tanjug (24 September 1986), trans. in Foreign Broadcast Information Service (FBIS), *Daily Report* (Eastern Europe), 25 September 1986, p. I7; and *Vecernji list* (Zagreb), 9 July 1987, p. 5.

22. *Komunist* (13 September 1985), p. 8.

23. See, for example, *Politika* (12 July 1984), p. 6; Tanjug (9 December 1985), trans. in Joint Publications Research Service (JPRS), *East Europe Report* No. EER-86-008 (21 January 1986), p. 101; *Politika* (25 December 1985), p. 6; and *Borba* (Zagreb edition), 16 September 1987, p. 4.

24. Dennison I. Rusinow, "Yugoslavia 1983: Between 'Continuity' and 'Crisis,'" *University Field Staff International Reports* (1983), no. 3, p. 10; and *Vjesnik* (7 February 1987), p. 3.

25. *Vjesnik* (3 November 1982), p. 5.

26. Tanjug (9 December 1985) [footnote 23], p. 102.

27. Tanjug (12 June 1981), and (6 June 1983), trans. respectively in FBIS, *Daily Report* (Eastern Europe), 16 June 1981, pp. 113–114, and 9 June 1983, p. I; and Louis Zanga, "News Media Coverage of Events in Kosovo," *Radio Free Europe Research* (20 November 1987), p. 2.

28. Tanjug (7 October 1985), trans. in FBIS, *Daily Report* (Eastern Europe), 17 October 1985, p. I3.

29. *Borba* (Belgrade edition), 22 August 1986, p. 3.

30. *Ibid.* (26 August 1986), p. 3.

31. Dragana Roter-Crkvenjakov, "Pokrajinska stampa o promenama ustava SR Srbije," in *Novinarstvo,* Vol. 24, Nos. 1–2 (1988), pp. 59–60.

32. *Vjesnik* (15 June 1987), p. 3.

33. Quoted in Tanjug (7 February 1983), trans. in FBIS, *Daily Report* (Eastern Europe), 8 February 1983, p. I16.

34. *Le Monde* (Paris), 11 May 1983, p. 6, trans. in FBIS, *Daily Report* (Eastern Europe), 11 May 1983, p. I9.

35. *Vjesnik* (16 September 1987), p. 5.

36. Stojanovic had only been on the job nine months. See *Politika* (13 October 1987), pp. 1, 5–7; and *Borba* (Zagreb ed.), 13 October 1987, pp. 1, 3.

37. Interview with staff members of *Delo,* Ljubljana, 1 September 1989.

38. As summarized in *Vjesnik* (21 February 1987), p. 3.

39. As summarized in *Politika* (23 February 1987), p. 6.

40. *Vjesnik* (21 February 1987), p. 3.

41. *Politika* (15 March 1987), p. 6.

42. Interviews, Ljubljana, July 1987. See also Tanjug (11 March 1987), trans. in FBIS, *Daily Report* (Eastern Europe), 6 April 1987, p. I8; *The Economist* (London), 11 April 1987, p. 50; and *Borba* (Zagreb edition), 11 September 1987, p. 3.

43. Tanjug (30 October 1986), trans. in FBIS, *Daily Report* (Eastern Europe), 6 November 1986, p. I5.

44. See the report of the session of the CC Presidium's Commission for Information and Propaganda Activity in *Vecernje novosti* (9 December 1986).

45. Discussed in *Vecernji list* (29 May 1987), p. 5.

46. See discussion in *Vjesnik* (9 July 1987), p. 3.

47. *Borba* is published in both Cyrillic and Latin-alphabet editions.

48. Tanjug (15 March 1979), trans. in FBIS, *Daily Report* (Eastern Europe), March 16, 1979, p. 110.

49. See, for instance, *Borba* (Zagreb edition), 17 January 1986, p. 3; also *Komunist* (19 June 1987), p. 6.

50. *Komunist* (26 July 1985), p. 4.

51. *Mladina* (1986), as quoted in *Borba* (Belgrade edition), 3 October 1986, p. 11.

52. Tanjug (9 December 1986), trans. in FBIS, *Daily Report* (Eastern Europe), 10 December 1986, p. 14, referring to a commentary published in *Vjesnik* on 3 December 1986.

53. Tanjug (9 December 1985), trans. in JPRS, *East Europe Report* No. EER-86-008 (21 January 1986), p. 103.

54. See *Borba* (Zagreb edition), 4 September 1987, p. 4; and *Ibid.* (13 October 1987), p. 3.

55. Quoted in *Christian Science Monitor* (23 March 1988), p. 2.

56. Tanjug Domestic Service (15 August 1988), trans. in FBIS, *Daily Report* (Eastern Europe), 16 August 1988, p. 24.

57. *Politika* (31 August 1988), p. 11.

58. Tanjug (28 October 1988), in FBIS, *Daily Report* (Eastern Europe), 31 October 1988, p. 71.

59. Interview, Ljubljana, 1 September 1989.

60. The examples I provided in "The Yugoslav Press in Flux" (pp. 111–112) in 1985 should be quite sufficient to justify this portrayal.

61. Interview with a staff member of *Mladina,* Ljubljana, July 1987.

62. *Ibid.*

63. And Radio Student.

64. Interview with a staff member of *Mladina,* Ljubljana, July 1987.

65. *Borba* (Zagreb edition), 1–2 August 1987, p. 6.

66. Interview, Ljubljana, July 1987.

67. *Delo* (Ljubljana), 19 September 1986, p. 6, trans. in FBIS, *Daily Report* (Eastern Europe), 1 October 1986, p. 19.

68. *Delo* (19 September 1986), p. 6, trans. in FBIS, *Daily Report* (Eastern Europe), 1 October 1986, pp. 19–110.

69. *Delo* (20 September 1986), p. 4, trans. in FBIS, *Daily Report* (Eastern Europe), 1 October 1986, pp. 110–111.

70. Translated in *South Slav Journal,* Vol. 10, No. 1 (Spring 1987), pp. 38–45.

71. *The Economist* (11 April 1987), p. 50.

72. *Vecernji list* (2 July 1987), p. 4.

73. *Christian Science Monitor* (9 March 1988), p. 2; *The Economist* (19 March 1988), p. 48; and *New York Times* (19 March 1988), p. 15.

74. "Slovenian Spring—Centralism or Democracy?," *Independent Voices from Slovenia,* Vol. 4, Special edition (October 1988), p. 6.

75. For a more detailed discussion of the effects of this trial, see chapter 2, above.

76. *Mladina* (Ljubljana), 9 December 1988), pp. 18–19, trans. in FBIS, *Daily Report* (Eastern Europe), 16 December 1988, pp. 57–58.

77. *Die Presse* (Vienna), 22 January 1982, p. 2.

78. *Borba* (Zagreb edition), 1 October 1987, p. 3.

79. Zagreb Domestic Service (8 December 1986), trans. in FBIS, *Daily Report* (Eastern Europe), 10 December 1986, p. 11; and *Politika* (December 11, 1985), p. 6.

80. Tanjug (9 October 1986), trans. in FBIS, *Daily Report* (Eastern Europe), 15 October 1986, p.17.

81. *Danas* (Zagreb), no. 333 (5 July 1988), p. 76.

82. *Nasi dani* (Sarajevo), no. 962 (3 March 1989), p. 25.

83. *Münchner Merkur* (Munich), 15–16 March 1986, p. 4; *Vecernji list* (14 September 1989), p. 5; and *Vecernje novosti* (14 September 1989), p. 19. See also *NIN,* no. 1840 (6 April 1986), pp. 22–23.

84. *Christian Science Monitor* (9 June 1988), p. 13; and report by Marinko Bulatovic, in *6. Sednica,* p. 53.

85. *Borba* (Zagreb edition), 6 February 1986), p. 3; and *Borba* (Belgrade edition), 28 October 1986, p. 3.

86. *Politika* (15 March 1986), p. 6.

87. Tanjug (24 July 1986), and (2 April 1987), trans. respectively in FBIS, *Daily Report* (Eastern Europe), 25 July 1986, p. 110, and 3 April 1987, p. 19; and *Politika* (21 February 1987), p. 6, and (19 March 1987), p. 6.

88. Tanjug (10 October 1986), trans. in FBIS, *Daily Report* (Eastern Europe), 22 October 1986, p. 113.

89. *Oslobodjenje,* as reprinted in *Borba* (Belgrade edition), 17 October 1986, p. 11, as summarized in FBIS, *Daily Report* (Eastern Europe), 13 November 1986, P. 16.

90. *Politika ekspres* (Belgrade), 25 June 1987, p. 2.

91. See *Duga* (Belgrade), 13–26 June 1987, p. 11.

92. *Vecernji list* (23 June 1987), p. 4.

93. *Borba* (Zagreb edition), 6 October 1987, p. 5.

94. *Duga* (5–18 October 1987), as trans. in *South Slav Journal,* Vol. 8, No. 3-4 (Autumn-Winter 1985), pp. 81–88.

95. Report by Sanije Hiseni, in *6. Sednica,* p. 101.

96. Tanjug (19 September 1986), trans. in FBIS, *Daily Report* (Eastern Europe), 22 September 1986, p. 14.

97. Quoted in *Danas,* no. 278 (16 June 1987), p. 8.

98. *Vjesnik* (24 December 1982), p. 14, trans. in FBIS, *Daily Report* (Eastern Europe), 3 January 1983, p. 17; *Los Angeles Times* (3 April 1983), Pt. I-A, pp. 8–9; and *Neue Zürcher Zeitung* (Zürich), 9 May 1984, p. 4.

99. *Knjizevne novine* (Belgrade), 1 September 1987, p. 3.

100. Tanjug (7 November 1985), trans. in FBIS, *Daily Report* (Eastern Europe), 8 November 1985, p. 17.

101. *Borba* (Belgrade edition), 15–16 September 1984, p. 9, trans. in JPRS, *East Europe Report* No. EPS-84-127 (12 October 1984), p. 109 (punctuation altered slightly).

102. *Politika* (18 February 1987), p. 6; and *Vjesnik* (26 February 1987), p. 4.

103. *Novi list* (Rijeka), 17 April 1987, as quoted in *Glas koncila* (26 April 1987), p. 2.

104. *Vjesnik* (5 April 1987), as cited in *Glas koncila* (12 April 1987), p. 2.

105. *Danas* no. 279 (23 June 1987), p. 25.

106. *Dnevnik* (Novi Sad), 8 September 1986, p. 5.

107. Interview, Zagreb, June 1987.

108. A copy of the decision (no. 132/87, dated 18 March 1987) is in the author's file.

109. Interview, Belgrade, July 1987.

110. Tanjug (5 July 1988), trans. in FBIS, *Daily Report* (Eastern Europe), 13 July 1988, p. 68.

111. *Vjesnik* (1 July 1988), p. 4.

112. Cited in *Los Angeles Times* (24 July 1990), p. H2.

113. *Vecernji list* (18 September 1989), p. 4.

114. *Vjesnik* (13 September 1990), p. 3.

115. *Ibid.* (6 October 1990), in FBIS, *Daily Report* (Eastern Europe), 26 October 1990, p. 51; and Tanjug (26 November 1990), trans. in FBIS, *Daily Report* (Eastern Europe), 30 November 1990, p. 70.

116. Tanjug (25 October 1990), in FBIS, *Daily Report* (Eastern Europe), 26 October 1990, p. 51; and Tanjug (26 November 1990), trans. in FBIS, *Daily Report* (Eastern Europe), 30 November 1990, p. 70.

117. Tanjug (14 March 1991), trans. in FBIS, *Daily Report* (Eastern Europe), 15 March 1991, p. 58.

118. Tanjug (13 March 1991) and (18 March 1991)—trans. respectively in FBIS, *Daily Report* (Eastern Europe), 14 March 1991, p. 49, and 19 March 1991, p. 59.

119. *Borba* (2 November 1990), p. 1.

120. Tanjug (28 March 1991), trans. in FBIS, *Daily Report* (Eastern Europe), 29 March 1991, p. 45; and Tanjug (29 March 1991), in FBIS, *Daily Report* (Eastern Europe), 12 April 1991, p. 28.

121. *Borba* (2 October 1989), p. 7.

122. According to the data reported in *Ibid.*

CHAPTER FIVE

1. Interview with Goran Bregovic, leader of Bijelo dugme, Sarajevo, 14 September 1989.

2. *Ibid.*

3. Conversation with Drazen Vrdoljak, Radio Zagreb music department, Zagreb, 10 September 1989.

4. Interview with Goce Dimovski (director of the House of Youth) and Pande Dimovski (music manager of the House of Youth), Skopje, 26 September 1989.

5. Quoted in Dusan Vesic, "Novi prilozi za istoriju Jugoslovenskog rock'n rolla": Part 1, "Josip Broz i rock'n roll," *Pop Rock* (10 May 1990), p. 2.

6. Quoted in *Ibid.,* p. 4.

7. Ljuba Trifunovic, *Vibracije* (Belgrade: Kultura, 1986), pp. 99–100.

8. *Ibid.,* p. 100.

9. Interview with Zoran Simjanovic, former leader of Elipse, Belgrade (telephone), 28 September 1989.

10. *Pop Rock* (21 February 1990), p. 35.

11. Trifunovic, *Vibracije,* p. 102.

12. Interview with Drazen Vrdoljak, Zagreb, 22 June 1987; and interview with Simjanovic [note 9].

13. Interview with Kornell Kovach, former leader of Korni Group, and Bora Djordjevic, leader of Riblja corba, Belgrade, 18 July 1988.

14. Vesic, "Novi prilozi," Part 1: "Josip Broz i rock'n'roll," p. 4.

15. Quoted in *Ibid.,* p. 13.

16. *Ibid.,* p. 12.

17. See Darko Glavan and Drazen Vrdoljak, *Nista mudro—Bijelo dugme: autorizirana biografija* (Zagreb: Polet Rock, 1981), pp. 13–18.

18. See, for instance, *Sarajevske novine* (22 March 1979).

19. This was emphasized and confirmed by several knowledgeable people, including Vrdoljak [note 3]; Simjanovic [note 9]; and Darko Glavan, free lance writer (in interview), Zagreb, 28 August 1989.

20. Interview with Vrdoljak [note 3].

21. Re. Leb i sol, see *Oko* (7–21 September 1989), p. 27.

22. Interview with Igor Vidmar, musical coordinator of Radio Student, Ljubljana, 30 June 1987; and interview with Glavan [note 19]. For articles on Buldozer, see *Vjesnik* (16 February 1985), p. 11; and *Pop Rock* (12 July 1989), p. 22.

23. *Pop Rock* (Belgrade), October 1988, p. 37.

24. *Pop Rock* (21 February 1990), pp. 16–17; and *Vjesnik* (6 October 1990), p. 18.

25. *Pop Rock* (3 May 1989), p. 20 (reporting the results of a survey conducted in 1988).

26. Interview with Dragan Todorovic, editor of *NON* and staff writer for *Rock* magazine, Belgrade, 10 July 1987.

27. See *Vjesnik* (19 July 1988), p. 7, (21 July 1988), p. 7, and (24 August 1988), p. 13.

28. See his interview in *Pop Rock* (24 January 1990), pp. 20–21.

29. Interview with Mimo Hajric, former member of Vatreni poljubac, Sarajevo, 15 September 1989.

30. Interview with Sasa Losic, in *Pop Rock* (March 1989), pp. 16–17.

31. Interview with Sasa Losic, in *Pop Rock* (28 June 1989), p. 16.

32. Interview with Jura Nolosevic and Srdjan 'Gul' Gulic, members of Dee Dee Mellow, Zagreb, 28 August 1989.

33. In interview with the author, Skopje, 25 September 1989.

34. Interview with Valentino Skenderovski, former member (1985–86) of Mizar, Sarajevo, 15 September 1989.

35. *Pop Rock* (17 May 1989), p. 22.

36. Re. the hostility confronted by early rockers in the United States, see John Orman, *The Politics of Rock Music* (Chicago: Nelson-Hall, 1984).

37. See, for instance, Tanjug (26 February 1985), trans. in Foreign Broadcast Information Service, *Daily Report* (Eastern Europe), 27 February 1985, p. 18.

38. Interview with Nele Karajlic, leader of Zabranjeno pusenje, Sarajevo, 16 September 1989.

39. See *Vecernje novosti* (Belgrade, 30 December 1987), p. 4.

40. Interview with Miha Kovac, former Editor-in-Chief of *Mladina,* Ljubljana, 3 July 1987.

41. *Pop Rock* (17 May 1989), p. 20.

42. *Ibid.,* (13 June 1990), p. 15.

43. *Ibid.,* p. 15.

44. *Ibid.*

45. *Sudba* means fate. OZNA and UDBa were successive incarnations of the Yugoslav secret police.

46. Quoted in *Pop Rock* (13 June 1990), p. 15.

47. The song lyrics were also subsequently published in Bora Djordjevic's second book, *Hej Sloveni* (Belgrade: Glas, 1987).

48. *Ibid.*

49. Bora Djordjevic, *Necu* (Belgrade: Knjizevna zadruga, 1989).

50. *Ibid.,* p. 123.

51. The story is recounted in Pedro Ramet, "Apocalypse Culture and Social Change in Yugoslavia," in Pedro Ramet (ed.), *Yugoslavia in the 1980s* (Boulder, Colo.: Westview Press, 1985), p. 14.

52. Vesic, "Novi prilozi," Part 1: "Josip Broz i rock'n'roll," p. 5.

53. Interview with Elvis J. Kurtovic, Sarajevo, 15 September 1989.

54. Interview with Nele Karajlic, Sarajevo, 14 September 1989.

55. Interview with Kurtovic [note 53].

56. Interview with Karajlic [note 54].

57. There was, in fact, a gang of "old primitives" in Sarajevo who terrorized young people who dressed in Western fashions.

58. These figures all date from 1987. Interview with Sinisa Skarica, Program Director of Jugoton, Zagreb, 24 June 1987; and interview with Aleksandar Pilipenko, Editor for Rock and Pop Records, PGP RTB, 20 September 1989.

59. Interview with Ilija Stankovic, free-lance manager, Belgrade, 18 September 1989.

60. Interview with Sasa Dragic, in *Rock* magazine [original title of *Pop Rock*], January 1988, p. 50.

61. Interview with Tanja Petrovic, Director of "U sred srede" show, Belgrade, 23 September 1989.

62. *Borba* (8 May 1989), pp. 1, 14; *NIN,* no. 2002 (14 May 1989), pp. 30–31; and *Danas,* no. 378 (16 May 1989), pp. 71–72.

63. *Oslobodjenje* (Sarajevo), 14 September 1989, p. 6; *Nedjeljna Dalmacija* (Split), 24 September 1989, p. 19; and *Pop Rock* (4 October 1989), p. 30.

64. *Danas,* no. 437 (3 July 1990), pp. 76–77; and *Pop Rock* (8 August 1990), pp. 1–5.

65. *Pop Rock* (11 July 1990), p. 12.

66. *Rock* (December 1987), p. 39.

67. *Vjesnik* (6 September 1990), p. 12, and (9 September 1990), p. 14.

68. *Ibid.* (9 October 1990), p. 8.

69. *Ibid.* (2 November 1990), insert.

70. For a brief article on Borghesia, see *Danas,* no. 347 (11 October 1988).

71. *Ibid.,* no. 405 (21 November 1989), p. 75.

72. *Pop Rock* (11 July 1990), p. 14.

73. *Ibid.* (20 September 1989), p. 20.

74. *Ibid.* (16 May 1990), pp. 20–21.

75. Tanjug (17 October 1990), trans. in FBIS, *Daily Report* (Eastern Europe), 19 October 1990, p. 56.

76. *Pop Rock* (11 July 1990), p. 14.

77. *Ibid.*

78. Telephone interview with Pero Lovsin, leader of Falcons and chief editor of *Gram,* Seattle-Ljubljana, 21 June 1991.

79. Quoted in *Pop Rock* (11 July 1990), p. 20.

80. For further discussion of rock music in Yugoslavia, see Pedro Ramet, "The Rock Scene in Yugoslavia," in *Eastern European Politics and Societies,* Vol. 2, No. 2 (Spring 1988); Pedro Ramet, "Yugoslavia 1987: Stirrings from Below," in *South Slav Journal,* Vol. 10, No. 3 (Autumn 1987), pp. 25–27, 29–30; and Sabrina Petra Ramet, *Social Currents in Eastern Europe: The Sources and Meaning of Contemporary Change* (Durham, N.C.: Duke University Press, 1991), chapter 9.

CHAPTER SIX

1. Bette S. Denich, "Sex and Power in the Balkans," in Michelle Zimbalist Rosaldo and Louise Lamphere (eds.), *Woman, Culture, and Society,* Stanford, Calif.: Stanford University Press, 1974), p. 253.

2. See the discussion in Sherry B. Ortner, "Is Female to Male as Nature is to Culture?," in Rosaldo and Lamphere (eds.), *Woman, Culture, and Society*; and Casey Miller and Kate Swift, *Words and Women* (Garden City, N.Y.: Anchor Press/Doubleday, 1977).

3. Denich, "Sex and Power," p. 250.

4. Andrei Simic, "Machismo and Cryptomatriarchy: Power, Affect, and Authority in the Contemporary Yugoslav Family," in *Ethos,* Vol. 11, Nos. 1–2 (Spring/Summer 1983), p. 67.

5. *Ibid.,* pp. 79–80.

6. Nancy Chodorow, "Being and Doing: A Cross-Cultural Examination of the Socialization of Males and Females," in Vivian Gornick and Barbara K.

Moran (eds.), *Woman in Sexist Society: Studies in Power and Powerlessness* (New York: Basic Books, 1971), p. 274, citing Karen Horney.

7. As cited in *Ibid.,* p. 271.

8. Carol Gilligan, *In a Different Voice: Psychological Theory and Women's Development* (Cambridge, Mass.: Harvard University Press, 1982), p. 8.

9. Chodorow, "Being and Doing," p. 280.

10. Denich, "Sex and Power," pp. 252–253.

11. As quoted in Bram Dijkstra, *Idols of Perversity: Fantasies of Feminine Evil in Fin-de-Siecle Culture* (New York: Oxford University Press, 1986), p. 220.

12. Dragan Radulovic, *Prostitucija u Jugoslaviji* (Belgrade: Filip Visnjic, 1986), pp. 21, 25.

13. *Ibid.,* p. 40.

14. B. Djukanovic, "Prostitucija," in *Socijalni problemi jugoslovenskog drustva* (1985), as cited in *Ibid.,* p. 48.

15. Radulovic, *Prostitucija u Jugoslaviji,* p. 47.

16. Denich, "Sex and Power," p. 256.

17. *Ibid.,* pp. 257–258.

18. Jasna A. Petrovic, "Zene na Kongresu sindikata Hrvatske," in *Zena,* Vol. 44 (1986), nos. 2–3, pp. 6–8.

19. *Statisticki godisnjak Jugoslavije 1989* (Belgrade: Savezni zavod za statistiku, 1989), p. 129.

20. Report by Branka Lazic, in *Dvanaesti kongres Saveza Komunista Jugoslavije, Beograd, 26–29 juni 1982.,* Magnetofonske beleske (Belgrade: Izdavacki centar Komunist, 1983), Vol. 3, p. 213.

21. *Statisticki godisnjak,* p. 158.

22. Report by Bahtije Abrasi, in *Dvanaesti kongres,* Vol. 3, p. 247.

23. *Statisticki godisnjak,* p. 131.

24. Report by Branka Lazic, p. 213.

25. Report by Bahtije Abrasi, p. 248.

26. Ruza First-Dilic, "Zena u socijalistickom razvoju poljoprivrede," in *Socijalizam,* Vol. 20, Nos. 7–8 (July–August 1977), p. 1398; and Eva Berkovic and Mirosinka Dinkic, "Ekonomski polozaj zene i ostvarivanje drustvene jednakosti polova," in *Socioloski pregled,* Vol. 14 (1980), nos. 3–4, p. 9.

27. Dusan Bilandzic, "The League of Communists of Yugoslavia on the Social Position of Women," in *Socialist Thought and Practice,* Vol. 21, No. 9 (September 1981), p. 44.

28. Berkovic and Dinkic, "Ekonomski polozaj zene," p. 9. See also Olivera Buric, "Polozaj zene u sistemu drustvene moci u Jugoslaviji," in *Sociologija,* Vol. 14 (1972), no. 1, pp. 61–76.

29. See Vesna Pusic, "Zene i zaposlenost," in *Sociologija,* Vol. 23 (1981), nos. 3–4, pp. 337–344.

30. *Statisticki godisnjak,* p. 123.

31. *Ibid.,* p. 124.

32. Report by Branka Lazic, p. 213.

33. These figures date from 1972. See Olivera Buric, "Izmena strukture drustvene moci: uslov za drustvenu ravnopravnost zene," in *Sociologija,* Vol. 17 (1975), no. 2, p. 208.

34. *Mladost* (Zagreb), 30 March–12 April 1987, p. 20.

35. *Borba* (Belgrade) 18 July 1977, p. 5.

36. Veljko Vlahovic, *Sabrani radovi,* Vol. 2 (Titograd: Pobjeda, 1981), p. 72.

37. Marko Bezer, in interview with *Vjesnik: Sedam dana* (Zagreb), 5 January 1980, p. 7.

38. *Ibid.* (11 April 1987), p. 8.

39. See, for example, *Borba* (28–30 November 1990), p. 20.

40. *Danas,* no. 308 (12 January 1988), p. 72.

41. The most important books in this vein are: Blazenka Despot, *Zensko pitanje i socijalisticko samoupravljanje* (Zagreb: Cekade, 1987); Slavenka Drakulic-Ilic, *Smrtni grijesi feminizma* (Zagreb: Znanje, 1984); Vjeran Katunaric, *Zenski eros i civilizacija smrti* (Zagreb: Naprijed, 1984); Nada Ler-Sofronic, *Neofeminizam i socijalisticka alternativa* (Belgrade: Radnicka stampa, 1986); Snezana Pejanovic, *Drustvena jednakost i emancipacija zene* (Belgrade: Prosvetni pregled, 1984); Lydia Sklevicky et al., *Zena i drustvo: Kultiviranje dijaloga* (Zagreb: Socijalisticko drustvo Hrvatske, 1987); and Slavka Veljkovic, *Feminizam i oslobodjenje zene* (Pirot: Grafika, 1982).

42. Barbara Jancar, "Neofeminism in Yugoslavia: A Closer Look," in *Women and Politics,* Vol. 8 (1988), no. 1, p. 26.

43. Tanjug (22 March 1990), trans. in Foreign Broadcast Information Service (FBIS), *Daily Report* (Eastern Europe), 23 March 1990, p. 89; and Tanjug (1 November 1990), trans. in FBIS, *Daily Report* (Eastern Europe), 2 November 1990, p. 71.

44. Interview with a feminist intellectual, Belgrade, September 1989.

45. Quoted in *New York Times* (25 November 1990), Section 4, p. 2.

46. See Zorica Raicevic, "Javna glasila o zenama," in *Zena,* Vol. 44 (1984), no. 4; and Dragomir Pantic and Ljiljana Bacevic, "Zena u informativno politickoj stampi," in *Novinartstvo,* Vol. 8 (1972), nos. 3–4.

47. Anto Knezevic, "Zena i jezik: Polozaj zene u drustvu," in *Zena,* Vol. 44 (1986), nos. 2–3.

48. Quoted in Bilandzic, "The League of Communists," pp. 48–49.

CHAPTER SEVEN

This chapter is a revised and updated version of my earlier chapter, "The Catholic Church in Yugoslavia, 1945–1989," originally published in Pedro Ramet (ed.), *Catholicism and Politics in Communist Societies* (Durham, N.C.: Duke University Press, 1990). The author wishes to thank Duke University Press for granting permission to reproduce the chapter here. I am grateful to Stella Alexander and Ivo Banac for their helpful comments on earlier drafts of this study.

1. *Keston News Service,* no. 357 (30 August 1990), p. 11.

2. *Ibid.,* no. 359 (27 September 1990), p. 8.

3. Zlatko Markus, "Sadasnji trenutak crkve u Hrvatskoj," in *Hrvatska revija* (Buenos Aires), Vol. 25, No. 2 (June 1975), pp. 223–224.

4. Frane Franic, *Putovi dijaloga* (Split: Crkva u svijetu, 1973), quoted in Markus, "Sadasnji trenutak," p. 219.

5. Ciril Petesic, *Katolicko svecenstvo u NOB-u 1941–1945* (Zagreb: VPA, 1982), p. 130.

6. *Ibid.,* p. 55.

7. AVNOJ = Anti-Fascist Council of the People's Liberation of Yugoslavia.

8. Petesic, *Katolicko svecenstvo,* pp. 32, 36.

9. See Ivo Banac, *The National Question in Yugoslavia: Origins, History, Politics* (Ithaca, N.Y.: Cornell University Press, 1984).

10. Fikreta Jelic-Butic, *Ustase i NDH* (Zagreb: S. N. Liber and Skolska Knjiga, 1977), p. 214.

11. Petesic, *Katolicko svecenstvo,* p. 95.

12. Richard Pattee, *The Case of Cardinal Aloysius Stepinac* (Milwaukee: Bruce Publishing Co., 1953), pp. 114, 276–281, 300–305. Stepinac's efforts on behalf of the Orthodox are noted in Ivan Cvitkovic's generally unsympathetic biography, *Ko je bio Alojzije Stepinac,* 2nd ed. (Sarajevo: Oslobodjenje, 1986), p. 209.

13. Quoted in Branko Bosnjak and Stefica Bahtijarevic, *Socijalisticko drustvo, crkva and religija* (Zagreb: Institut za drustvena istrazivanja Sveucilista u Zagrebu, 1969), p. 159.

14. O. Aleksa Benigar, *Alojzije Stepinac, Hrvatski Kardinal* (Rome: Ziral, 1974), p. 492.

15. Quoted in *Ibid.,* pp. 502–503.

16. See Pedro Ramet, *Cross and Commissar: the Politics of Religion in Eastern Europe and the USSR* (Bloomington, Ind.: Indiana University Press, 1987), p. 29.

17. Rastko Vidic, *The Position of the Church in Yugoslavia* (Belgrade: Jugoslavija, 1962), pp. 69–70.

18. Giuseppe Masucci, *Misija u Hrvatskoj 1941–1946* [Diary] (Madrid: Drina, 1967), pp. 204–205.

19. Benigar, *Alojzije Stepinac,* p. 508.

20. See article by Dragoljub Petrovic, in *Knjizevne novine* (October 15, 1985).

21. Quoted in Benigar, *Alojzije Stepinac,* p. 536.

22. *Ibid.,* pp. 540–541.

23. *Ibid.,* pp. 519, 542–543.

24. *Ibid.,* p. 555; confirmed in *New York Times* (September 20, 1946), p. 9.

25. *New York Times* (September 24, 1946), p. 11.

26. *Ibid.* (September 28, 1946), p. 5.

27. Benigar, *Alojzije Stepinac,* p. 578; and *New York Times* (September 26, 1946), p. 7.

28. Jakov Blazevic, *Mac a ne mir. Za pravnu sigurnost gradjana* [Vol. 3 of Memoirs, 4 vols.] (Zagreb/Belgrade/Sarajevo: Mladost/Prosveta/Svjetlost, 1980), pp. 208–209.

29. Benigar, *Alojzije Stepinac,* p. 601.

30. Blazevic, *Mac a ne mir,* pp. 211, 234–236.

31. *Ibid.,* pp. 237–238. Pattee (*The Case,* p. 129) estimates that some 200,000 former Catholics who had been pressured into Orthodoxy were among those converting to Catholicism during the war.

32. Blazevic, *Mac a ne mir,* pp. 360, 284–285.

33. *L'Osservatore Romano* (September 30, 1946), summarized in *New York Times* (October 1, 1946), p. 15.

34. Blazevic, *Mac a ne mir,* pp. 210–211.

35. *Ibid.,* p. 374.

36. Stella Alexander, *The Triple Myth: A Life of Archbishop Alojzije Stepinac* (Boulder, Colo.: East European Monographs, 1987), p. 178.

37. *L'Osservatore Romano* (October 12, 1946), translated in Croatian in Benigar, *Alojzije Stepinac,* pp. 635–638; and *L'Osservatore Romano* (October 31, 1946), excerpted in *New York Times* (November 1, 1946), p. 17.

38. Quoted in Benigar, *Alojzije Stepinac,* p. 639.

39. *Polet* (February 8 and 15, 1985), as quoted in *Glas koncila* (February 24, 1985), p. 3.

40. *Borba* (October 24, 1945), p. 3.

41. This latter story seems to have been a complete fabrication, however, since on December 10, 1945, 20 priests from the Bar archdiocese sent a letter to Stepinac objecting that Archbishop Dobrecic had made no such statements to the press as had been claimed. See Benigar, *Alojzije Stepinac,* p. 546.

42. Stella Alexander, *Church and State in Yugoslavia since 1945* (Cambridge: Cambridge University Press, 1979), p. 126.

43. Report in *Borba* (December 18, 1952), reprinted in Vladimir Dedijer (ed.), *Dokumenti 1948.,* Vol. 3 (Belgrade: Rad, 1979), pp. 466–468.

44. Fra Ignacije Gavran, *Lucerna Lucens? Odnos vrhbosanskog ordinarijata prema bosanskim Franjevcima (1881–1975)* (Visoko: N.P., 1978), p. 155.

45. Rudolf Grulich, *Kreuz, Halbmond und Roter Stern: Zur Situation der katholischen Kirche in Jugoslawien* (Munich: Aktion West-Ost, 1979), p. 62.

46. E.g., Gavran, *Lucerna Lucens,* pp. 158–159; and Grulich, *Kreuz, Halbmond,* p. 62.

47. Quoted in Gavran, *Lucerna Lucens,* p. 158n.

48. *Vjesnik* (July 15, 1978), trans. in Joint Publications Research Service (JPRS), *East Europe Report* No. 72058 (October 17, 1978).

49. *NIN,* no. 1900 (March 22, 1987), p. 32.

50. Interview, Ljubljana, July 1982.

51. Quoted in Alexander, *Church and State,* p. 229.

52. Paul Mojzes, "Religious Liberty in Yugoslavia: A Study in Ambiguity," in Leonard Swidler (ed.), *Religious Liberty and Human Rights in Nations and in Religions* (Philadelphia: Ecumenical Press, 1986), pp. 25–26.

53. Quoted in Zdenko Roter, "Relations between the State and the Catholic Church in Yugoslavia," in *Socialist Thought and Practice,* Vol. 18, No. 11 (November 1974), p. 69.

54. *New York Times* (June 26, 1966), p. 4.

55. Quoted in Zdenko Roter, *Katoliska cerkev in drzava v Jugoslaviji 1945–1973* (Ljubljana: Cankarjeva zalozba, 1976), p. 203.

56. *Ibid.,* p. 206.

57. For details, see Pedro Ramet, "Catholicism and Politics in Socialist Yugoslavia," in *Religion in Communist Lands,* Vol. 10, No. 3 (Winter 1982), pp. 261–262.

58. *Borba* (October 9, 1970), p. 6. For further discussion of the Catholic Church's association with Croatian nationalism, see Pedro Ramet, "Religion and Nationalism in Yugoslavia," in Pedro Ramet (ed.), *Religion and Nationalism in Soviet and East European Politics,* Revised and expanded ed. (Durham, N.C.: Duke University Press, 1989).

59. "Vjernost Alojziju Stepincu—za reviziju sudskog procesa i kanonizaciju!," in *Hrvatska revija,* Vol. 20, No. 1 (March 1970), pp. 85–87.

60. *Borba* (January 14, 1973), p. 7, trans. in JPRS, *Translations on Eastern Europe* No. 58221 (February 13, 1973).

61. *Nedjeljna Dalmacija* (Varazdin, December 9, 1972), quoted in *Glas koncila* (January 7, 1973), p. 12, trans. in JPRS, *Translations on Eastern Europe* No. 58479 (March 14, 1973).

62. *Glas koncila* (December 25, 1980).

63. *Frankfurter Allgemeine* (November 2, 1987), p. 4.

64. Tanjug (November 15, 1987), quoted in *Keston News Service,* No. 290 (December 17, 1987), p. 14.

65. *Glas koncila* (December 6, 1987), p. 2, and (December 13, 1987), p. 2; and *AKSA Bulletin,* Catholic news summary translation service edited by Stella Alexander with Muriel Heppell and Kresimir Sidor (January 26, 1988), pp. 5–6.

66. *Druzina* (August 1, 1971), cited in *Borba* (August 1, 1971), p. 5.

67. Interview with Franjo Cardinal Kuharic, in *Veritas* (March 1987), excerpted in *Glas koncila* (March 8, 1987), p. 3.

68. Dionisie Ghermani, "Die katholische Kirche in Kroatien/Slowenien," in *Kirche in Not,* Vol. 27 (1979), p. 93; *Glas koncila* (February 19, 1984), p. 4, and (June 16, 1985), p. 3.

69. *Delo* (Ljubljana, February 20, 1988), as reported in AKSA (February 26, 1988), in *AKSA Bulletin* (April 14, 1988), p. 4.

70. *Keston News Service* No. 274 (April 30, 1987), pp. 16–17.

71. *Glas koncila* (October 25, 1981), p. 3.

72. Interview with Archbishop of Belgrade Dr. Franc Perko, in *Danas* no. 260 (February 10, 1987), p. 26; and source listed in note 64.

73. Drago Simundza, "Ustavni i stvarni polozaj vjernika u drustvu," in *Crkva u svijetu* (1987), no. 4, reprinted in *Glas koncila* (December 25, 1987), p. 5; *Frankfurter Allgemeine* (March 17, 1988), p. 1; and *Glas koncila* (April 3, 1988), p. 5.

74. *Glas koncila* (January 7, 1973), p. 12.

75. *Ibid.* (January 22, 1978), p. 3, trans. in JPRS, *East Europe Report* No. 70836 (March 24, 1978).

76. See Pedro Ramet, "Factionalism in Church-State Interaction: the Croatian Catholic Church in the 1980s," in *Slavic Review,* Vol. 44, No. 2 (Summer 1985): reprinted as chapter 6 of Ramet, *Cross and Commissar.*

77. Zlatko Frid, *Religija u samoupravnom socijalizmu* (Zagreb: Centar za drustvene djelatnosti omladine RK SOH, 1971), p. 118.

78. *Ibid.,* pp. 109–113. Yet there were churches in the diocese of Kotor which, even in the 1980s, continued to be used by both Catholics and Orthodox.

79. Viktor Novak, *Velika optuzba* (Sarajevo: Svjetlost, 1960), 3 vols., Vol. 1, pp. 20–34; and *Glas koncila* (March 27, 1983), p. 8.

80. *Glas koncila* (December 15, 1985), p. 6.

81. *Frankfurter Allgemeine* (July 23, 1980), p. 5; and *Vjesnik: Sedam dana* (April 24, 1982), p. 17.

82. *Glas koncila* (April 19, 1981), pp. 7, 9.

83. *Vjesnik: Sedam dana* (April 30, 1982), p. 10; and *Frankfurter Allgemeine* (February 8, 1983), p. 10, (July 5, 1983), p. 8, and (February 21, 1985), p. 12.

84. *Vjesnik: Sedam dana* (July 31, 1982), p. 14.

85. Rudolf Grulich, *Die Katholische Kirche in der Sozialistischen Foderativen Republik Jugoslawien* (Zollikon: Glaube in der 2. Welt, 1980), p. 11.

86. Gavran, *Lucerna Lucens,* p. 146.

87. See *Ibid.,* pp. 146–151.

88. Rene Laurentin and Ljudevit Rupcic, *Is the Virgin Mary Appearing at Medjugorje?* (Washington D.C.: Word Among Us Press, 1984), pp. 113–114.

89. *Duga* (August 25, 1984), as reported AKSA (August 31, 1984), in *AKSA Bulletin* (November 28, 1984), p. 5.

90. Manojlo Brocic, "The Position and Activities of the Religious Communities in Yugoslavia with Special Attention to the Serbian Orthodox Church," in Bohdan R. Bociurkiw and John W. Strong (eds.), *Religion and Atheism in the USSR and Eastern Europe* (London: Macmillan, 1975), pp. 364-365.

91. Srdjan Vrcan, "Omladina osamdesetih godina, religija i crkva," in S. Vrcan et al., *Polozaj, svest i ponasanje mlade generacije Jugoslavije: Preliminarna analiza rezultata istrazivanja* (Zagreb: IDIS, 1986), p. 159.

92. AKSA (February 22, 1985), as extracted in *AKSA Bulletin* (April 17, 1985), p. 5.

93. *Nedjeljna Dalmacija* (April 21, 1985), reported in AKSA (April 26, 1985), as extracted in *AKSA Bulletin* (July 25, 1985), p. 5.

94. AKSA (June 6, 1986), in *AKSA Bulletin* (August 5, 1986), p. 4; and *Keston News Service* No. 257 (August 21, 1986), p. 12.

95. *Borba* (Zagreb ed., February 6, 1986), p. 3.

96. Grulich, *Kreuz, Halbmond,* pp. 58–59.

97. Bosnjak and Bahtijarevic, *Socijalisticko drustvo,* p. 33.

98. *Ibid.,* p. 134.

99. *Ibid.,* p. 83.

100. *Ibid.,* pp. 83–84.

101. *Ibid.,* p. 63.

102. *Nedjeljna borba* (Zagreb, February 14–15, 1987), summarized in AKSA (February 20, 1987), in *AKSA Bulletin* (May 26, 1987), p. 2.

103. Quoted in Bosnjak and Bahtijarevic, *Socijalisticko drustvo,* p. 133.

104. Bishop Nikodim Milas, *Pravoslavna Dalmacija* (Belgrade: Sfairos, 1989).

105. This suggestion was made indirectly, by publishing an old Chetnik map of Yugoslavia in the pages of *Glas koncila.* See *Glas koncila* (24 September 1989), p. 3; also *Ibid.* (30 July 1989), p. 5, and (8 October 1989), p. 2.

106. *NIN* no. 1879 (January 4, 1987), pp. 15–16; and *Frankfurter Allgemeine* (January 2, 1987), p. 4.

107. Interview, Ljubljana, July 1987.

108. *Borba* (Zagreb ed., October 31–November 1, 1987), p. 3; *Dnevnik* (Novi Sad, November 13, 1987), summarized in AKSA (November 13, 1987), as reported in *AKSA Bulletin* (January 26, 1988), p. 7; and *Glas koncila* (January 3, 1988), p. 3.

109. *Delo* (January 6, 1988), reported in AKSA (January 8, 1988), in *AKSA Bulletin* (March 9, 1988), p. 10; and *Ilustrovana politika* (Belgrade, February 2, 1988), reported in AKSA (February 19, 1988), in *AKSA Bulletin* (April 14, 1988), p. 8.

110. *Glas koncila* (8 January 1989), p. 6.

111. *Ibid.* (26 February 1989), p. 3.

112. *Ibid.* (18 June 1989), p. 6.

113. *Keston News Service,* no. 342 (25 January 1990), p. 23.

114. *Ibid.,* no. 348 (20 April 1990), p. 11, and no. 360 (11 October 1990), p. 11.

115. *Vjesnik: Panorama subotom* (6 October 1990), p. 6.

116. *Danas,* no. 464 (8 January 1991), p. 25.

CHAPTER EIGHT

This chapter is a revised and updated version of my earlier chapter, "The Serbian Orthodox Church," originally published in Pedro Ramet (ed.), *Eastern Christianity and Politics in the Twentieth Century* (Durham, N.C.: Duke University Press, 1988). The author wishes to thank Duke University Press for granting permission to reproduce the chapter here.

1. Blagota Gardasevic, "Organizaciono ustrojstvo i zakonodavstvo pravoslavne crkve izmedju dva svetska rata", in *Srpska Pravoslavna Crkva 1920–1970: Spomenica o 50-godisnjici vaspostavljanja Srpske Patrijarsije,* hereafter *SPC 1920–1970* (Belgrade: Kosmos Publishers, 1971), pp. 37–39.

2. Miodrag B. Petrovich, "A Retreat from Power: The Serbian Orthodox Church and its Opponents, 1868–1869," in *Serbian Studies,* Vol. 1, No. 2 (Spring 1981), pp. 4–12.

3. Quoted in Gardasevic, "Organizaciono ustrojstvo," p. 41.

4. James L. Sadkovich, "Il regime di Alessandro in Iugoslavia, 1929–1934: Un'interpretazione," in *Storia Contemporanea,* Vol. 15, No. 1 (February 1984), p. 11.

5. *Ibid.,* p. 25.

6. Bertold Spuler, *Gegenwartslage der Ostkirchen,* 2nd ed. (Frankfurt: Metopen Verlag, 1968), p. 122.

7. Viktor Pospischil, *Der Patriarch in der Serbisch-Orthodoxen Kirche* (Vienna: Verlag Herder, 1966), p. 55; and Sadkovich, "Il regime," p. 25.

8. *Primedbe i prigovori na projekat Konkordata izmedju nase drzave i vatikana* (Sremski Karlovci: Patrijarsija stamparija, 1936).

9. *Ibid.,* pp. 9, 22, 34, 35, 41, 43, 50, 52–53, 56.

10. *Ibid.,* p. 36.

11. *Ibid.,* p. 33.

12. Joseph Rothschild, *East Central Europe between the Two World Wars* (Seattle, Wash.: University of Washington Press, 1974), p. 254.

13. Ivan Lazic, "Pravni i cinjenicni polozaj konfesionalnih zajednica u Jugoslaviji," in *Vjerske zajednice u Jugoslaviji* (Zagreb: NIP "Binoza," 1970), pp. 50–54; and Viktor Novak, *Velika optuzba* (Sarajevo: Svjetlost, 1960), Vol. 2, pp. 131–36.

14. Bosnia's Metropolitan Petar Zimonjic, Banja Luka's Bishop Platon Jovanovic, Gornji Karlovac's Bishop Sava Trlajic, Zagreb's Metropolitan Dositej, Bishop Nikolaj of Herzegovina, and Vicar-Bishop Valerijan Pribicevic of Sremski Karlovci.

15. *Katolicki tjednik* (Sarajevo), 26 June 1941, as quoted in Dusan Lj. Kasic, "Srpska crkva u tzv. Nezavisnoj Drzavi Hrvatskoj," in *SPC 1920–1970,* p. 184.

16. *Ibid.,* p. 196.

17. Marko Dimitrijevic, "Srpska crkva pod bugarskom okupacijom," in *SPC 1920–1970,* p. 213.

18. See Vaso Ivosevic, "Srpska crkva pod italijanskom okupacijom," in *SPC 1920–1970,* pp. 217–20.

19. Milisav D. Protic, "Izgradnja crkava u poratnom periodu," in *SPC 1920–1970,* p. 253.

20. Djoko Slijepcevic, *Istorija srpske pravoslavne crkve* (Munich: Iskra, 1966), Vol. 2, p. 687.

21. Risto Grdjic, "Opsta obnova crkvenog zivota i ustrojstva," in *SPC 1920–1970,* p. 243; and interview, Belgrade, July 1987.

22. Stella Alexander, *Church and State in Yugoslavia since 1945* (Cambridge: Cambridge University Press, 1979), pp. 164–73.

23. *Ibid.,* p. 189.

24. *Borba* (3 July 1952), cited in *Ibid.*

25. Trevor Beeson, *Discretion and Valour,* Rev. ed. (Philadelphia, Pa.: Fortress Press, 1982), p. 315; and letter to the author from Stella Alexander, 17 October 1983.

26. Robert Lee Wolff, *The Balkans in Our Time* (Cambridge, Mass.: Harvard University Press, 1956), p. 551.

27. Alexander, *Church and State,* p. 224.

28. *Borba* (22 August 1953), cited in *ibid,* pp. 200–201.

29. *Ibid,* pp. 213, 219. Also *Politika* (Belgrade), 1 June 1982, trans. into German under the title, "Die Serbisch-Orthodoxe Kirche und ihre Beziehungen zum jugoslawischen Staat," in *Osteuropa,* Vol. 33, No. 1 (January 1983), pp. A53–A54.

30. Radomir Rakic, "Izdavacka delatnost crkve od 1945. do 1970. godine," in *SPC 1920–1970,* p. 291n; and interview, Belgrade, July 1982.

31. Protic, "Izgradnja crkava," pp. 254, 271–72.

32. Stevan K. Pavlowitch, "The Orthodox Church in Yugoslavia: Rebuilding the Fabric," in *Eastern Churches Review,* Vol. 2, No. 2 (Autumn 1968), p. 171.

33. Rastko Vidic, *The Position of the Church in Yugoslavia* (Belgrade: Jugoslavija, 1962), p. 53; Pavlowitch, "The Orthodox Church," p. 170; *Europa Year Book 1972,* Vol. 1, pp. 1435–36, cited in Burton Paulu, *Radio and Television Broadcasting in Eastern Europe* (Minneapolis: University of Minnesota Press, 1974), p. 463; Beeson, *Discretion and Valour,* p. 291; and interview, Belgrade, July 1982.

34. For details, see Branko A. Cisarz, "Crkvena stampa izmedju dva svetska rata," in *SPC 1920–1970,* pp. 141–155.

35. Rakic, "Izdavacka delatnost," pp. 291–95; and interviews, Belgrade, July 1982 and July 1987.

36. See *NIN* (Belgrade), no. 2031 (3 December 1989), pp. 26–28.

37. Alexander, *Church and State,* p. 169.

38. Fred Singleton, *Twentieth Century Yugoslavia* (New York: Columbia University Press, 1976), p. 229.

39. Alexander, *Church and State,* pp. 270–271.

40. *ibid,* p. 265.

41. For a fuller discussion of these political currents and of Rankovic's role in the 1960s, see Sabrina P. Ramet, *Nationalism and Federalism in Yugoslavia, 1962–1991,* Second ed. (Bloomington, Ind.: Indiana University Press, forthcoming in 1992).

42. Interview, Belgrade, July 1987.

43. *Nova Makedonija, Sabota* supplement, 10 October 1981, p. 5, trans. in Joint Publications Research Service (JPRS), *East Europe Report* (29 December 1981); and *Borba* (Belgrade), 6–7 May 1989, p. 6.

44. E.g., *Politika* (6 October 1981), p. 6.

45. E.g., Tanjug (19 June 1981), in Foreign Broadcast Information Service (FBIS), *Daily Report* (Eastern Europe), 22 June 1981.

46. Tanjug (25 February 1982), trans. in FBIS, *Daily Report* (Eastern Europe), 26 February 1982.

47. Quoted in *Vjesnik* (Zagreb), 15 July 1978, trans. in JPRS, *East Europe Report* (17 October 1978).

48. *ibid.*

49. *Vesnik* (Belgrade), 1–15 January 1971, p. 1.

50. Interview with Patriarch German, *NIN,* no. 1637 (16 May 1982), p. 18; and *Keston News Service,* no. 232 (22 August 1985), p. 10.

51. "Informationsdienst," in *Glaube in der 2. Welt* (February 1978), p. 5, as summarized in "News in Brief," in *Religion in Communist Lands,* Vol. 6, No. 4 (Winter 1978), pp. 272–273.

52. *Ilustrovana politika* (Belgrade), 20 November 1984, pp. 24–25.

53. *Keston News Service,* no. 229 (11 July 1985), pp. 8–9.

54. *ibid,* no. 244 (20 February 1986), p. 11.

55. *ibid,* no. 251 (29 May 1986), p. 12.

56. Stella Alexander, "The Serbian Orthodox Church Speaks Out in Its Own Defence," in *Religion in Communist Lands,* Vol. 10, No. 3 (Winter 1982), pp. 331–332.

57. *Pravoslavlje* (Belgrade), 15 May 1982, p. 1.

58. I have examined the nationalism of the Serbian Orthodox Church in more detail in my chapter, "Religion and Nationalism in Yugoslavia," in Pedro Ramet (ed.), *Religion and Nationalism in Soviet and East European Politics,* Rev. and expanded ed. (Durham, N.C.: Duke University Press, 1989).

59. *Pravoslavlje* (1 July 1990), p. 1.

60. *Politika* (2 September 1990), p. 18.

61. *Süddeutsche Zeitung* (Munich), 23/24 June 1990, p. 8.

62. *Pravoslavlje* (1 November 1990), p. 2.

63. *ibid* (15 May 1991), p. 1.

64. *Yugoslav Life* (April 1990), p. 3.

65. *Pravoslavlje* (1–15 August 1990), p. 1.

66. Quoted in *Los Angeles Times* (18 December 1980), Pt. I-B, p. 5.

CHAPTER NINE

This chapter is a revised and updated version of an earlier article, "Islam in Yugoslavia Today," originally published in *Religion in Communist Lands,* Vol. 18, No. 3 (Autumn 1990). The author wishes to thank the editor of *Religion in Communist Lands* and Keston College, the journal's publisher, for granting permission to reproduce the chapter here.

1. *Intervju* (Belgrade), no. 216 (15 September 1989), pp. 15–16.

2. *Nedjeljna Borba* (Zagreb ed.), 5–6 September 1987, p. 4; *Vjesnik* (Zagreb), 7 September 1987, p. 3; and *Danas* (Zagreb), no. 290 (8 September 1987), pp. 23–24.

3. Tanjug (30 April 1991), trans. in Foreign Broadcast Information Service (FBIS), *Daily Report* (Eastern Europe), 1 May 1991, p. 53.

4. *Statisticki kalendar Jugoslavije 1982* (Belgrade: Savezni zavod za statistiku, February 1982), p. 37.

5. Ahmed Smajlovic, "Muslims in Yugoslavia," in *Journal Institute of Muslim Minority Affairs,* Vol. 1, No. 2 and Vol. 2, No. 1 (Winter 1979/Summer 1980), p. 132; and Rudolf Grulich, "Der Islam in Jugoslawien," in *Glaube in der 2. Welt,* Vol. 7 (1979), No. 4, p. 6. See also Sabrina P. Ramet, "Primordial Ethnicity or Modern Nationalism: the Case of Yugoslavia's Muslims, Reconsidered," in *South Slav Journal,* Vol. 13, No. 1/2 (Spring/Summer 1990).

6. Smajlovic, "Muslims in Yugoslavia," pp. 135–136.

7. *Ibid.,* pp. 141–142.

8. *Keston News Service,* no. 336 (19 October 1989), p. 14.

9. See, for example, *Pravoslavlje* (Belgrade), 15 May 1982, p. 1.

10. Re. Tsar Lazar, see *NIN* (Belgrade), no. 2020 (17 September 1989), pp. 42–43.

11. *Aktuelnosti krscanske sadasnjosti* (AKSA), 13 November 1987, summarized in *AKSA Bulletin,* No. 8 (26 January 1988), p. 14. See also *Vjesnik* (12 November 1987), p. 4.

12. *Radio Free Europe Research* (30 June 1986), pp. 21–22.

13. *Nova Makedonija* (Skopje), 19 June 1973, p. 2.

14. *Start* (Zagreb), 19 April 1986, as cited in *Radio Free Europe Research* (30 June 1986), p. 21.

15. *Preporod* (Sarajevo), 15 November 1981), p. 10.

16. Quoted in *Radio Free Europe Research* (30 June 1986), p. 23.

17. *Preporod* (1 September 1989), p. 14.

18. For discussion, see Muhamed Hadzijahic, *Od tradicije do identiteta: Geneza nacionalnog pitanja bosanskih muslimana* (Sarajevo: Svjetlost, 1974); and Ramet, "Primordial Ethnicity or Modern Nationalism" (cited in note 5).

19. In February 1990, Muslim nationalist leaflets, supporting Kosovo's secession and vilifying Serbian leader Slobodan Milosevic, appeared in Novi Pazar. See Belgrade Domestic Service (6 February 1990), trans. in Foreign Broadcast Information Service, *Daily Report* (Eastern Europe), 8 February 1990, pp. 74–75.

20. Tehran IRNA (10 March 1991), in FBIS, *Daily Report* (Eastern Europe), 12 March 1991, p. 60.

21. Tanjug (16 January 1991), trans. in FBIS, *Daily Report* (Eastern Europe), 22 January 1991, pp. 38–39.

22. Tanjug (16 January 1991), trans. in FBIS, *Daily Report* (Eastern Europe), 23 January 1991, p. 43.

EPILOGUE

1. Quoted in *Radio Free Europe Research* (25 November 1983), p. 2.

2. Pedro Ramet, "Yugoslavia and the Threat of Internal and External Discontents," in *Orbis,* Vol. 28, No. 1 (Spring 1984), p. 114. (The article was written in November 1983.)

3. Sabrina P. Ramet, "The Breakup of Yugoslavia," in *Global Affairs,* Vol. 6, No. 2 (Spring 1991), p. 97.

4. Dennison Rusinow, "To be or Not to be? Yugoslavia as Hamlet," *UFSI Field Staff Reports,* No. 18 (1990–91), p. 1.

5. James Gow, "The Yugoslav Crisis and the Role of the Military: In Search of Authority," in *South Slav Journal,* Vol. 13, No. 1–2 (Spring–Summer 1990), pp. 56, 59.

6. Re. one such attempt, see *Politika International Weekly* (Belgrade), 3–16 August 1991, p. 2.

7. Tanjug (27 May 1991), trans. in FBIS, *Daily Report* (Eastern Europe), 29 May 1991, p. 41.

8. Tanjug (29 May 1991), in FBIS, *Daily Report* (Eastern Europe), 30 May 1991, p. 25.

9. *Neue Zürcher Zeitung* (2 July 1991), p. 1.

10. *Ibid.* (5 July 1991), p. 5.

11. Misa Milosevic, official representative of Serbs in Slavonia, Baranja, and western Srem, as quoted in *Politika* (Belgrade), 9 October 1991, p. 1.

12. *Neue Zürcher Zeitung* (10/11 August 1991), p. 7, and (22 August 1991), p. 2.

13. *Danas* (16 July 1991), p. 9.

14. *New York Times* (18 October 1991), p. A4.

15. Quoted in *Ibid.* (8 September 1991), p. 6.

16. Ministry of Information, Republic of Croatia, Press Release (20 September 1991), p. 1.

17. Re. Serbian proposals, see *Neue Zürcher Zeitung* (27 July 1991), p. 3, and (14 August 1991), p. 2.

18. *Politika* (10 August 1991), p. 1.

19. *Ibid.* (14 August 1991), p. 1.

20. *Ibid.* (13 August 1991), p. 1.

21. *Ibid.* (14 August 1991), p. 1.

22. Reprinted in *Ibid.* (17 August 1991), p. 10.

23. *Süddeutsche Zeitung* (26/27 October 1991), p. 6.

24. Radio Slovenia Network (Ljubljana), 15 July 1991, trans. in FBIS, *Daily Report* (Eastern Europe), 15 July 1991, p. 35.

25. *Financial Times* (13 September 1991), p. 2; confirmed in *New York Times* (13 October 1991), p. 6.

26. *New York Times* (13 October 1991), p. 6.

27. Quoted in *Ibid.*

28. *New York Times* (12 September 1991), p. A3.

29. See *Neue Zürcher Zeitung* (7 August 1991), p. 17.

30. *Ibid.* (27 September 1991), p. 3.

31. *Financial Times* (8 November 1991), p. 2.

32. For details, see Sabrina P. Ramet, *Nationalism and Federalism in Yugoslavia, 1962–1991* (Bloomington, Ind.: Indiana University Press, 1991), chapter 13.

33. Quoted in Michael Dobbs, "Serbian Leader Looks Vulnerable in the Long Term," in *Washington Post,* reprinted in *Manchester Guardian Weekly* (29 September 1991), p. 18.

34. Quoted in *Ibid.*

35. Quoted in *Ibid.*

36. See any issue of *Pravoslavlje* in 1991 for documentation and confirmation; also *Politika International Weekly* (22–28 June 1991), p. 6.

37. See *Politika* (18 August 1991), p. 3.

38. *Ibid.* (8 August 1991), p. 5.

39. Both quoted in *Politika International Weekly* (3–16 August 1991), p. 7.

40. *Politika* (17 August 1991), p. 3.

41. *Politika International Weekly* (27 July–2 August 1991), p. 1.

42. Andrei Simic, "Obstacles to the Development of a Yugoslav National Consciousness: Ethnic Identity and Folk Culture in the Balkans," in *Journal of Mediterranean Studies,* Vol. 1 (1991), No. 1, p. 31.

43. *Ibid.*

For Further Reading

FOR A COUNTRY OF JUST OVER 20 million people, Yugoslavia has attracted a great deal of attention. Needless to say, among the various books that have addressed themselves to the scrutiny of this polyglot country, there have been some truly splendid books, and some utterly wretched and profoundly misleading books. I do not propose hereunder to weigh the merits of all those books which have received attention in recent years, but merely to highlight some of those books and other writings, appearing in English, which I consider to be among the best and the most useful.

GENERAL STUDIES, HISTORIES

Among books of a more general nature, Dusko Doder's *The Yugoslavs,* published in 1978, still stands as one of the most readable accounts of modern-day Yugoslavia. Its age is no fault, and it has weathered the years well. As a general introduction to this country, especially for someone with no previous knowledge of Yugoslavia, it is without equal.

Two other works of an introductory nature are Fred Singleton's *A Short History of the Yugoslav Peoples* and his *Twentieth Century Yugoslavia* (1976).

Three outstanding works of history should also be mentioned. Ivo Banac's *The National Question in Yugoslavia,* published in 1984, won the Wayne Vucinich Prize for that year. Its subject is the formation of the Yugoslav state in 1918 and the experiences of the various parties in the subsequent two decades. Banac highlights, especially well, the reasons for Croatian disillusionment with the Serbian-dominated state apparatus. Jozo Tomasevich's *The Chetniks: War and Revolution in Yugoslavia, 1941–1945* (1975) is a painstakingly researched account of the war years and well deserves its reputation as the single most reliable source for its subject. Finally, a newer book, by Aleksa Djilas, *The Contested Country: Yugoslav Unity and Communist Revolution, 1919–1953* (1991), covers the evolution of the Yugoslav communist party from its founding through its first eight years in power.

Finally, a general book for a more advanced reader is *Yugoslavia in the 1980s,* edited by Pedro Ramet in 1985. This book brings together writings by a variety of authors on such subjects as politics, economics, foreign policy, the environment, the military, women's status, the media, and religion.

POSTWAR POLITICS

The classic treatment of the early post-war period is Dennison I. Rusinow's *The Yugoslav Experiment, 1948–1974* (1977). Generally sympathetic to Tito, Rusinow sketches the major crises of this period, both in internal politics and in foreign relations, starting with the expulsion of Yugoslavia from the Cominform and ending with the adoption of a new constitution in 1974.

For the more recent period, I would refer the reader to my own book, *Nationalism and Federalism in Yugoslavia, 1962–1991,* Second ed. (1992). In its second edition, the book traces the role that nationalism played in producing political crises and in finally plunging the country into civil war in summer 1991. The book also highlights the cultural aspects of the attendant political problems.

Among the several biographies of Tito, my own favorite is Milovan Djilas's *Tito,* published in 1980. Djilas has a keen mind, and the book contains many insights into Tito's character and strategies.

Aside from these three books, I might add that I continue to be impressed by the argument offered by Gary K. Bertsch and M. George Zaninovich in their 1974 article for *Comparative Politics*: "A Factor-Analytic Method of Identifying Different Political Cultures: The Multinational Yugoslav Case."

THE MEDIA

The only book ever written about the media in Yugoslavia is Gertrude Joch Robinson's *Tito's Maverick Media: The Politics of Mass Communications in Yugoslavia* (1977), although Paul Lendvai's *The Bureaucracy of Truth: How Communist Governments Manage the News* (1981) also contains material germane to the Yugoslav case. Of the two books, the Lendvai book is the more useful. Aside from these two books, further information about the Yugoslav media may also be obtained by looking at my earlier essay, "The Yugoslav Press in Flux," published as chapter 5 in my *Yugoslavia in the 1980s.*

ROCK MUSIC

There is almost no scholarly literature devoted to rock music in Yugoslavia. I am responsible for what English-language material exists. Here the chief sources are my "The Rock Scene in Yugoslavia," published in *Eastern European Politics and Societies* in Spring 1988, and my "Bora Djordjevic: Vanguard of Rock Protest (An Interview with Pedro Ramet)," published in *South Slav Journal* in Winter 1987/88. Aside from that, I have included some additional material about the Yugoslav rock scene in my introductory essay to *Yugoslavia in the 1980s,* "Apocalypse Culture and Social Change," in my essay "Yugoslavia 1987: Stirrings from Below" for *South Slav Journal* (Autumn 1987), and, within the context of a broader discussion of rock music in Eastern Europe generally, in chapter 9 of my book, *Social Currents in Eastern Europe: The Sources and Meaning of the Great Transformation* (1991).

WOMEN

The only book-length treatment of Yugoslav women of which I am aware is Vida Tomsic's fine book, *Woman in the Development of Socialist Self-Managing Yugoslavia.* Published in Belgrade in 1980, the book traces the fortunes of Yugoslav women from their experiences in the Partisan war to their gains under the self-management system, and contains ample statistical data. Barbara Wolfe Jancar's *Women under Communism* (1978), although covering all of Eastern Europe and the Soviet Union, is also useful in this regard.

Among shorter studies one might mention Bette S. Denich's "Sex and Power in the Balkans," which was included in the collection, *Woman, Culture, and Society* (1974), edited by Michelle Zimbalist Rosaldo and Louise Lamphere; Barbara Jancar's sensitive treatment in "The New Feminism in Yugoslavia," included in the collection, *Yugoslavia in the 1980s*; my own discussion of "Feminism in Yugoslavia," included as chapter 8 in my *Social Currents in Eastern Europe*; Obrad Kesic's chapter on women in Yugoslavia, scheduled for inclusion in the forthcoming collection, *Women and Revolution,* edited by Mary Ann Tetreault; and several chapters in the collection, *Women, State, and Party in Eastern Europe* (1985), edited by Sharon L. Wolchik and Alfred G. Meyer.

RELIGION

Stella Alexander's *Church and State in Yugoslavia since 1945* (1979) is a highly detailed and immensely useful discussion of the Catholic Church and the Serbian Orthodox Church during the years 1945–1970. The same author subsequently wrote a biography of Stepinac, which is as good as any other. Its title is *The Triple Myth: A LIfe of Archbishop Alojzije Stepinac* (1987). Also useful is my essay, "Religion and Nationalism in Yugoslavia," included in the collection, *Religion and Nationalism in Soviet and East European Politics,* Revised and expanded ed. (1989), edited by Pedro Ramet. That collection also includes a useful essay by Zachary T. Irwin on Muslims of the Balkans. Aside from those sources, the reader will be best served by consulting the journal, *Religion in Communist Lands,* which regularly published articles dealing with Yugoslavia.

THE ECONOMY

There are a number of excellent treatments of the Yugoslav economy. Among the best known are: Deborah D. Milenkovitch's *Plan and Market in Yugoslav Economic Thought* (1971); Svetozar Pejovich's *The Market-Planned Economy of Yugoslavia* (1966); Fred Singleton and Bernard Carter's *The Economy of Yugoslavia* (1982); and Branko Horvat's *The Political Economy of Socialism: A Marxist Social Theory* (1984).

Index

Abbas, Abu, 60
Absurdities of Historical Reality
  (Tudjman), 41
Adultery, dealing with, 112
Adzic, General, 50
Aesthetic culture, 105
Agnosticism, increase in, 141
Agriculturalists, 111–112
  pastoralists and, 112
Agriculture, feminization of, 113
Agrokomerc scandal, 39, 72, 95
"AKSA" news bulletin, 122
Albanians
  control by, 17
  frictions with, 12, 39
  independence for, 46
  number of, 1
  riots by, 10, 15
  self-defense units of, 47
Alexander, Crown Prince, 31, 181
Alexander, King, 30
  Serbian Orthodox Church and, 148
Alexander, Stella: on priests'
  associations, 153
Ali drugog puta nema (Sagi-Bunic), 143
"Alternative outlet" syndrome, 58
Amadeus, Rambo 89
Andjeo cuvar, 127
Andric, Ivo, xii, 29
Anti-bureaucratic revolution, 27–28
Anti-Fascist Council of the People's
  Liberation of Yugoslavia (AVNOJ),
  64, 200(n7)
Aporea (Apocryphal Reality), 29, 30, 91–
  92
Apostolov, Nikola, 156

Artukovic, Andrija: *Ustasha* movement
  and, 123
Arzensek, Vladimir, 13
AS, 76
Association of Catholic Priests of
  Montenegro, 131–132
Association of Journalists, 60
Association of Kosovo Journalists, 62
Asymetric federation, 25, 33
Atheists, 141, 142
Atomic Shelter (Atomsko skloniste), 88,
  103
Autonomism, 16, 48
Autopsija, 29
Avala Rock Festival, 103
AVNOJ. *See* Anti-Fascist Council of the
  People's Liberation of Yugoslavia
Azra, 87

Baby Doll (Dragana Saric), 89
Baez, Joan, 98
Bahtijarevic, Stefica, 141
Bajaga and the Instructors, 88
Bakamovic, Salih-beg, 173
Bakaric, Vladimir, 124, 125
Baker, James, 37, 52
Bakocevic, Aleksandar, 179
Balasevic, Djordje, 86, 89
Baljak, Momcilo, 63
Bans. *See* Censorship; News bans
Bardin, Tomislav, 72
Barter economy, 10
Bastards (Pankrti), 88, 97, 100
Bastina, 76
Battle of Kosovo (1389), 28
  anniversary of, 30, 161, 169

Bauer, Archbishop: concordat and, 148
Beach Boys, 84
Beatles, 84
Bebek, Zeljko, 85, 86
Beckovic, Matija, 29
Belgrade Protocol, 133
Belgrade Television, 75
  rock music on, 101
Believers, 140–143
  discrimination against, 135
Berry, Chuck, 83
Biber, Dusan, 175
*Bibliography of Croatian Writers of
  Bosnia-Herzegovina between the
  Two Wars,* Muslims in, 172–173
Big Rock n' Roll Party (Velika Rokenrol
  Partija), 103
Bilic, Jure, 16, 60
Bill Haley and the Comets, 83
Binicki, Stanislav, 27
Black Sabbath, 102
Blagovest, 132
Blazevic, Jakov, 127–129
Blue Orchestra (Plavi Orkestar), 90, 103
Boardwalk, award for, 102
Bogdanovic, Radmilo: resignation of, 49
Bogoslovlje, 155
Boja, 88
Bombarder, 88
"Boom" rock festivals, 87
Bora i Ramiz Hall, rock concerts at, 101
"Borba" publishing house, 63
Borba, 59, 63, 65, 67, 73, 129, 153,
  191(n47)
  articles in, 16
  influence of, 76, 77, 78
  on rock music, 92
Borghesia, 102
Borstner, Ivan: trial of, 24
Bosnia
  confederalism and, 50
  ethnic Muslims in, 166
  inter-communal relations in, 170–171
  secession of, 179
  sovereignty of, 38
Bosnia-Herzegovina, ethnic division of,
  22
Bosnjak, Branko, 141
Bowie, David, 102

Boyfriends (Rdecki decki), 84
Bread and Salt (Leb i sol), 87, 88, 92
Bregovic, Goran, 86, 89, 96, 97, 103
  lyrics of, 81
  on religion, 95
  threats against, 93
Brijeg, Siroki, 128
Brkic, Milovan: persecution of, 70
Brothels, 111
Brown, Arthur, 84
Buble, Marin: on multi-party system, 32
Budak, Mile, 150
Bukatko, Gabrijel, 137
Bukcevic, Risto, 179
Bulatovic, Momir, 179
Bulgarian Orthodox Church, 151, 155
Bulldozer (Buldozer), 87
Bush, George: on Yugoslav unity, 51
Byzantine rock, origins of, 91–92

Cacadou Look, 88
Caldarevic, M.: democratic centralism
  and, 12
Cankar, Ivan, 29
Cao, 101
Car, Pavlo, 68–69
Caric, Mirjana, 74
Catholic Action, 123, 126
Catholic Church
  adherents of, 2, 140
  communism and, 123–126, 135
  concordat with, 148–149
  criticism of, 40, 73–74
  Croatizing by, 179
  divisions within, 136–140
  human rights and, 135
  Islam and, 169, 170
  modernization of, 121–122, 144
  nationalism and, 121
  Partisans and, 123
  publications of, 132
  Serbian Orthodox Church and, 150,
    161–162
  Serbo-Croat issue and, 143
  symbology of, 121–122
  Ustasha movement and, 74, 122–124,
    126–127, 143
  vernacular and, 121–122, 137
  See also Vatican

Catholic Faculty of Theology, 143
  establishment of, 134
  state subsidies for, 130
Cavoski, Kosta, 69
Ceasefires, failure of, 178–179
Ceausescu, Nicolae, 51
Cekada, Smiljan, 122, 137
Censorship, 58–61
  abolition of, 76
  rock music and, 95–99
  See also News bans
Center for the Social Activities of Youth,
  94, 101
Centralization, 18, 21, 157
  revolutionary, xi
  See also Decentralization;
  Recentralization
Chameleons (Kameleoni), 84
Chauvinism
  ethnic, 32
  male, 106, 109, 110, 116
  Serbian Orthodox Church and, 145
  See also Machismo
Checker, Chubby, 83
Chodorow, Nancy: on women's role, 109
Christianity Today Publishing House,
  136, 172
Christianity Today Theological Society
  controversy surrounding, 137, 139
  publication by, 122–123
  Vatican II and, 138
Church-state relations, 132–136, 139,
  157–158
Church of St. Sava, construction of, 159
Cicak, Ranka, 73, 85
Citizens' militias, formation of, 44
Civil war, 39, 42–45, 175–177
  casualties of, 178
  fears of, 42, 49, 53
  rock music and, 104
Codex, 85
Colakovic, Enver, 173
Collaboration, 74, 125, 152
Collective presidency, 50, 53
Cominform, 38, 82
Commission for Ideological Work, 59
Commission for Political-Propaganda
  Activity in Information, 59

Commission for Relations with Religious
  Communities, 161
Committee for Press, Radio and
  Television (SAWPY), 60
Committee for the Protection of Human
  Rights, formation of, 24
Communist Party of Yugoslavia (CPY)
  Serbian Orthodox Church and, 152,
  156
  See also League of Communists of
  Yugoslavia
Communists
  Catholic Church and, 123–126, 135
  national groups and, xi–xii
  nationalization and, xiii
  Serbian Orthodox Church and, 151–
  155, 160
Community of the Islamic Alia Dervish
  Monastic Order, 171–172
Confederalization, xi, 33, 48, 50, 144
Constitution (1974)
  Catholic Church and, 136, 162
  problems with, 16
  review of, 16–19
  Serbian Orthodox Church and, 162
Constitutional Court of Serbia, 17
Cooper, Alice, 102
Corruption, 8, 32
Cosic, Dobrica, 29, 63
CPY. *See* Communist Party of Yugoslavia
"Creators and Creatures" (Kreatori i
  kreature), 102
Crime, increase in, 23
Criticism, inward and outward, 72–75
Crkva u svijetu, 135
Crkveni zivot, 30
Crnjanski, Milos, 29
Croatia
  confederalism and, 50
  independence for, 37, 38, 46, 176, 178
  JNA and, 50–51
  mobilization in, 52–53
  nationalism in, 21, 42
  Serbs in, 43–44
  tensions in, 176, 178
Croatian Commission for Religious
  Affairs, 123
Croatian League of Women, 116
Croatian Orthodox Church, 155, 162

Croatian Peasant Party, 125, 128, 148
Croats
    agriculturist, 111–112
    number of, 1
Cukvas, Veselin, 158
Cultural autonomy, elements of, 30
Cultural diversity, ix–xi
Cvijic, Jovan: work of, ix–x
Cvitkovic, Ivan, 33
Cyrillic, 65, 175
Czechoslovak Orthodox Church, 155

Dabcevic-Kucar, Savka: removal of, 41–
    42
Dalmatia, autonomy of, 48
Danas, 72, 103
    outward criticism in, 73
    readership of, 78
Dapcevic, Peko: on Leninism, 13
Decentralization, 10, 18, 157
    recentralization and, 12, 17
    See also Centralization;
        Recentralization
Dedijer, Vladimir: on jazz, 82
Dee Dee Mellow, 88, 90
Del Masochistas, 88
Delo, 67, 71
    influence of, 76, 78
Democratic centralism, 12, 13, 18, 67
Democratic Movement of Women, 116
Democratization, 15, 42
Demolition Group, 88
Denich, Bette, 107, 108, 112
Denis and Denis, 89
Department Store (Robna kuca), 88
Dervish order, introduction of, 171–172
Devils, 103
Dimovski, Pande, 101
Diplomatic service, women in, 114–115
Dirty Theater (Prljavo kazaliste), 88, 103
Discipline of the Spine (Disciplina
    kicme), 102
Disintegration, 176
    roots of, 38–40, 175
Disko selektor, 101
Divljan, Vlada, 102
Dizdarevic, Abdulatif, 173
Djilas, Milovan, 66, 82
    interview of, 69

restoration of, 28
    on Stepinac trial, 129
Djingic, Zoran, 180
Djogo, Gojko, 22, 28
Djogo, Husein Dubravic, 173
Djordjevic, Bora, 28, 87, 181
    Big Rock n' Roll Party and, 103
    criticism of, 92–93, 98
    impact of, 86
    nationalism of, 97
Djordjevic, Irinej: collaboration by, 152
Djordjevic, Jovan, 16
Dmitrovic, Ratko: persecution of, 70
Dnevnik, 62, 74, 75
    influence of, 77
Dobrecic, Nikola, 130, 201(n41)
Dobri pastir, 131
Dobri pastir (periodical), 132
Dolanc, Stane, 15
Dositej, Archbishop, 156
Dr. Steel, 88
Dragic, Sasa, 101
Dragosavac, Dusan, 17
Draskovic, Vuk, 29
Dreamers (Sanjalice), 84
Druzina, 135
    circulation of, 78
Duga, 79
    investigative journalism of, 72
    outward criticism in, 73
Dusan, Tsar, 169
Dylan, Bob, 98

Earthquake (Zemljotres), 88
Economic crisis, 10, 21, 34, 38, 44–46,
    114, 175
    crime and, 23
    women and, 114
Ecumenical Patriarchate, 147
Education
    Serbian-language, 40
    women and, 113–114
Edukataiislam, 168
Eighth Party Congress, 181
Eighth Traveler (Osmi putnik), 88
Electric Orgasm (Elektricni orgazam),
    88, 103
El-Hilal, 168
Elipse, 84

El-Islam, 168
Elvis J. Kurtovic Band, 98–99
  popularity of, 100
Epidemic, 88
Episcopal Conference of Slovenia,
  Provincial, 135
Episcopal Conference of Yugoslavia, 138
  repluralization and, 144
Episcopal Synod, concordat and, 148
Etatism, 9, 82
Ethnic culture, 105
Ethnic keys, dropping, 17
Ethnocentrism, reinforcing, 30
European Community
  mediation by, 178
  sanctions by, 177
  Slovene question and, 37

Falcons, 88
Fall of Byzantium (Padat na Vizantija),
  91
"Fall of Rock 'n' Roll, The," 102
Fascism, 40, 41, 52
Federal Constitutional Court, Slovenian
  amendments and, 24
Federal Executive Council, military
  budget and, 46
Federalization, xi, 13, 33–34
Female culture
  behavior and, 107
  understanding, 105–106
Femininity, assimilation of, 109
Feminism, 106
  challenge of, 116–117
  gender relations and, 107
  opposition to, 110, 115
Fiery Kiss (Vatreni poljubac), 88
  performance art of, 89–90
Fish Soup (Riblja corba), 87, 88, 92, 103
  Veterans Association of Macedonia
    and, 96, 98
Fit, 103
Five Flames (Plamenih pet), 84
Flaka e Vellazerimit, 47
Flight 3 (Let 3), 89
Folk music, 83, 90, 101
  bourgeois nationalism in, 88–89
  rock music and, 91
Foreign debt, 44, 114

Formula 4, 88
Fourteenth Central Committee Plenum,
  15
  resolution of, 9
Fourth Reich (4–R), 88, 93
Francetic, Jure, 128
Franciscan Order, 137, 139
Franciscan Province, subsidies for, 130
Franic, Frane, 122, 137
  priests' associations and, 131
Franklin, Aretha, 84

Galija, 100, 103
Gavric, Svetozar, 75
Gavrilo, Patriarch, 151
Gender culture, 105–106, 115, 117
Genocide, 50, 178
German, Patriarch, 156, 159, 160
Gilligan, Carol, 109
Glas crkve, 28
Glas koncila, 58, 133, 135, 136, 138, 169
  circulation of, 78
  on communism, 74
Glasnik, 154, 168
Glasnik Srca Isusova, 127
Glasnik sv. Antuna, 127
Gligorov, Kiro, 42
Goati, Vladimir, 13
Gogov, Metodije, 156
Gojkovic, Srdjan 'Gele,' 102
Golden Boys (Zlatni decaci), 84
Goli Otok prison camp, discussion of, 57
Goljevsek, Alenka, 64
Gorbachev, Mikhail, 52
Gow, James: quote of, 176–177
Grabcanovic, Mustafa H., 173
Gradac monastery, reconstruction of, 160
Gram, 101
Grbic, Cedo, 14
Green Party, 25, 70
Grlickov, 14, 16
Group 220, 84
Gujic, Kasim, 173
Gulic, Srdjan 'Gul,' 90
Gypsies, 1

Hadzic, Osman Nuri, 173
Hadzijahic, Muhamed, 173
Haley, Bill, 83

Hallyday, Johnny, 83
Handzic, Mehmed, 173
Happy Guys, 92
Hard currency, loss of, 45, 179–180
Hare Krishnas, 2
Haustor, 90, 103
Heavy Company, 88
Heavy metal, 88
Helidon, 100
Helsinki Act, 35
Helsinki Watch, 49
Hendrix, Jimmy, 84, 85
Heroina, 101
Hieng, Andrej, 29
Historical memory, length of, 40–41
Holly, Buddy, 83
Horvat, Branko, 13
Houra, Jasenko, 103
Hribar, Tine, 64
Human rights issues, 170
  Catholic Church and, 24, 135
Hungarians, 1
Hurricanes, 84

ICCPR. *See* International Covenant on
  Civil and Political Rights
Illiteracy, women and, 113, 115
Ilmija, SAWPY and, 168
Ilustrovana politika, 72
IMF loans, 52
INA petrochemical company, 45
Independent State of Croatia (*Nezavisna
  Drzava Hrvatska,* NDH), 124, 126,
  127
  Serbian Orthodox Church and, 150–
  151
Indexes (Indeksi), 84, 85, 87
Industrial production, decline of, 44
Inflation, 10, 45, 114
Inter-cultural contact, breakdown of, 3,
  35, 40
Internal Macedonian Revolutionary
  Organization-Democratic Party for
  Macedonian National Unity, 48, 50
International Covenant on Civil and
  Political Rights (ICCPR), 49
Intervju, 73, 76, 165, 179
Investigative journalism, 11, 72–73
Irinej, Bishop, 153

Isakovic, Antonije, 181
  novels of, 24
Iskra, on rock music, 102
Islam, x
  adherents of, 1, 2, 140, 166
  national question and, 165–174
  social presence of, 169–172
  women and, 172
  See also Muslims
Islamic Central Board, 172
Islamic community
  administrative regions of, 167–168
  emigres and, 168–169
  suppressing, 173
  See also Muslims
Islamic fundamentalism, 42, 170
Islamicization, fear of, 166, 173
Islamic Supreme Assembly, 174
Islamic Theological Faculty, 168
  women at, 172
Islamska misao, 168
Ismaili, Isa: on female imams, 172
Istria, 188(n39)
  autonomy of, 48
Iustitia et Pax Commission,
  repluralization and, 144
Ivanovic, Predrag: popularity of, 83
Izetbegovic, Alija, 42, 43, 47, 179

Jancar, Barbara: on feminism, 116
Jancar, Drago, 29
Janic, Vojislav, 147
Jansa, Janez: trial of, 24
Jasarevic, Nermina, 172
Jazz
  criticism of, 82
  musicians' association for, 83
Jedinstvo, 62
Jedretic, Kuzma: Partisans and, 123
Jehovah's Witnesses, 2, 140
Jelacic, Ban Josip, 31
Jelacic, Bonaventura, 128
Jelic, Ratko, 158
Jews, 2
JNA. *See* Yugoslav National Army
Johnny and the Hurricanes, 83
John Paul II, 74
Josef II, political modernization and, 33

Journalists
  associations of, 60, 62, 66, 71, 75, 144
  Catholic, 144
  censorship and, 60
  independence for, 76
  instructions for, 58
  party membership of, 61
  prosecution of, 69–70, 71
  protest by, 75
  solidarity fund of, 71
  See also Press
Jovanovic, Dusan, 11
Jovanovic, Jovan, 146
Jovic, Borisav, 50
Jugoton, 83, 84, 96, 100

Kadijevic, Veljko, 44
Karadjordjevic, Jelena, 30
Karadjordjevic dynasty, 181
Karadzic, Radovan, 47
Karadzic, Vuk, ix, 169
Karajlic, "Dr." Nele, 99–100
  on rock music, 92
Karamazovs, The (Jovanovic), 11
Kardelj, Edvard, 39, 156
  rock music and, 85
Katedra, 67, 68, 69
Katolicki tjednik, 127
Kavcic, Stane, 42
Kerber, 88
Kersovani, Otokar, 63
Kingdom of Serbs, Croats, and Slovenes, 31, 33, 181
Knjizevne novine
  banning, 75
  controversy about, 64
  Philosophical Society of Serbia and, 73
Kojic, Dusan 'Koja,' 102
Komunist, 60, 61, 65
  termination of, 72, 75
Koncar, Rade, 184(n15)
  proposal of, 12
Korni Group, 85, 86
Kosovo, 1, 32–33, 39
  autonomy of, 11–12, 26, 179
  inter-communal relations in, 170–171
  reconquest of, 28
  tensions in, 21, 35, 43, 47
Kosovo Assembly, arrest of, 39

Kosovo Socialist Youth Federation, 70
Kovac, Josip, 84
Kovach, Kornell, 85, 86
Krajgher Commission for the Reform of the Economic System, 9, 10, 16
Krajisnik, Momcilo, 179
Krizari (Crusaders), 126
Krleza, Miroslav, xii
Kucan, Milan, 25, 49
Kuharic, Franjo Cardinal, 134, 135, 162, 169
  on confederalization, 144
  criticism of, 73–74
Kurtovic, Elvis J.: new primitivism and, 98–100
Kuzmanovic, Jasmina, 178
Kvaternik, Slavko, 127

Labor force, women in, 112–114
Lach, Josip, 124
Laibach, 29, 67, 88, 181
  art rock of, 93–94
Langer, Bruno, 103
Law on Agrarian Reform and Colonization (1945), religious organizations and, 154
Law on Press and Information (1985), 66
Law on the Legal Status of Religious Communities (1953), 153, 154
  passage of, 132–133
Lazar, Tsar, 169
  reinterment of, 30
LCY. *See* League of Communists of Yugoslavia
League of Communists of Croatia
  Seventh Congress of, 112
  women and, 112
League of Communists of Serbia, 25
League of Communists of Yugoslavia (LCY), 7, 65
  Catholic Church and, 135
  Central Committee of, 11, 13, 17, 59–60, 112
  decay of, 8–10
  Information Commission of, 62
  press and, 59–60, 61, 71
  religion and, 134, 135, 141
  Seventh Congress of, 117
  women and, 112, 117

See also Communist Party of
  Yugoslavia
Legion (Legija), 88
Lekovic, Zdravko: on censorship, 60
Leninism, ineffectiveness of, 13
Leo XIII, 125
Lesbianism, 115
  See also Feminism
Lewis, Jerry Lee, 83, 102
Liberalism, 11, 23, 32, 133
  Catholic Church and, 144
  retrenchment and, 10
Licht, Sonja, 116
Lilith (feminist organization), 115
Lisac, Josipa, 89
Lisica, Goran "Fox," 101
Little Richard, 83
Ljevar, Bosiljko: Partisans and, 123
Ljubljana Military District, 176
Local party organizations, concerns
  about, 18
Losic, Sasa: musical philosophy of, 90
L'Osservatore Romano, Stepinac trial
  and, 128, 129
Lovsin, Pero, 101
Lukac, Sergij, 87

Macedonia
  confederalism and, 50
  independence for, 46, 38, 50, 179
  nationalism in, 21, 48
  status of, 22
Macedonian Orthodox Church, 156, 157,
  159, 162
Macedonians, 1
Macedonian schism, 156
Macek, Vlatko: concordat and, 128, 148
Machismo, 108–111
  See also Chauvinism
Magazines. *See* Periodicals
Magyar Szo, 62
Majnaric, Dubravko, 96
Makoter, Andrea, 89
Male complex, pastoralism and, 107–110
Male culture
  behavior and, 107
  understanding, 105–106
Male democracies, 116
Mamula, Branko, 44, 69

Mancevski, Veljo, 156
Mandic, Oliver, 89
"March to the Drina" (Binicki), 27
Marcone, Ramiro, 125
Maric, Misa, 85
Marinc, Andrej, 15–16
Market economy, 32, 34
Markovic, Ante, 22
  economic plan of, 42, 45
Markovic, Dragoslav, 15
Markus, Zlatko, 122
Marx, Karl, 31
Marxism, accepting, 141
Masculinity, proving, 109
Masucci, Don Giuseppe, 125
Mead, Margaret: on female identity, 109
Medrasas, religious instruction at, 168
Memory, 103
Mesic, Stipe, 50
  confirmation of, 53
  speech by, 177–178
Metikos, Karlo, 83
Metropolie Trans, 29
Mihailo, Metropolitan, 146–147
Mihailovic, Draza, 22, 27
  rehabilitation of, 28
  trial of, 153
Mikulic, Branko, 39, 68
Milacic, Vladimir, 102
Milanovic, Bozo, 130
Military budget, 44, 46, 179
Milivojevic, Dionisije, 155
Milosevic, Mirjana, 44
Milosevic, Sladjana Aleksandra, 87
Milosevic, Slobodan, xiii, 7, 15–16, 21,
    33, 42–43, 46, 50–52, 96, 146, 178
  anti-bureaucratic revolution and, 27–
    28
  citizens' militias and, 44
  civil war and, 39
  criticism of, 49, 180, 208(n19)
  ethnic chauvinism and, 115
  Helsinki Act and, 35
  Helsinki Watch and, 49
  Muslims and, 170–171
  press and, 63, 65, 73, 75
  reform of, 39–40, 179
  rise of, 22, 27, 32, 175–176
  rock music and, 103

Serbian Orthodox Church and, 152, 161, 180
Slovene question and, 37
supporters of, 81, 110
unity and, 26, 53
Milosevic, Vladimir: arrest of, 51
Ministry of Faiths, concordat and, 148
Minorities, rights of, xiii
Miric, Jovan: on 1974 Constitution, 16
Misic, Alojzije: *Ustasha* movement and, 123
Mizar, 101, 103
Orthodox music and, 91–92
Mlad Borec, on rock music, 102
Mladenovic, Tanasije: poem by, 162–163
Mladina, 69, 70, 94, 135
banning, 66–68, 75
influence of, 67–68, 76
poll by, 188(n39)
on rock music, 102
Mladost, 65, 67
banning, 59
Mlinarec, Drago, 84
Modesty, 88
Mojzes, Paul, 132
Monarchy, revived interest in, 30–31
Montano, Tonny, 89
Montenegrin Central Committee, 11
Montenegrin Party Congress, unity and, 18
Montenegrins, 1
Montenegrin schism, 156
Montenegro, changes in, 47–48
Montenegro (film), 100
Moral field, creating, 182
Mosques, construction of, 171
Mother, centrality of, 108
Movement for All-Macedonian Action, 48
Movement for the Unification of Serbia and Montenegro, 48
Multi-party system, 14, 23, 70
semi-, 32
Muradbegovic, Ahmed, 173
Muslim republic
fear of, 166
pressures for, 173
Music festivals, 84, 87, 102, 103
Muslims
Albanian, 171–173

confessional, 167
emigration of, 168–169
ethnic, 166, 167
national question and, 165–174
number of, 1, 2, 140, 166
See also Islam; Islamic community
Muslim writers, Croatization of, 173

Nadj, Kosta, 96
Nasi dani, 67
banning, 70
National Assembly, Orthodox clergy in, 147
National Bank of Yugoslavia, 46
Nationalism, 19
Catholic Church and, 121
economic interests and, 45
press and, 61–65
revival of, ix, 21–22
Serbian, 26–31
Serbian Orthodox Church and, 145, 152, 160
Nationalities
communists and, xi–xii
cultural diversity within, ix–x
press and, 60, 62
protection of, xiii
Nationalization
Catholic schools and, 132
Serbian Orthodox Church and, 154
National Liberation Struggle, 64
National question, xi, 40
repercussions about, 19
rock music and, 103, 104
Serbo-Croat relationship and, 43
Slovenian, 64
NDH. *See* Independent State of Croatia
Nedjeljna Dalmacija, 136
banning, 66, 75
Nektarije, Bishop, 154
Nemanjic, Sava, 123
Nesa, 103
Neue Slowenische Kunst (New Slovenian Art), 29, 30, 93
Neue Zürcher Zeitung, 45
"New art" groups, 29
New Primitivism, origins of, 99–100
News bans, 60
controversy about, 64

overturning, 66, 68
  See also Censorship
Newspapers
  banning, 59
  circulation of, 78, 79
  number of, 57
  Serbian Orthodox, 154–155
  See also Periodicals
New wave music, 88
Nikola I, reinterment of, 31
Nikolaj, Bishop, 153
NIN, 11, 72, 76
  changes at, 75, 79
  outward criticism in, 73
  readership of, 78
  on rock music, 87
Njegos, 29
Nolosevic, Jura, 90
NON, 67
Nonalignment, 7, 8
Nonbelievers, 140–143
Nova Makedonija, 171
  influence of, 76
Nova revija, 24, 63–64, 69
  controversy about, 64
Novi Evropski Poredak (New European
  Order), 29
Novi tjednik, 76
NSK. *See Neue Slowenische Kunst*

Office of the State Prosecutor, censorship
  and, 59
Oil, increased prices for, 39
Olbina, Zivana: nationalism of, 63
Old Catholic Church, 124–125
Omladinska Iskra, banning, 66
Opacic, Jovo, 22, 43
Organizing Committee for the Founding
  of an Independent Church in
  Macedonia, 156
Orthodox Association, 159
Orthodox clergy
  CPY and, 156
  imprisonment of, 151, 152
  resistance and, 151
  social activism of, 146, 147
  See also Serbian Orthodox Church
Orthodox seminaries, opening, 154
Oslobodjenje, 71, 74, 76, 99

Otok, Goli, 11
OZNA, 96, 196(n45)
Oznanilo, 132

Pacem in Terris, 138
Paldum, Hanka, 90
Panegyric rock, 86
Pantic, Miroslav: interview with, 179
Paraga, Dobroslav, 169
  plea for, 135
Paroski, Milan, 181
Partisans
  Catholic Church and, 123
  massacre of, 124
  mythology of, 182
Party Breakers (Partibrejkers), 88
Party of Democratic Action of Kosovo,
  demands of, 41
Pastoralists
  agriculturists and, 112
  male complex and, 107–110
Patriarchate of Pec, suppression of, 146
Patrimonial system, 32
  See also Male culture
Pavelic, Ante, 126, 127, 128, 150, 181
Pavicevic, Miso: interview of, 72
Pavle, Patriarch, 162, 180
Pavlitza, Igor, 90
Peace plans, unacceptable, 178–179
Perezic, Marina, 89
Periodicals
  Catholic, 127, 132, 133
  influential, 77, 78
  Islamic, 168
  JNA, 57
  number of, 57
  rock music, 101–102
  SAWPY, 67
  Serbian Orthodox, 154–155
  women's, 77
  See also Newspapers
Petar II, reinterment of, 31
Petesic, Ciril, 123
Petrovic, Milutin, 158
Petrovic, Tanja, 101
Petrovski, Metodi, 64
PGP RTB, 83, 100
Philosophical Society of Serbia, banning,
  73

Pichler, Alfred, 137
Pickett, Wilson, 84
Pigeonhole (Radulovic), 11
Pius XII, anti-communism of, 124
Planinc, Milka, 60
Plitvice National Park, attempted
    annexation of, 47, 50
Pluralization, 7, 29, 32, 33, 75
    democratic, 116
    political, 13, 23, 34, 35
    press and, 79
    regional, 22–23
    rock music and, 103
    Slovenian, 25
    See also Repluralization
Pobjeda, 71, 75
Polet, 72, 129
    on rock music, 102
Political debate, phases of, 7
Political organizations, malfunction of,
    8–10
Politika, 59, 63, 65, 71, 72, 76, 181
    control of, 75
    influence of, 77, 78
    on rock music, 92
    Serbian Orthodox Church and, 161
Politika ekspres, 76
    circulation of, 78
    on rock music, 102
"Politika" publishing house, 27, 63
    changes at, 75, 76
    subjugation of, 65
Pop festivals, 84
Popit, France, 16
Popovic, Davorin, 85
Popovic, Dusan, 16
Popovic, Gorica, 86
Popovic, Mihailo, 14
Popovic, Petar, 101
Pop Rock magazine, 86
    criticism of, 101–102
    survey by, 89
Pornographic press, leeway for, 58
Pos, Franjo: Partisans and, 123
Pozderac, Hamdija, 16
Pravoslavlje, 155, 158, 160, 161, 162
    Serbian nationalism and, 169
Pravoslavna misao, 155
Pravoslavni misionar, 154

Preporod, 168, 169, 173
Preseren, France, 29
Presley, Elvis, 83
Press
    Albanian-language, 62
    critical, 71–75
    JNA and, 61
    nationalism and, 61–65
    new law on, 65–67
    pornographic, 58
    purpose of, 57, 58–61
    republicanization of, 57, 58, 61–65,
        76–80
    rock music and, 87
    struggle for, 75–76
    women's, 58
    youth, 57, 58, 61, 67–70, 79
    See also Journalists
Priests' associations, 157–159
    government control of, 153
    health insurance and, 131, 132
    Orthodox, 152, 153, 156
    promotion of, 129–132
Prostitution, 110–111
Protestants, 2
Provincial Committee for Information,
    62
Prusina, Ivan, 139
Psychomodo Pop, 103
Publications. *See* Newspapers;
    Periodicals
Punk, 90, 93, 103
    development of, 87–88

Qaddafi, Muamar, Yugoslav Muslims and,
    165
"Quidam Episcopi," 138
Quotas, dropping, 17

Rabzelj, Vladimir, 24
Radio Luxemburg, 84
Radio Mileva, 22
Radio stations, number of, 58
Radio Student, 67
Radio Studio B, rock music on, 101
Radio-Television Titograd, 71
Radio Zagreb, 127
Radulovic, Jovan, 11
Rankovic, Aleksandar, 156–157

centralism of, 41
Rap music, 102
Rasic, Mihailo: on news bans, 60
Raskovic, Jovan, 165
Ratkovic, Radoslav, 13
Recentralization, 10–13, 21
    decentralization and, 12, 17
    risks of, 18–19
    See also Centralization;
        Decentralization
Red Corals (Crveni koralji), 84
Redding, Otis, 84
Regional party organizations
    concerns about, 18
    reform by, 15
Regional state monopolies, 34
Reis-ul-ulema, 167, 173
Religiosity, decline in, 140–143
Religious culture, x–xi, 105
Religious instruction, 142
    Catholic, 126, 132, 141, 144, 149, 160
    elimination of, 125
    Islamic, 168, 170
    laws on, 136, 153
    LCY and, 134
    Orthodox, 159, 160
Religious Law of 1953, Catholic Church
    and, 136
Repluralization, 144
    Islamic community and, 173
    See also Pluralization
Reporter, 72
    outward criticism in, 73
Reprivatization, 23, 34, 35, 42, 45
Republican Conference of the Socialist
    Alliance of Working People of Serbia
    Duga and, 73
    Islamic community and, 170
Republic Committee for Information of
    SR Serbia, 62
Revival literature, 29
Ribicic, Ciril, 16, 23, 26
Ribicic, Mitja, 143
Rijeka publishing house, 63
Rilindja, 39, 62
Ristic, Ljubisa, 73
Ritam, 101
RI Telefax, 76
Rittig, Svetozar, 124

Partisans and, 123
Robots (Roboti), 84
Rock festivals, 84, 87, 103
Rock groups
    important, 84, 88–89
    protests by, 98
Rock magazine, 101
Rock managers, free-lance, 101
Rock music
    criticism of, 87, 92
    development of, 82, 83, 89–90, 104
    folk music and, 91
    liturgical music and, 91–92
    national question and, 103
    Naziism and, 93
    pluralization and, 103
    political messages in, 81
    politicians and, 92–95
    promoting, 100–102
    Serbian Orthodox Church and, 91–92
    transnationality of, 102–103
Rock musicians, role of, 81–82, 85
Rock operetta, 102
Rock videos, 95
Rolling Stones, 84
Romanian Orthodox Church, 155
Rossi, Carlo Alberto, 85
Roter, Zdenko: on Catholic Church, 121
Royal Council, Serbian patriarch and,
    147
RTV Ljubljana, 100
Rusinow, Dennison, 176

Sagi-Bunic, Tomislav: quote of, 143
Sakic, Viktor: Partisans and, 123
Salamun, Tomas, 29
Salesians, 139
Salis-Seewis, Franjo, 124
Samoupravne interesne zajednice
    (SIZ), 9
Sanctions, 177
Saric, Dragana, 89
Saric, Ivan: *Ustasha* movement and, 123
Satan Panonski band, 103
SAWPY. *See* Socialist Alliance of Working
    People of Yugoslavia
Scandals, probing, 72–73
Secessionist movements, 47

Second Vatican Council. *See* Vatican II
  Council
Secularization, 140–143, 146
Seks, Vladimir, 68
Self-determination, 22, 40
  opposition to, 37
  rock music and, 92
  Slovenian, 44
Self-management, 7, 8, 9, 13, 34, 138, 172
  criticism and, 73
  press and, 58, 61
Seligo, Rudi, 29
Selimoski, Jakub, 173
Separatism, xi, 16
Seper, Franjo, 137
Serbian army
  establishing, 43, 180
  siege by, 178
Serbian Assembly, 66
Serbian Association of Writers, 93
Serbian Central Committee, 16
Serbian language, education in, 40
Serbian League of Journalists, 66
Serbian National Council, 43
Serbian Orthodox Church, 11
  accommodation by, 152, 153, 161
  adherents of, 1–2, 140
  Catholic Church and, 150, 161–162
  communists and, 151–155, 160
  confrontations with, 146, 148
  converting to, 127–128, 201(n31)
  internal opposition in, 158
  Islam and, 169, 170
  nationalism and, 145, 152, 160
  NDH and, 150–151
  persecution of, 74, 145, 146, 154, 162
  privileges for, 146–148
  rapprochement with, 21, 149–150, 161–
    162
  rebuilding, 27, 145, 151–155, 159, 161
  rock music and, 91–92
  schism and, 156
  Ustasha movement and, 150–151
  wartime losses for, 151
Serbian Patriarchate, 30
  reestablishment of, 147
Serbian Socialist Youth Federation, 160
Serbian Writers' Association, 28, 29
Serbs
  non-Serbs and, 1, 40–42
  number of, 1
Seselj, Vojislav, 69
Seventh Day Adventists, 140
Seventh Festival of the European Radio
    Diffusion Union, 102
Sex and Character (Weininger), 110
Shadows, 83, 84
Shehu, Sheikh Jemaly Haxhi-, 172
Silhouettes (Siluete), 84
Simic, Andrei
  on extended family, 108
  moral field and, 182
Simrak, Janko, 126
Siroki Brijeg monastery, massacre at, 124
Sisters of Mercy, 102
SIZ. *See Samoupravne interesne
    zajednice*
Sliska, J., 85
Slobodna Dalmacija, 32, 77, 78
Slovenes
  agriculturist, 111–112
  number of, 1
Slovenia
  confederalism and, 50
  independence for, 25, 37, 38, 52, 178
  JNA and, 37, 52–53
  mobilization in, 24–26, 52–53
  nationalism in, 21, 24
  pluralization in, 25
  tensions in, 178
Slovenian Assembly, amendments by, 24,
  26
Slovenian Bishops' Conference of the
    Catholic Church, 24
Slovenian Christian Socialist Movement,
  25
Slovenian Commission for the Protection
    of Thought and Writing, 69
Slovenian-Croatian federation, 40
Slovenian Democratic Union, 25
Slovenian Journalists' Association, 71
Slovenian Party Congress, 17–18
Slovenian Peasant Union, growth of, 25
Slovenian Territorial Militia, JNA and, 37
Slovenian Writers' Association, 69
Smiljkovic, Rados, 14

Smoking Forbidden (Zabranjeno
pusenje), 92, 99
popularity of, 100
rock video by, 95
Smole, Joze, 64
Smuggling, 10
Social democracy, call for, 14
Social Democratic Alliance, 25
Socialist Alliance of Slovenia, 25
Socialist Alliance of Working People of
Croatia, criticism of, 65–66
Socialist Alliance of Working People of
Serbia, Republican Conference of,
73, 170
Socialist Alliance of Working People of
Yugoslavia (SAWPY), 9, 12, 65, 158,
168
end of, 14, 25
LCY control of, 14
periodicals of, 67
priests' associations and, 131
religion and, 135, 141
Section for Information and Public
Opinion of, 60
Socialist Youth Federation, 65
Socialist Youth Organization of Slovenia,
67
Society of Catholic Journalists in
Yugoslavia, 144
Society of Journalists of Croatia, protest
by, 75
Society of Journalists of Slovenia,
Catholic journalists and, 144
Socijalizam, 13
problems for, 8–9
Sogor rock, origins of, 91
Soul music, 85
Spencer Davies Group, 84
Sporazum (Cvetkovic-Macek), 8,
183(n2)
Srskic, Milan, 148
Stalin, 38, 83
Stambolic, Ivan, 96–97, 161
nationalism and, 39
removal of, 21, 26
Stankovic, Ilija, 101
Start, 79
banning, 75
outward criticism in, 73

readership of, 78
State Secretariat for Information, news
bans by, 60
Stav, 62
Stepinac, Alojzije Cardinal, 122, 143, 169,
201(n41)
concordat and, 148
Croatian nationalism and, 121
death of, 133–134
rehabilitation for, 134, 144
sentence for, 129
Tito and, 125–126, 129
trial of, 41, 126–129
Ustasha movement and, 74, 123, 125
Stojadinovic, Milan, 149, 150
Stojanov, Kiril, 156
Stojanovic, Ivan: nationalism of, 63
Stojanovic, Svetozar, 13, 14
Storm Cloud (Storm klaud), 88
Strossmayer, Bishop Josip Juraj, 121, 122,
123, 131, 143
Student, 67
anti-Marxism, of, 70
Studentski list, 67
Stvarno i moguce (The Real and the
Possible) (Cosic), 63
Subotica Festival, 84
Supreme Court of Croatia, news bans
and, 66
Supreme Court of Slovenia, news bans
and, 68
Sustar, Archbishop, 143
Svet, 73
Svetosavsko zvonce, 155
Sympho-rock, 90

Takvim, 168
"Tamo daleko" (song), banning, 27
Tanjug, 17
on religious instruction, 134
Tasic, David: trial of, 24
Techno-pop, 102
Television, rock music and, 101
Television centers, number of, 58
Teoloski pogledi, 155
Terzic, Dragan, 162
Theological Faculty (Serbian Orthodox
Church), 154, 155
Thirteenth Party Congress, 13, 18, 19

Vlaskalic Commission and, 17
34th Eurovision Music Festival, 102
Tito, Josip Broz, 7, 23, 27–28, 32, 33
  as arbiter, 38–39
  Catholics and, 124–126, 132–133, 143
  criticism of, 73, 92, 97
  on jazz, 82
  press and, 57, 95
  rock music and, 83, 85, 86, 98, 99
  Stepinac and, 125–126, 129
Tito, Jovanka: musical satire about, 87,
  90
Titoists, 181
  moral field and, 182
  press and, 58
Tomac, Zdravko, 23
Toran, Jean-Louis, 180
Traditional values, promoting, 115
Trailovic, Dragoljub: resignation of, 63
Trajkovski, Goran: Byzantine rock and,
  91–92
Trash of Civilization, 88
Tren I and II (Isakovic), 24
Trifunovic, Ljuba, 86
Tripalo, Miko
  removal of, 41–42
  Tito and, 28
Trubar, Primos, 29
Tudjman, Franjo, 42, 50, 75, 178
  on Catholicism, 121
  writing of, 41
Tupurkovski, Vasil: pluralization and, 32
Turks, 1
Turner, Tina, 102
TV Politika, 76
Twelfth Party Congress, 10, 17
  accomplishments of, 12

UDBa, 96, 196(n45)
Ukraden, Neda, 89
Underground music, 88
Unemployment, 44, 114
Union of Yugoslav Journalists, 66
Unitarianism, xi, xii, 26
"U sred srede" (In the Middle of
  Wednesday), rock music on, 101
Ustasha movement, 41, 125, 129, 169
  Catholic Church and, 74, 122–124,
  126–127, 143

Serbian Orthodox Church and, 150–
  151

Valter, 67
  on rock music, 102
Vasic, Milos: criticism by, 180
Vatican, 41
  priests' associations and, 130
  protocol with, 133
  Stepinac trial and, 126, 128
  See also Catholic Church
Vatican II Council, 121, 122
  Christianity Today and, 138
  responses to, 137
Vecer, influence of, 76
Vecernje novosti, 63, 74, 78
Vecernji list, 76, 78
Vego, Ivica, 139
Velimirovic, Bishop Nikolaj
  collaboration by, 152
  imprisonment of, 151
Veritas, 135
Veselinov, Dragan, 180
Vesic, Dusan, 85, 98
Vesnik, 153, 158, 159
Veterans Association of Macedonia
  Fish Soup and, 96, 98
Videosex, 101
Vidik, 67
  anti-Marxism of, 70
Viktorija, Snezana Miskovic, 89
Vjesnik, 19, 59, 67, 76, 144
  criticism of, 65–66
  on rock music, 92
Vlahovic, Veljko: on woman question,
  115
Vlaskalic, Tihomir, 16–17
Vlaskalic Commission, report by, 17
Vojvodina, autonomy of, 26, 48
Vojvodina Journalists' Federation, 71
Voodoobuddah, 102
Vrcan, Srdjan, 134
Vreme, 76, 180
Vrhovec, Josip, 18
Vukasinovic, Milic, 90
Vukov, Vice, 95–96

Walker Brothers, 84
We (Mi), 84

Weber, Vinko: priests' associations and, 131
Weininger, Otto, 110
White Arrows (Bijele strijele), 84
White Button (Bijelo dugme), 81, 88, 89, 93, 95, 97, 103
   criticism of, 87, 98
   popularity of, 86–87
Woman question, solution to, 115
Women
   agriculture and, 113
   culture and, 105
   fear of, 110
   leadership by, 112–116
   political organizations of, 115–116
   population of, 112–113
   as socializers, 109
   subordination of, 110, 112, 116
Women's Party of Belgrade, 116
Women's press, leeway for, 58
World War Two, impact of, 41
Writers. *See* Journalists; Press

Youth press, 57, 67–70, 79
   JNA and, 61
   leeway for, 58
YU-Group, 88, 91
YU-Madonna (Andrea Makoter), 89

Yugoslavism, 22, 121, 181–182
   integral, 156
   organic, 156
Yugoslav Journalists' Charter, 71
Yugoslav League of Journalists, 66
Yugoslav National Army (JNA), 37, 43, 45, 177, 178
   Croatia and, 50–51
   Macedonia and, 48
   musical satire about, 87
   periodicals of, 57
   press and, 61
   recruiting problems for, 47, 180
   restructuring of, 176
   Slovenia and, 52–53
Yugoslav synthesis, xii
   advocation of, 32

Zagreb Eparchy, 154
Zagreb Military District, 176
Zanic, Bishop Pavao, 139
Zavrl, Franci, 24, 69
Zbornik radova, 155
Zemzem, 168
Zeri i Renise, 47, 70
Zivkovic, Miroslav: social democracy and, 14
Zvan, Antun, 12, 13